应用语言学方法导论

刘辉 编著

黑龍江大學出版社
HEILONGJIANG UNIVERSITY PRESS
哈尔滨

图书在版编目（CIP）数据

应用语言学方法导论 / 刘辉编著. -- 哈尔滨 : 黑龙江大学出版社, 2019.6
ISBN 978-7-5686-0373-7

Ⅰ. ①应… Ⅱ. ①刘… Ⅲ. ①应用语言学－教材
Ⅳ. ①H08

中国版本图书馆 CIP 数据核字 (2019) 第 115342 号

应用语言学方法导论
YINGYONG YUYANXUE FANGFA DAOLUN
刘 辉 编著

责任编辑 张微微
出版发行 黑龙江大学出版社
地 址 哈尔滨市南岗区学府三道街 36 号
印 刷 哈尔滨市石桥印务有限公司
开 本 720 毫米 ×1000 毫米 1/16
印 张 19.25
字 数 276 千
版 次 2019 年 6 月第 1 版
印 次 2019 年 6 月第 1 次印刷
书 号 ISBN 978-7-5686-0373-7
定 价 58.00 元

目　录

第一章

语言与语言学

导 读

语言是人类生活中不可或缺的部分，是人类最重要的交际工具，也是人类和动物分道扬镳的最后标志。古代中国、古印度和古希腊等国家的人们很早就开始关注语言问题。对语言进行系统和科学研究的语言学(Linguistics)同样经历了漫长的发展过程——从最初的语文学(Philology)到历史比较语言学(Historical Comparative Linguistics)。而语言学家的语言观也在不断地发展——从语言工具论到语言非工具论。

20 世纪初，索绪尔(F. Saussure)开创了现代语言学，揭开了人类语言研究的新篇章。他的结构主义思想影响了当时的很多学科，最终成为 20 世纪上半叶的时代精神。而且他的区分：能指与所指、历时与共时、语言与言语等至今仍是语言研究中的重要概念。

20 世纪中叶，乔姆斯基(N. Chomsky)提出转换生成语法，掀起了语言研究的另一场革命，并对计算语言学等学科的发展提供了理论根基。20 世纪 80 年代，我国也出现了研究转换生成语法的热潮。与此同时，韩礼德(M. A. K. Halliday)提出系统功能语法。这位与中国有着不解渊源的语言学家十分重视语言的社会性特征，因此他的理论对社会语言学、话语分析和文体学等都有很强的指导意义。

随着语言研究的深入，语言学必将迎来更加辉煌的明天。

1. Definitions

1.1 Language

Language is a purely human and non-instinctive method of communicating ideas, emotions, and desires by means of a system of voluntarily produced symbols.

(Sapir 1921: 8)

Language is a form of human communication by means of a system of symbols principally transmitted by vocal sounds.

(Robins 1942: 12)

Vehicle for the expression or exchanging of thoughts, concepts, knowledge, and information as well as the fixing and transmission of experience and knowledge. It is based on cognitive processes, subject to societal factors and subject to historical change and development. In this definition, language refers to a specific form of expression that is restricted to humans, and differs from all other possible languages, such as **animal communication** and **artificial languages** through **creativity**, the ability to make conceptional abstractions, and the possibility of metalinguistic reflection.

(Bussmann 1996: 627)

Webster's new World Dictionary offers several most frequently used senses of the word "language", namely, [1] (a) human speech; (b) the ability to communicate by this means; (c) a system of vocal sounds and combinations of such sounds to which meaning is attributed, used for the expression or communication of thoughts and feelings; (d) the written representation of such a system; [2](a) any means of expressing or communicating, as gestures, signs, or animal sounds; (b) a special set of symbols, letters, numerals, rules etc. used for the transmission of information, as in a computer.

(*Webster's new World Dictionary*, 759)

1.2 General linguistics

Scientific discipline with the goal of describing language and speech in all relevant theoretical and practical aspects and their relation to adjoining disciplines.

(Bussmann 1996: 693)

General linguistics may be defined as the science of language.

(Robins 2000: 1)

1.3 Phonetics

That part of linguistics that deals with the material of speech itself is called phonetics.

(Robins 2000: 19)

Linguistic subdiscipline that studies the phonetic aspect of speech with regard to the following processes: (a) articulatory-genetic sound production (articulatory phonetics); (b) structure of the acoustic flow (acoustic phonetics); and (c) neurological-psychological processes involved in perception (auditory phonetics). An understanding of anatomy, physiology, neurology, and physics is fundamental to these studies. In contrast to phonology, phonetics studies the concrete articulatory, acoustic, and auditory characteristics of all the possible sounds of all languages.

(Bussmann 1996: 895)

1.4 Phonology

Linguistic subdiscipline concerned with semantically relevant speech sounds (phoneme) and their pertinent characteristics, relations, and systems viewed synchronically and diachronically.

(Bussmann 1996: 897)

Phonology is concerned with the patterns and organization of languages in terms of the phonetic features and categories involved.

(Robins 2000: 20)

1.5 Morphology

The central focus of those who study morphology is how language users understand complex words and how they create new ones.

(Strazny 2005: 715)

The study of the grammatical structure of words.

(Robins 2000: 182)

1.6 Semantics

Meaning is an attribute not only of language but of all sign and symbols systems, and the study of meaning is called semantics.

(Robins 2000: 19)

Semantics is the study of the meaning of signs and representations, both mental and linguistic. The ultimate target of semantics is the construction of a general theory of meaning.

(Strazny 2005: 947)

1.7 Syntax

Subcategory of the grammar of natural languages: a system of rules which describe how all well-formed sentences of a language can be derived from basic elements (morphemes, words, part of speech).

(Bussmann 1996: 1169)

The study of the grammatical structure of sentences as built up of words, though the relations between the two need careful consideration.

(Robins 2000: 182)

2. Classical theories

Language is such an integral part of our life and humanity that too much about it has been taken for granted. To give the barest of definition, language is a means of verbal communication. It is instrumental in that communicating by speaking or writing is a purposeful act. It is social and conventional in that language is a social semantic and communication can only take place effectively if all the users share a broad understanding of human interaction including such associated factors as nonverbal cues, motivation, and socio-cultural roles. Now we will introduce some main theories in linguistics in order to see how they deal with language.

2.1 The beginning of modern linguistics

Modern linguistics began from the Swiss linguist F. de Saussure (1857 –

1913), who is often described as "father of modern linguistics" and "a master of a discipline which he made modern" (Culler, 1976:7).

From the year 1907 to 1911, Saussure lectured on general linguistics in the University of Geneva. After he died in 1913, two of his students, C. Bally and A. Sechehaye, collected lecture notes from students and put them together to produce the great work, *Course in General Linguistics*, in 1916.

Saussure was the first to notice the complexities of language. He believed that language is a SYSTEM OF SIGNS. Noises count as language only when they serve to express or communicate ideas; otherwise they are nothing but noise. To communicate ideas, they must be part of a system of conventions, part of a system of signs. This sign is the union of a form and an idea, which Saussure called the signifier and the signified. Though we may speak of the signifier and the signified as if they were separate entities, they exist only as components of the sign. The sign is the central fact of language, and therefore or incidental we must start fron the nature of the sign itself.

Saussure's answers to these questions serve to direct our attention to essentials of language and make clear the object of study for linguistics as a science. His ideas on the arbitrary nature of sign, on the relational nature of linguistic units, on the distinction of LANGUE and PAROLE and of SYNCHRONIC and DIACHRONIC linguistics, etc. pushed linguistics into a brand new stage. In short, all linguistics in the twentieth century are Saussurean linguistics.

2.2 Transformational-Generative Grammar

In the late 1950s, a new theory appeared in America and violently punched the prevailing structuralist descriptive linguistics. The founder of this new theory was A. N. Chomsky (1928 –). As a student of Hebrew with the structuralist methodology, Chomsky tried to open up a new route when he found that the classification of structural elements of language according to distribution and substitution had its limitations. From this practice Chomsky gradually established the well-known **Transformational-Generative (TG) Grammar.** The publication of his *Syntactic Structures* (1957) marked the beginning of the Chomskyan Revolution.

From its birth to the present day, TG Grammar has seen five stages of development. The Classical Theory aims to make linguistics a science. The Standard Theory deals with how semantics should be studied in a linguistics theory. The Extended Standard Theory focuses discussion on language universals and universal grammar. The Revised Extended Standard Theory (or GB) focuses discussion on government and binding. The latest is the Minimalist Program, a further revision of the previous theory. Since there are too many aspects of Chomsky's theory to be discussed and not all of them can be taken up within the space of a few pages, we have to content with a brief discussion of some important points.

Chomsky's TG Grammar differs from the structural grammar in a number of ways: (1) rationalism; (2) innateness; (3) deductive methodology; (4) emphasis on interpretation; (5) formalization; (6) emphasis on linguistic competence; (7) strong generative powers; (8) emphasis on linguistic universals.

First, Chomsky defines language as a set of rules or principles. Second, Chomsky believes that the aim of linguistics is to produce a generative grammar which captures the tacit knowledge of the native speaker of his language. This concerns the question of learning theory and the question of linguistic universals. Third, Chomsky and his followers are interested in any data that can reveal the native speaker's tacit knowledge. They seldom use what native speakers actually say; they rely on their own intuition. Fourth, Chomsky's methodology is hypothesis-deductive, which operates at two levels: (a) the linguist formulates a hypothesis about language structure-a general linguistic theory; this is tested by grammars for particular languages, and (b) each such grammar is a hypothesis on the general linguistic theory. Finally, Chomsky follows rationalism in philosophy and mentalism in psychology.

2.3 Systemic-Functional Grammar

M. A. K. Halliday (1925 –) has developed the ideas stemming from Firth's theories in the London School. His Systemic-Functional (SF) Grammar is a sociologically oriented functional linguistic approach and one of the most influential linguistic theories in the twentieth century, having great effect on various disciplines related to language, such as language teaching, sociolinguistics, discourse analysis, stylistics, and machine translation.

SF Grammar has two components: SYSTEMIC GRAMMAR and FUNCTIONAL GRAMMAR. They are two inseparable parts for an integral framework of linguistic theory. Systemic grammar aims to explain the internal relations in language as a system network, or meaning potential. And this network consists of subsystems from which language users make choices. Functional grammar aims to reveal that language is a means of social interaction, based on the position that language system and the forms that make it up ate inescapably determined by the uses or functions which they serve.

Systemic-Functional grammar is based on two facts: (1) language users are actually making choices in a system of systems and trying to realise different semantic functions in social interaction; and (2) language is inseparable from social activities of man. Thus, it takes actual uses of language as the object of study, in opposition to Chomsky's TG Grammar that takes the ideal speaker's linguistic competence as the object of study.

In Systemic Grammar, the notion of system is made of a central explanatory principle, the whole of language being conceived as a "system of systems".

Systemic Grammar is concerned with establishing a network of systems of relationships, which accounts for all the semantically relevant choices in the language as a whole.

The system network in Systemic Grammar chiefly describes three components of function, or three METAFUNCTIONS. Each of the metafunctions is a complex system consisting of other systems, and choices are simultaneously made from the three metafunctions. This is the close relationship between Systemic Grammar and Functional Grammar.

Halliday's Systemic Grammar contains a functional component, and the theory behind his Functional Grammar (Halliday, 1985/1994) is systemic. According to Halliday, the adult's language becomes much more complex and it has to serve many more functions, and the original functional range of the child's language is gradually reduced to a set of highly coded and abstract functions, which are metafunctions: the ideational, the interpersonal and the textual functions. These metafunctions appear at a new level in the linguistic system, taking the form of "grammar." The grammatical system has, as it were, a functional input and a structural output; it provides the mechanism for different functions to be combined in one utterance in the way the adult requires.

3. Original selecting

The Object of Linguistics

3.1 Definition of Language

What is both the integral and concrete object of linguistics? The question is especially difficult; later we shall see why; here I wish merely to point up the difficulty.

Other sciences work with objects that are given in advance and that can then be considered from different viewpoints; but not linguistics. Someone pronounces the French word nu "bare": a superficial observer would be tempted to call the word a concrete linguistic object; but a more careful examination would reveal successively three or four quite different things, depending on whether the word is considered as a sound, as the expression of an idea, as the equivalent of Latin *nudum*, etc. Far from it being the object that antedates the viewpoint, it would seem that it is the viewpoint that creates the object; besides, nothing tells us in advance that one way of considering the fact in question takes precedence over the others or is in any way superior to them.

Moreover, regardless of the viewpoint that we adopt, the linguistic phenomenon always has two related sides, each deriving its values from the other. For example:

1) Articulated syllables are acoustical impressions perceived by the ear, but the sounds would not exist without the vocal organs; an n, for example, exists only by virtue of the relation between the two sides. We simply cannot reduce language to sound or detach sound from oral articulation; reciprocally, we cannot define the movements of the vocal organs without taking into account the acoustical impression.

2) But suppose that sound were a simple thing: would it constitute speech? No, it is only the instrument of thought; by itself, it has no existence. At this point a new and redoubtable relationship arises: a sound, a complex acoustical-vocal unit, combines in turn with an idea to form a complex physiological-psychological unit. But that is still not the complete picture.

3) Speech has both an individual and a social side, and we cannot conceive of one without the other.

4) Speech always implies both an established system and an evolution; at

every moment it is an existing institution and a product of the past. To distinguish between the system and its history, between what it is and what it was, seems very simple at first glance ; actually the two things are so closely related that we can scarcely keep them apart. Would we simplify the question by studying the linguistic phenomenon in its earliest stages—if we began, for example, by studying the speech of children? No, for in dealing with speech, it is completely misleading to assume that the problem of early characteristics differs from the problem of permanent characteristics. We are left inside the vicious circle.

From whatever direction we approach the question, nowhere do we find the integral object of linguistics. Everywhere we are confronted with a dilemma: if we fix our attention on only one side of each problem, we run the risk of failing to perceive the dualities pointed out above; on the other hand, if we study speech from several viewpoints simultaneously, the object of linguistics appears to us as a confused mass of heterogeneous and unrelated things. Either procedure opens the door to several sciences—psychology, anthropology, normative grammar, philology, etc.—which are distinct from linguistics, but which might claim speech, in view of the faulty method of linguistics, as one of their objects.

As I see it there is only one solution to all the foregoing difficulties: from the very outset we must put both feet on the ground of language and use language as the norm of all other manifestations of speech. Actually, among so many dualities, language alone seems to lend itself to independent definition and provide a fulcrum that satisfies the mind.

But what is language [*langue*]? It is not to be confused with human speech [*langage*], of which it is only a definite part, though certainly an essential one. It is both a social product of the faculty of speech and a collection of necessary conventions that have been adopted by a social body to permit individuals to exercise that faculty. Taken as a whole, speech is many-sided and heterogeneous; straddling several areas simultaneously—physical, physiological, and psychological—it belongs both to the individual and to society; we cannot put it into any category of human facts, for we cannot discover its unity.

Language, on the contrary, is a self-contained whole and a principle of classification. As soon as we give language first place among the facts of speech, we introduce a natural order into a mass that lends itself to no other classification.

One might object to that principle of classification on the ground that since the use of speech is based on a natural faculty whereas language is something acquired and conventional, language should not take first place but should be subordinated to the natural instinct.

That objection is easily refuted.

First, no one has proved that speech, as it manifests itself when we speak, is entirely natural, i. e. that our vocal apparatus was designed for speaking just as our legs were designed for walking. Linguists are far from agreement on this point. For instance Whitney, to whom language is one of several social institutions, thinks that we use the vocal apparatus as the instrument of language purely through luck, for the sake of convenience: men might just as well have chosen gestures and used visual symbols instead of acoustical symbols. Doubtless his thesis is too dogmatic; language.

is not similar in all respects to other social institutions; moreover, Whitney goes too far in saying that our choice happened to fall on the vocal organs; the choice was more or less imposed by nature. But on the essential point the American linguist is right: language is a convention, and the nature of the sign that is agreed upon does not matter. The question of the vocal apparatus obviously takes a secondary place in the problem of speech.

One definition of articulated speech might confirm that conclusion. In Latin, *articulus* means a member, part, or subdivision of a sequence; applied to speech, articulation designates either the subdivision of a spoken chain into syllables or the subdivision of the chain of meanings into significant units;

gegliederte Sprache is used in the second sense in German. Using the second definition, we can say that what is natural to mankind is not oral speech but the faculty of constructing a language, i. e. a system of distinct signs corresponding to distinct ideas.

Broca discovered that the faculty of speech is localized in the third left frontal convolution; his discovery has been used to substantiate the attribution of a natural quality to speech. But we know that the same part of the brain is the center of everything that has to do with speech, including writing. The preceding statements, together with observations that have been made in different cases of aphasia resulting from lesion of the centers of localization, seem to indicate: (1) that the various disorders of oral speech are bound up in a hundred ways with those of written speech; and (2) that what is lost in all cases of aphasia or agraphia is less the faculty of producing a given sound or writing a given sign than the ability to evoke by means of an instrument, regardless of what it is, the signs of a regular system of speech. The obvious implication is that beyond the functioning of the various organs there exists a more general faculty which governs signs and which would be the linguistic faculty proper. And this brings us to the same conclusion as above.

To give language first place in the study of speech, we can advance a final argument: the faculty of articulating words—whether it is natural or not—is exercised only with the help of the instrument created by a collectivity and provided for its use; therefore, to say that language gives unity to speech is not fanciful.

3.2 Place of Language in the Facts of Speech

In order to separate from the whole of speech the part that belongs to language, we must examine the individual act from which the speaking-circuit can be reconstructed. The act requires the presence of at least two persons; that is the minimum number necessary to complete the circuit. Suppose that two people, A andB, are conversing with each other:

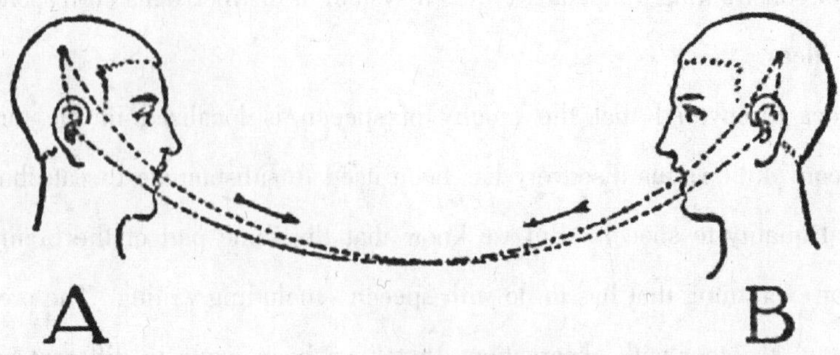

Suppose that the opening of the circuit is in A's brain, where mental facts (concepts) are associated with representations of the linguistic sounds (sound-images) that are used for their expression. A given concept unlocks a corresponding sound-image in the brain; this purely psychological phenomenon is followed in turn by a physiological process: the brain transmits an impulse corresponding to the image to the organs used in producing sounds. Then the sound waves travel from the mouth of A to the ear of B: a purely physical process. Next, the circuit continues in B, but the order is reversed: from the ear to the brain, the physiological transmission of the sound-image; in the brain, the psychological association of the image with the corresponding concept. If B then speaks, the new act will follow—from his brain to A's—exactly the same course as the first act and pass through the same successive phases, which I shall diagram as follows

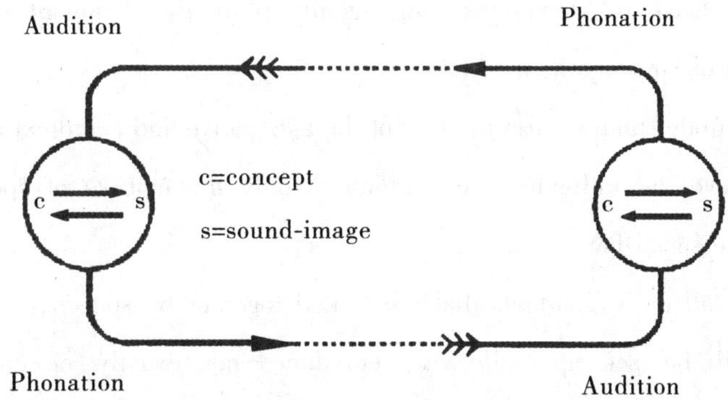

The preceding analysis does not purport to be complete. We might also single out the pure acoustical sensation, the identification of that sensation with the latent sound-image, the muscular image of phonation, etc. I have included only the elements thought to be essential, but the drawing brings out at a glance the distinction between the physical (sound waves), physiological (phonation and audition), and psychological parts (word-images and concepts). Indeed, we should not fail to note that the word-image stands apart from the sound itself and that it is just as psychological as the concept which is associated with it.

The circuit that I have outlined can be further divided into:

a) an outer part that includes the vibrations of the sounds which travel from the mouth to the ear, and an inner part that includes everything else;

b) a psychological and a nonpsychological part, the second including the physiological productions of the vocal organs as well as the physical facts that are outside the individual;

c) an active and a passive part: everything that goes from the associative center of the speaker to the ear of the listener is active, and everything that goes from the ear of the listener to his associative center is passive;

d) finally, everything that is active in the psychological part of the circuit is executive (c —> s), and everything that is passive is receptive (s —> c).

We should also add the associative and coordinating faculty that we find as soon as we leave isolated signs; this faculty plays the dominant role in the organization of language as a system.

But to understand clearly the role of the associative and coordinating faculty, we must leave the individual act, which is only the embryo of speech, and approach the social fact.

Among all the individuals that are linked together by speech, some sort of average will be set up: all will reproduce—not exactly of course, but approximately—the same signs united with the same concepts.

How does the social crystallization of language come about? Which parts of the circuit are involved? For all parts probably do not participate equally in it.

The nonpsychological part can be rejected from the outset. When we hear people speaking a language that we do not know, we perceive the sounds but remain outside the social fact because we do not understand them.

Neither is the psychological part of the circuit wholly responsible: the executive side is missing, for execution is never carried out by the collectivity. Execution is always individual, and the individual is always its master: I shall call the executive side speaking [*parole*].

Through the functioning of the receptive and coordinating faculties, impressions that are perceptibly the same for all are made on the minds of speakers. How can that social product be pictured in such a way that language will stand apart from everything else?

If we could embrace the sum of word-images stored in the minds of all individuals, we could identify the social bond that constitutes language. It is a storehouse filled by the members of a given community through their active use of speaking, a grammatical system that has a potential existence in each brain, or, more specifically, in the brains of a group of individuals. For language is not complete in any speaker; it exists perfectly only within a collectivity.

In separating language from speaking we are at the same time separating:

(1) what is social from what is individual; and (2) what is essential from what is accessory and more or less accidental.

Language is not a function of the speaker; it is a product that is passively assimilated by the individual. It never requires premeditation, and reflection enters in only for the purpose of classification, which we shall take up later.

Speaking, on the contrary, is an individual act. It is wilful and intellectual. Within the act, we should distinguish between: (1) the combinations by which the speaker uses the language code for expressing his own thought; and (2) the psychophysical mechanism that allows him to exteriorize those combinations.

Note that I have defined things rather than words; these definitions are not endangered by certain ambiguous words that do not have identical meanings in different languages. For instance, German *Sprache* means both "language" and "speech"; *Rede* almost corresponds to "speaking" but adds the special connotation of "discourse." Latin *sermo* designates both "speech" and "speaking," while lingua means "language," etc. No word corresponds exactly to any of the notions specified above ; that is why all definitions of words are made in vain; starting from words in defining things is a bad procedure.

To summarize, these are the characteristics of language:

1) Language is a well-defined object in the heterogeneous mass of speech facts. It can be localized in the limited segment of the speaking-circuit where an auditory image becomes associated with a concept. It is the social side of speech, outside the individual who can never create nor modify it by himself; it exists only by virtue of a sort of contract signed by the members of a community. Moreover, the individual must always serve an apprenticeship in order to learn the functioning of language; a child assimilates it only gradually. It is such a distinct thing that a man deprived of the use of speaking retains it provided that he understands the vocal signs that he hears.

2) Language, unlike speaking, is something that we can study separately.

Although dead languages are no longer spoken, we can easily assimilate their linguistic organisms. We can dispense with the other elements of speech; indeed, the science of language is possible only if the other elements are excluded.

3) Whereas speech is heterogeneous, language, as defined, is homogeneous. It is a system of signs in which the only essential thing is the union of meanings and sound-images, and in which both parts of the sign are psychological.

4) Language is concrete, no less so than speaking; and this is a help in our study of it. Linguistic signs, though basically psychological, are not abstractions; associations which bear the stamp of collective approval—and which added together constitute language —are realities that have their seat in the brain. Besides, linguistic signs are tangible; it is possible to reduce them to conventional written symbols, whereas it would be impossible to provide detailed photographs of acts of speaking [*actes de parole*]; the pronunciation of even the smallest word represents an infinite number of muscular movements that could be identified and put into graphic form only with great difficulty. In language, on the contrary, there is only the sound-image, and the latter can be translated into a fixed visual image. For if we disregard the vast number of movements necessary for the realization of sound-images in speaking, we see that each sound-image is nothing more than the sum of a limited number of elements or phonemes that can in turn be called up by a corresponding number of written symbols. The very possibility of putting the things that relate to language into graphic form allows dictionaries and grammars to represent it accurately, for language is a storehouse of soundimages, and writing is the tangible form of those images.

3.3 Place of Language in Human Facts: Semiology

The foregoing characteristics of language reveal an even more important characteristic. Language, once its boundaries have been marked off within the speech data, can be classified among human phenomena, whereas speech cannot.

We have just seen that language is a social institution; but several features set it apart from other political, legal, etc. institutions. We must call in a new type of facts in order to illuminate the special nature of language.

Language is a system of signs that express ideas, and is therefore comparable to a system of writing, the alphabet of deaf-mutes, S5Tnbolic rites, polite formulas, military signals, etc. But it is the most important of all these systems.

A science that studies the life of signs within society is conceivable; it would be a part of social psychology and consequently of general psychology; I shall call it *semiology* (from Greek sēmeîon "sign"). Semiology would show what constitutes signs, what laws govern them. Since the science does not yet exist, no one can say what it would be ; but it has a right to existence, a place staked out in advance. Linguistics is only a part of the general science of semiology; the laws discovered by semiology will be applicable to linguistics, and the latter will circumscribe a well-defined area within the mass of anthropological facts.

To determine the exact place of semiology is the task of the psychologist. The task of the linguist is to find out what makes language a special system within the mass of semiological data. This issue will be taken up again later; here I wish merely to call attention to one thing: if I have succeeded in assigning linguistics a place among the sciences, it is because I have related it to semiology.

Why has semiology not yet been recognized as an independent science with its own object like all the other sciences? Linguists have been going around in circles: language, better than anything else, offers a basis for understanding the semiological problem; but language must, to put it correctly, be studied in itself; heretofore language has almost always been studied in connection with something else, from other viewpoints.

There is first of all the superficial notion of the general public: people see nothing more than a name-giving system in language, thereby prohibiting any research into its true nature.

Then there is the viewpoint of the psychologist, who studies the sign-mechanism in the individual; this is the easiest method, but it does not lead beyond individual execution and does not reach the sign, which is social.

Or even when signs are studied from a social viewpoint, only the traits that attach language to the other social institutions—those that are more or less voluntary—are emphasized; as a result, the goal is by-passed and the specific characteristics of semiological systems in general and of language in particular are completely ignored. For distinguishing characteristic of the sign—but the one that is least apparent at first sight—is that in some way it always eludes the individual or social will.

In short, the characteristic that distinguishes semiological systems from all other institutions shows up clearly only in language where it manifests itself in the things which are studied least, and the necessity or specific value of a semiological science is therefore not clearly recognized. But to me the language problem is mainly semiological, and all developments derive their significance from that important fact. If we are to discover the true nature of language we must learn what it has in common with all other semiological systems; linguistic forces that seem very important at first glance (e. g., the role of the vocal apparatus) will receive only secondary consideration if they serve only to set language apart from the other systems. This procedure will do more than to clarify the linguistic problem. By studying rites, customs, etc. as signs, I believe that we shall throw new light on the facts and point up the need for including them in a science of semiology and explaining them by its laws. ①

① 摘自索绪尔. 普通语言学教程[M]. 北京：中国社会科学出版社，1999.

References

[1] Bussmann H. Routledge Dictionary of Language and Linguistics. Translated and edited by Gregory Trauth and Kerstin Kazzazi. London: Routledge, 1996.

[2]Lyons J. Semantics (Vol. 2) [M]. Cambridge: Cambridge University Press, 1977.

[3]罗宾斯. 普通语言学概论[M]. 北京: 外语教学与研究出版社, 2000.

[4]索绪尔. 普通语言学教程[M]. 北京: 外语教学与研究出版社, 2001.

[5]胡壮麟. 语言学教程[M]. 北京:北京大学出版社,2002.

第二章

应用语言学

导　读

应用语言学是一门涉猎范围很广的学科,到目前为止还没有明确的范围和定义。通常的理解分广义和狭义两种:狭义的应用语言学专指外语教学,广义的应用语言学是语言学在各方面的应用以及各有关实际领域的学问的统称。"应用语言学所关心的是如何应用语言学理论、方法和成果来阐释其他应用领域所遇到的跟语言有关的问题。"(齐沪扬 2004:2)

1871 年,波兰语言学家博杜恩·德·库尔特内(J. Baudouin de Courtenay)首次提出"应用语言学"这个术语,并提出要区分"纯粹语言学"和"应用语言学"。但是,库尔特内的努力并没有引起人们的重视,直到 20 世纪 40 年代,外语教学的蓬勃发展才使人们意识到了应用语言学的重要性。

1958 年,英国爱丁堡大学建立了应用语言学学院,以培养应用语言学的专门人才。目前,爱丁堡大学仍然是应用语言学研究的主要阵地,他们出版的系列教材在世界通用。应用语言学是一个相对独立的学科,它有明确的研究任务和对象。其次,应用语言学具有实用性的特点,它可以指导语言康复、语言规划和语言政策等实际问题。另外,应用语言学还具有实验性和综合性等特点。我们可以结合实验数据和问卷调查等方式对语言的各种应用现象进行综合研究。

作为一个同现实紧密联系的语言学分支,应用语言学在未来的语言研究中必将扮演越来越重要的角色。

1. Definitions

1.1 applied linguistics

Term covering several linguistic subdisciplines as well as certain interdisciplinary areas that use linguistic methods: language pedagogy, psycholinguistics, language acquisition, second language acquisition, translation, contrastive analysis, language planning, lexicography, computational linguistics, ethnolinguistics, sociolinguistics, and others. Applied linguistics differs from theoretical linguistics in that the latter is concerned with the formal structure of language as an autonomous system of signs. The term "applied linguistics" is in some cases misleading, since in many of the subdisciplines language is studied from both a theoretical and practical (i. e. applied) perspective. Moreover, some areas should be considered "applications" of linguistics. Applied linguistics has become a field of growing linguistic interest, as evidenced by the many journals devoted to these allied studies which have been launched since the 1960s.

(Bussmann 1996: 77)

In a broad sense, applied linguistics is concerned with increasing understanding of the role of language in human affairs and thereby with providing the knowledge necessary for those who are responsible for taking language-related decisions whether the need for these arises in the classroom, the workplace, the law court, or the laboratory.

(Wilkins 1999:7)

The applications of linguistics to other activities serving particular purposes in the world are collective known as applied linguistics.

(Robins 2000: 11)

Applied linguistics is the study of second and foreign language learning and teaching; the study of language and linguistics in relation to practical problems, such as LEXICOGRAPHY, TRANSLATION, SPEECH PATHOLOGY, etc. Applied linguistics uses information from sociology, psychology, anthropology, and INFORMATION THEORY as well as from linguistics in order to develop its own theoretical models of language and language use, and then uses this information and theory in practical areas such as syllabus design, SPEECH THERAPY, LANGUAGE PLANNING, STYLISTICS, etc.

(Richards 2005: 36)

1.2 lexicography

Theory and practice of compiling dictionaries. Lexicography provides the principles necessary for documenting the **vocabulary** of a language, a dialect or a profession by drawing on **lexicology** with its theoretical bases and materials for lexicographic codification and by taking practical concerns such as marketability, userfriendliness, etc. into consideration.

(Bussmann 1996: 682)

Lexicography is the art of dictionary making. Foreign language lexicography involves the development of dictionaries for language learners.

(Richards 2005: 397)

1.3 speech pathology

It is the study of abnormalities in the development and use of language in children and adults (such as STUTTERING and APHASIA). Speech pathology includes the diagnosis of such disorders and the development of techniques (including clinical techniques) to treat them. Speech therapists (see SPEECH THERAPY) are sometimes called **speech pathologists or speech/language pathologists**, especially in the USA.

(Richards 2005: 645)

1.4 language planning

It is often carried out by a government or government agency, concerning choice of national or official language(s), support for minority and community languages, ways of spreading the use of one or more languages, spelling reforms, the addition of new words to the language, and other language problems. Through language planning, an official language policy is established and/or implemented. For example, in Indonesia, Malay was chosen as the national language and was given the name Bahasa Indonesia (Indonesian language). It became the main language of education. There were several spelling reforms and a national planning agency was established to deal with problems such as the development of scientific terms. In pluralistic countries or in federal states, language planning may not be monolithic and several "plans" may coexist. Teachers' implementation of programmes such as BILINGUAL EDUCATION or resistance to such plans may also have an effect on language planning at the local or micro-level.

(Richards 2005: 377)

2. Classical theories

2.1 Origin and definition of applied linguistics

The term "applied linguistics" was first introduced as early as 1871 by the

Polish linguist J. Baudouin de Courtenay, who drew attention to the necessity for the distinction between pure linguistics and applied linguistics, and pointed out that applied linguistics aimed to solve problems in various fields by applying the knowledge of linguistics. But applied linguistics was a sub-discipline of linguistics for decades; it was not until 1946 that it was established as an independent discipline at the University of Michigan in the United States, and it was not until the 1960s that it began to develop vigorously.

The birth of applied linguistics as a discipline is closely associated with foreign language teaching. During World War II the global commitments thrust upon the United States and many of its citizens, military as well as civilian, required them to learn foreign languages. When the army called upon the linguists for help, they responded not only by compiling language guides and military phrase books, but also by setting up a series of intensive courses in many languages. They established a method especially for the solders, which was known as the "army method" or "oral-aural method", and later the method was applied with great success to the teaching of English as a foreign language (TEFL) to non-native speakers of English. We can see that at first, applied linguistics referred to the application of linguistics to teaching foreign languages. In October, 1964, the first World Congress of Applied Linguistics was held in Nancy, France, and the Association Internationale de Linguistique Appliquée (AILA) was set up. This marked the recognition of the status of applied linguistics as an independent discipline.

Considering that applied linguistics as a unified field of study came into being only in the late 1950s, it has blossomed and diversified in a remarkably rapid way. In 2002, the American Association of Applied Linguistics (AAAL) conference lists 18 topic areas for applied linguistics:

1. language and its acquisition
2. language and assessment

3. language and the brain
4. language and cognition
5. language and culture
6. language and ideology
7. language and instruction
8. language and interaction
9. language and listening
10. language and media
11. language and policy
12. language and reading
13. language and research methodology
14. language and society
15. language and speaking
16. language and technology
17. language and translation/interpretation
18. language and writing

Grabe and Kaplan say, "it is a central feature of applied linguistics that it is task-related, problem-oriented, project-centered, and demand-led." They think the term *applied linguistics* (AL) has been in use at least since the founding of the University of Edinburgh School of Applied Linguistics in 1956, and of the Center for Applied Linguistics in Washington, D. C., in 1957.

2.2 Source and target of applied linguistics

The urgent question mark against applied linguistics is this: just what is its source, what exactly is being applied? If the interpretation of applied linguistics is very narrow so that what is being applied is only linguistics, then because linguistics, like other theoretical disciplines, deals with idealisations, it appears to have very little to say about the language-related problems in what we call the real world. If applied linguistics is interpreted very broadly, then it must concern itself with everything to do with language. Neither position is tenable. Linguistics, it seems, must play an important role in applied linguistics but by no means the only role. Applied linguistics must also draw on psychology, sociology, education, measurement theory and so on.

It may be that we shall gain a clearer picture of the nature of applied linguistics if we turn our attention away from the source (what applied linguistics draws on) to its target (what applied linguistics equips you to do). The target clearly cannot be anything and everything to do with language. Corder's solution was to focus on language teaching, widely interpreted and therefore including, for example, speech therapy, translation and language planning. Such narrowing of the target still makes sense today, which is why most of the entries in the *Glossary of Applied Linguistics* (Davies 2005) have some connection with language teaching. My reasoning is that it remains true that many of those who study applied linguistics have been and will continue to be involved at some level in language teaching, which is, after all, the largest profession involved in language studies. This is not to say, once a language teacher always one: some, perhaps many, of those who engage with applied linguistics move on to research, administration and so on. But in preparing the *Glossary* I have found it helpful to provide myself with this constraint on what it is we claim as applied linguistics.

What that means is that, while we accept Brumfit's definition —"A working definition of applied linguistics will then be the theoretical and empirical investi gation of real-world problems in which language is a central issue" — I avoid the danger of the "science of everything" position by targeting language teaching, at the same time recognising that the world of language learning and teaching is not an artificial world but one that must engage every day with Brumfit's real-world problems. These real-world problems involve success and failure, ability and disability, ethical, cultural and gender issues, technology and lack of resources, the difficult and the simple, and the child and the adult.

2.3 language learning

The journal *Language Learning: A Journal of Applied Linguistics*, published from the University of Michigan, is an important chronicle of the development of applied linguistics over the past sixty years (Catford 1998). In a 1993 editorial the journal gave late recognition to the range of coverage beyond linguistics which applied linguistics embraced. Such recognition is significant. Coming out of the tradition of Charles Fries and Robert Lado at the University of Michigan, *Language Learning*, founded in 1948, was 'the first journal in the world to carry the term "applied linguistics" in its title' (*Language Learning* 1967:1). But by "applied linguistics" what was meant was the application of linguistics.

In the 1990s, the journal seems to have finally accepted a more catholic view. The 1993 editors remark on "the wide range of foundation theories and research methodologies now used to study language issues" (Cumming 1993) and they state that they intend to:

> Encourage the submission of more manuscripts from (a) diverse disciplines, including applications of methods and theories from linguistics, psycholinguistics, cognitive science, ethnography, ethnomethodology, sociolinguistics, sociology, semiotics, educational inquiry and cultural or historical studies, to address (b) fundamental issues in language learning, such as multilingualism, language acquisition, second and foreign language education, literacy, culture, cognition, pragmatics and intergroup relations.

However, the official recognition of "the wide range of foundation theories and research methodologies now used to study language issues" comes at a price. That price is the abandoning of the term "applied linguistics" as a sub-heading in the journal's title. The explanation for this removal is that its replacement title,

Language Learning: *A Journal of Research in Language Studies*, is now seen to be wider. What the editor appears to have meant by this change of title is to declare his interpretation of what applied linguistics is, knowing full well that the readers of the journal will understand "a journal of research in language studies" as a functional interpretation of "applied linguistics."

Getting rid of the label "applied linguistics" has been widely canvassed, on the grounds that it was the wrong term in the first place, introduced only to give academic respectability to degrees, courses and departments. Such was the view taken in the 1960s by the authors of the key text (Halliday, McIntosh and Strevens 1964). They recognised the oddity of the label "applied linguistics" but seemed prepared to live with it. The label was, they opined, misleading. It was misleading because (at the time of writing) it excluded many activities of linguistics (for example, machine translation, sociolinguistics) as well as activities which had a bearing on language teaching (for example psychology, educational theory). They wrote: "the aim of courses in applied linguistics, such as are now available, for example at Edinburgh, Leeds and London, is not to produce specialists in linguistics and phonetics ... but to give a solid grounding in those aspects of these and other subjects which lie behind the language class."

In consequence, the label "applied linguistics" was not used in the title of their book: *The Linguistics Sciences and Language Teaching*. Shades of the *Language Learning* unease about the term?

2.4 Restricting the scope

The Edinburgh Course in Applied Linguistics (Allen and Corder 1973 - 5, Allen and Davies 1977) did not have as a subtitle: "in language teaching." It was taken for granted in the 1960s and 1970s that applied linguistics was about language teaching. That was Pit Corder's view (Corder 1973) and at the time it mattered. It mattered because after the Second World War the expansion of language teaching (especially of English) revealed that many teachers and trainers and supervisors of teachers lacked knowledge about language. That gap is what applied linguistics was set up to fill. Over the next fifty years it became more likely that those entering teaching had already studied aspects of linguistics. They no longer needed post-experience knowledge of language. Linguistics had become mainstream. That was its success. At the same time applied linguistics had also been successful. Its dedication to language teaching had been remarked in other areas of language use, especially institutional language use (Howatt 1984), leading to an explosion of applied linguistics training, methodology and, perhaps above all, labeling in those other areas. Thus in the Anniversary Issue of the ALAA Newsletter (January 2001: No. 44) we read of developments over the past twenty years which "draw on a greater range of disciplines in our research" (Lewis 2001: 19): "applied linguistics is trying to resolve language-based problems that people encounter in the real world" (Grabe 2001: 25); "Applied Linguistics ... has undergone a significant broadening of its scope and now contributes its theoretical perspectives to a range of areas" (Baynham 2001: 26).

Of course, if the source of applied linguistics (the training, student curricula for beginners) is generally agreed, there is no reason in principle why applied linguistics should not take an interest in anything to do with language. That no doubt is the position taken by a publisher such as Mouton de Gruyter by devoting a forty-fivepage brochure to its applied linguistics list. Applied linguistics, according to this grouping, encompasses: Language Acquisition (L1 and L2), Psycho/Neuro-linguistics, Language Teaching, Sociolinguistics, Humor Studies, Pragmatics, Discourse Analysis/Rhetorics, Text/Processing/Translation, Computational Linguistics — Machine Translation, Corpus Linguistics, and Language Control/Dialectology.

3. Original selecting

Chapter 1 History and "definitions"

"In Anna Karenina and Onegin not a single problem is solved but they satisfy you completely just because all the problems are correctly presented."

(Anton Chekov, letter to Alexei Suvorin, 27 October 1888,
in L. Hellman (ed.), *Selected Letters of Anton Chekov*, 1955,
translated by S. Lederer)

3.1 DEFINITIONS

Applied linguistics does not lend itself to an easy definition, perhaps because, as Vivian Cook remarks: "Applied Linguistics means many things to many people" (Cook 2006). This absence of certainty is much bemoaned by those who practice applied linguistics but the lack of consensus can be found in other academic enterprises, especially those in the humanities and social sciences, where frag-mentation is rife, sometimes acting as an escape from disagreement and entrenched epistemological disputes as to the nature of the enterprise. Applied linguistics has a further definitional problem because, if the nature of the enterprise is disputed, what agreement can there be as to what it is that is being applied? A mediation between theory and practice (Kaplan and Widdowson 1992: 76); a synthesis of research from a variety of disciplines, including linguistics (Hudson 1999); "it presupposes linguistics ... one cannot apply what one does not know" (Corder 1973: 7); it is "understood as an open field, in which those inhabiting or passing through simply show a common commitment to the potential value of dialogue with people who are different" (Rampton 1997: 14). And taking up what some will regard as an extreme position: "critical applied linguistics ... opens up a whole new array of questions and concerns, issues such as identity, sexuality, access, ethics, disparity, difference, desire, or the reproduction of Otherness that have hitherto not been considered as concerns related to applied linguistics" (Pennycook 2004: 803 – 804).

What most introductions and collections try to do is to use applied linguistics concerns and activities in order to illustrate and then analyse what applied linguistics methods and purposes are (see for example van Els et al. 1984, Davies et al. 1999, Spolsky 1999, Schmitt 2002, Cook 2003, Davies and Elder 2004, Sealey and Carter 2004, Kaplan and Baldauf 2005). This is the approach by ostensive definition: if you want to know about applied linguistics, "look around you" (as the inscription on Wren's memorial in St Paul's Cathedral exhorts). Extreme versions of this approach can be found in Rampton (1997), postgraduate courses which operate as à la carte and even the anti-arguments of Pennycook (2004). The trouble with such views is that they offer no help in constructing introductory syllabuses in applied linguistics for initiates and they lack clarity as to how a determination can be made on those initiates' success in demonstrating that they should be admitted to the profession.

The ostensive view is defended by Spolsky:

> the definition of a field can reasonably be explored by looking at the professionals involved in its study ... Applied Linguistics [is now] a cover term for a sizeable group of semi-autonomous disciplines, each dividing its parentage and allegiances between the formal study of language and other relevant fields, and each working to develop its own methodologies and principles.
>
> (Spolsky 2005: 36)

Robert Kaplan, founding editor of the *Annual Review of Applied Linguistics*, whose career has been spent championing applied linguistics and whose

Handbook (Kaplan 2005) has been followed by a Festschrift (Bruthiaux et al. 2005), has long been concerned about the status of applied linguistics, convinced that what it had to offer was not always understood or valued. This was a way of speculating about the nature of applied linguistics.

Ostensive definitions are rejected by those who argue for a dictionary definition, who maintain that there is, indeed, an applied linguistics core which should be required of all those attempting the *rite du passage*. Widdowson, for example, argues strongly for the coherence of applied linguistics, dismissing as illogical the commonly held view that applied linguistics is a gallimaufry, a coming-together in an *adhoc* way of different disciplines (Widdowson 2005). Cook agrees with Widdowson: 'the task of applied linguistics is to mediate' between linguistics and language use (Cook 2003: 20).

Guy Cook defines applied linguistics as "the academic discipline concerned with the relation of knowledge about language to decision making in the real world" (ibid: 5). He recognises that 'the scope of applied linguistics remains rather vague' but attempts to delimit its main areas of concern as consisting of language and education; language, work and law; and language information and effect (ibid 7/8). Delimi -tations of this kind are helpful, even if they remain contestable. What is important is that applied linguistics is protected from the sneer that because language is everywhere, applied linguistics is the science of everything. In the thirty-two contributions to the *Handbook of Applied Linguistics* (Davies and Elder 2004) we attempted to provide a wide coverage, ranging from an interest largely in language itself (for example language descriptions, lexicography) to a concern for interventions in institutional language use (for example language maintenance, language teacher education). In presenting the edited volume we offered an overall schema, accepting that while there probably is a cline from the most theoretical to the most practical, our initial plan to oppose linguistics applied with applied linguistics (Davies and Elder 2004) was not tenable.

Lexicography typically makes use of the ostensive approach in the sense that inclusion in a dictionary provides an incremental defining of the area. This is particularly the case with the glossary or encyclopedic type of dictionary which describes the key terminology in an area of interest (for example politics, biology, applied linguistics) and by doing so defines it. This is what I attempted in my *Glossary of Applied Linguistics* (Davies 2005a), which offers an account of the field but of course has all the weakness of being only one person's view.

3.2 ETAL SERIES AND APPLIED LINGUISTICS CURRICULA

Corder (1973) was well aware that in limiting the coverage of applied linguistics to language teaching he was open to criticism. To some extent his defence was the mirror image of the *Language Learning* change of name. There the rationale was that the input was too undefined and therefore it was sensible to remove the label of applied linguistics. Corder argues that it is the output or target that is without shape and therefore it makes sense to limit the area of concern to one main object, that of language teaching.

Spolsky (1978) has proposed a different solution, that is to limit the name of the output to Corder's area of concern and to call it "educational linguistics," a proposal he has put into action in his *Concise Encyclopedia of Educational Linguistics* (Spolsky 1999 and Spolsky and Hult in press and see Chapter 4 below).

There are voices insisting that applied linguistics should fulfil a role wider than language teaching (for example Kaplan 1980a). There is a seductive appeal in such a view, an appeal which slips all too easily into a science of everything position. M. Bloomfield appears to beckon to this:

> This volume, then, concentrates on the human problems of language and tries to identify some of them and so indicate what is being done about them.

> The rise of ethnic consciousness and militancy as well as a general dissatisfaction with the "way things are" have led to a new stress on what may be called applied linguistics and the social dialect problems ... Problems of literacy, translation, bilingualism, language teaching, language and nationalism, the role of dialects and so forth have become urgent and some of our best minds have begun to turn towards these matters.
>
> (M. Bloomfield 1975: xviii)

What Bloomfield is suggesting is no different from what others (for example Brumfit) have proposed but the magnitude of the responsibility he lays on applied linguistics makes the modest scope proposed by Corder quite appealing.

The extent to which applied linguists see themselves as agents of change is controversial (Pennycook 2001, Davies 2003b, Sealey and Carter 2004). As current concerns with the ethics of the human sciences remind us, there is a tension for social scientists between their role as objective students of society and as agents of change. Such an opposition was noted in the 1960s in the area of cultural anthropology. Commenting on the field, Margaret Mead wrote:

> There is some difference at present between (a) those who would regard applied anthropology as a profession for which anthropologists, in addition to a theoretical education in some branch of anthropology, must be specially trained and within which professional standards should prevail; and (b) those who identify applied anthropology with a form of anthropological research which either continuously or at some point becomes part of and affects, the process of change which it studies. It must be stressed that either view involves a search for values, rooted in the discipline of anthropology, which can guide the applied anthropologist in any use of his knowledge at any level of interaction in human affairs.
>
> (Mead 1964: 33)

The more involved with human affairs the scholar becomes, the more difficult it is, as Mead argues, to resist the second alternative, which means that scientific objectivity is no longer possible (Skutnabb-Kangas, Phillipson and Bannut 1994, Searle 1995). Like applied cultural anthropology, applied linguistics has also felt the tug of the particular and the urge to identify locally. We take up this dilemma in Chapter 2 and again in Chapter 7 where I discuss critical discourse analysis and critical applied linguistics.

A glossary, with all its limitations, is one way of defining the field. Another is to survey the volumes that have followed the first edition of this Introduction to Applied Linguistics in the series Edinburgh Textbooks in Applied Linguistics. Since 1999, when ETAL 1 was published, eight volumes have appeared. These are, in order of publication:

Teaching Literature in a Second Language (Brian Parkinson and Helen Reid Thomas) 2000

Materials Evaluation and Design for Language Teaching (Ian McGrath) 2002

The Social Turn in Second Language Acquisition (David Block) 2003

Language Assessment and Programme Evaluation (Brian Lynch) 2003

Linguistics and the Language of Translation (Kirsten Malmkjaer) 2005

Pragmatic Stylistics (Elizabeth Black) 2006

Language Planning and Education (Gibson Ferguson) 2006

Language and Politics (John Joseph) 2006

The idea throughout the series has been that an author should explore a problem area of language use in which applied linguistics can take an informed position, informed both by understanding of the context, widely interpreted, and of the language involved. In addition, we attempted to link specialisms as a way of examining our premise that there is a general field of applied linguistics which is not just an agglomeration of unconnected interests. Let us look briefly at the eight volumes.

In the Preface to *Teaching Literature in a Second Language*, *the authors write*:

Although the book contains practical ideas, the emphasis is on principles rather than on specific recipes or model lessons, and the aim is to inform teacher choice rather than promote a particular method.

(Parkinson and Reid Thomas 2000: ix)

In his *Materials Evaluation and Design for Language Teaching*, McGrath maintains:

Those with a responsibility for the development and administration of languagelearning programmes in either educational or workplace settings will need little persuading that materials evaluation and design, along with, for example, syllabus design, learner assessment and the study of classroom processes are centrally important applied-linguistic activities.

(McGrath 2002: 1)

In *The Social Turn in Second Language Acquisition*, Block sets out to:

explore the extent to which Second Language acquisition researchers ... might adopt a more interdisciplinary and socially informed approach to their research [taking] a cue from recent debate about the present and future of applied linguistics.

(Block 2003: 1)

Lynch's purpose in *Language Assessment and Programme Evaluation* is to:

present the range of paradigms, perspectives, designs, purposes, methods, analyses and approaches to validity and ethics that commonly define language assessment and programme evaluation.

(Lynch 2003: vii)

Malmkjaer in *Linguistics and the Language of Translation* writes that the:

book is for students of translation, languages and linguistics who would like to enhance their understanding of the relationships between translation studies and linguistics-of how linguistics can be applied to the creation, description and constructive criticism of translation.

(Malmkjaer 2005: ix)

Black attempts to show in *Pragmatic Stylistics* that:

> Applied Linguistics can make a contribution to the study of literature ... The ways in which we interpret ordinary language use are relevant to the ways in which we interpret literary discourse-which is only the language of the time, written by people who are more adept at manipulating its nuances than most of us. But I shall try to show that we follow roughly the same procedures whether we are listening to a friend, reading a newspaper or reading a literary work.
>
> (Black 2006: 1)

Ferguson maintains in *Language Planning and Education* that his book:

> is approached from an applied linguistics perspective, meaning that educational concerns and the relationships of language planning to education feature prominently ... [L] anguage planning/language policy is an interdisciplinary field with a very wide scope, geographically as well as conceptually.
>
> (Ferguson 2006: ix)

In his *Language and Politics*, Joseph writes that:

> in the last decade, applied linguistics has abandoned the structuralist view of language as a self-contained, neutral system, in favour of a conception of language as political from top to bottom. This book examines the consequences of that conceptual shift, as it draws together key topics including language choice, linguistic correctness, (self-) censorship and hate speech, the performance of ethnic and national identity in language, gender politics and 'powerful' language, rhetoric and propaganda, and changing conceptions of written language, driven in part by technological advances.
>
> (Joseph 2006: ix)

The socialisation of both the child and the adult is an acculturation process: for the child, the initiating into the language and culture of the group, and for the adult, the introducing into the responsibilities of being an adult within his or her community. Independent actors engage in various domains, one of the most important being that of work. Much of the professionalising process is made up of acculturation into the shared knowledge and skills of the profession the initiate is entering. This is the case of applied linguistics and a clue to the requirements made of the neophyte can be found in the curricula of institutions offering qualifications in applied linguistics. What these show (the sample surveyed including institutions in Europe, the USA, Australia and Asia) is a degree of similarity. In the core curriculum, all institutions required a course in linguistic analysis, over half in research methods and again in sociolinguistics, and just under half in SLA and in psycholinguistics. The options on offer, of which students were expected to take one, two or three, ranged very widely, from statistics to translation. But in all cases, one core or one option in each institution had the term "teaching" in its title (TESOL, Teacher Education and so on).

3.3 APPLIED FIELDS

The doubt as to its role and uncertainty as to its status that trouble applied linguistics, along with its uneasy relationship with linguistics (theoretical or general), may seem uniquely distressing to applied linguists but they are not uncommon among the applied disciplines. Of the lack of status there is no doubt. Even the utility of applied disciplines is called into account. The famous scientist T. H. Huxley (known as Darwin's Bulldog) asserted before the Cowper Commission of 1892 that "the primary business of the universities is with pure knowledge and pure art-independent of all application to practice; with progress in culture not with increase in wealth" (Bibby 1956: 377).

It seems that "applied" disciplines are still struggling for academic status. We see this in an array of applied disciplines, for example, mathematics, physics, philosophy, sociology, engineering and anthropology. In each case some criterion is appealed to as making the distinction between the pure and the applied. In mathematics it is proof. Pure mathematics, according to those who profess it, is what is proved. Applied physics is marked by technological or practical use. Applied sociology relates to the world of work outside academia. Applied engineering requires input from a range of disciplines outside engineering. Applied anthropology makes a similar point. It is defined as the elucidation of practical problems in, for example, the fields of public health, clinical medicine and psychiatry (Barnard and Spencer 1996: 359). It has its roots, Barnard and Spencer tell us, "in work on behalf of colonial administrations but is now firmly established in contexts as diverse as development agencies, health education and social work, as well as work for private sector corporations" (ibid: 595 – 596).

Both applied engineering and applied anthropology, then, make the case for their applied discipline in terms of the target. Whether these varied "applied" targets have an influence on the training/education that is given is unclear but it seems reasonable to assume there is no differentiation, certainly not at the undergraduate level. The "source," that is the training provided, is the same. Where there is differentiation is at the postgraduate level. A general undergraduate training/education is followed by a range of specialisms. This assumes that the different specialisms can all draw equally on the same preparation. To an extent, this explains the proliferation in British universities of taught one-year Master's degrees which can provide the variety of specialist inputs (including in applied linguistics).

Applied linguistics began life in the 1950s as a postgraduate qualification. Its initial target, largely language teaching, has always been practical, policy-oriented. Its preparation at postgraduate level has been multidisciplinary and, as in mathematics, there is a continuing tension between pure (general, theoretical) linguistics and applied linguistics. It does not expect its conclusions to be buttressed with certainty (and it is unclear whether theoretical linguistics or any other social science can expect that, either). For applied linguistics, there is no finality: the problems such as how to assess language proficiency, what is the optimum age to begin a second language, what distinguishes native and non-native speakers, how we can treat memory loss, these problems may find local and temporary solutions but the problems recur. No doubt, once again, the same may be said of theoretical linguistics: whether all grammars are fundamentally one grammar; what the relation is between the sign and the referent; answers are partial, never final-the problems remain.

For the other applied subjects we have mentioned, it appears that those wishing for an applied outcome are normally expected to have followed the general under-graduate programme. This cannot be expected in applied linguistics, for two reason. First, because in spite of the availability of undergraduate courses in general or theoretical linguistics (or often just linguistics), it is normal to admit students to an applied linguistics postgraduate course without that training. A degree is required but often there is flexibility as to its area of study. The second reason, which probably impacts on the first, is the centrality to applied linguistics of the English language and of teaching English. The majority of entrants to an applied linguistics course will still have first-hand experience of TEFL and that means that students, both native and non-native English speakers, bring to their applied linguistics degree course their awareness and understanding of the English language and their proficiency in it. Nowadays, the insistence on previous practical language teaching experience may well be relaxed in the case of a student who has other relevant experience, in journalism, publishing, translating and so on. But in the majority of cases, experience of teaching English or another language or both is still the norm.

3.4 APPLIED LINGUISTICS THE UNMARKED FORM

The influence of English on the development of applied linguistics cannot be exaggerated (Phillipson 1992). In the medieval university Latin played the same role. In order to develop an educated work-force for whom Latin then (as English now) was the lingua franca, training in Latin structure and in logic, discourse and trans- ation was necessary. Hence the emphasis on grammar in the *trivium* (an analogue of which remains today in the Honours Moderations at Oxford University as the first part of the degree of *Literae Humaniores* or classics). Should we regard that type of interest as a form of applied linguistics? Would it perhaps be more accurate to see it as a precursor of linguistics?

If that is accepted, then we could extend the argument, first by suggesting that investigations (and teaching) are always prompted by socio-political and economic imperatives, which in the middle ages demanded the provision of an educated professional class of clerics and lawyers. That imperative, we might suggest, is what drives speculation ("pure research") rather than the other way round. Applied disciplines, it follows, develop in order to provide the necessary training in newly emerging technical and professional occupations.

This again suggests that the relation between theoretical linguistics and applied linguistics should place applied linguistics in the pole position. Applied linguistics can then be seen to be the driver, with linguistics following behind to respond to the practical questions applied linguistic raises, attempting to answer them and by doing so widening its range of coverage. Take second language acquisition, now firmly within theoretical linguistics but itself in origin a very practical study of error analysis in TEFL; or critical discourse analysis and other areas of stylistics or LSPs, now drawn into the wider study within sociolinguistics of language variation; or translation a seriously practical pursuit and now slowly becoming absorbed into comparative linguistics.

Of course, there are important and continuing distinctions between general or theoretical linguistics and applied linguistics. They may be summarised by:

- the immediate and the distant, with applied linguistics concerned with the former; and
- the need to expand to other disciplines because of the involvement of factors outside the scope of language. Applied linguistics is clearly multi-factorial in that in addition to linguistics, it draws on other disciplines, psychology, sociology, education, politics and so on. Ironically, as has become clear in the last period, linguistics also needs to do the same and cannot isolate itself from the daily uses of language.

3.5 CONCLUSION

In this chapter I have considered recent attempts to define applied linguistics, emphasising the importance of various ostensive methods of definition and comparing the lack of clarity about applied linguistics to that of other applied disciplines. The chapter ends with the unorthodox suggestion that all linguistic study is basically applied linguistics, with applied linguistics seeking out and working on language problems which linguistics responds to by idealising and then analysing in terms of current linguistic theory. ①

References

[1] Baynham M. Anniversary Newsletter of the Applied Linguistics Association of Australia, 2001.

[2] Bussmann H. Routledge Dictionary of Language and Linguistics. Translated and edited by Gregory Trauth and Kerstin Kazzazi. London:

① 摘自 Davies A. An Introduction to Applied Linguistics [M]. Edinburg: Edinburgh University Press, 2007.

Routledge, 1996.

[3] Catford J. C. Language Learning and the Applied Linguistics: A Historical Sketch[J]. Language Learning, 1998,48(4).

[4] Corder S. Pit. Introducing Applied Linguistics[M]. Harmondsworth: Penguins, 1973.

[5] Grabe William. Anniversary Newsletter of the Applied Linguistics Association of Australia, 2001.

[6] Howatt Anthony P. R. A History of English Language Teaching[M]. Oxford: Oxford University Press, 1984.

[7] Lewis P. Anniversary Newsletter of the Applied Linguistics Association of Australia, 2001.

[8]理查兹.朗文语言教学及应用语言学辞典[M].北京:外语教学与研究出版社,2005.

[9]齐沪扬,陈昌来.应用语言学纲要[M].上海:复旦大学出版社,2004.

第三章

语用学

导　读

早在古希腊时期人们就开始关注语言的使用,而现代意义上的语用研究则脱胎于语言哲学,特别是后期维特根斯坦(Ludwig Wittgenstein)“意义即使用”的思想。1938 年,美国符号学家莫里斯(Charles Morris)提出语用学(Pragmatics)这一术语,用来指研究符号①与符号解释者之间关系的学科。显然,它最初主要是研究语言和解释语言的人之间的关系。目前,语用学的理论主要包括言语行为理论(Speech Act Theory)、合作原则(Cooperative Principle)、礼貌原则(Politeness Principle)和关联理论(Relevance Theory)等。

1962 年,奥斯汀(John Austin)提出的言语行为理论是语用学的第一个经典理论。该理论将我们的日常会话看作是一种行为,应该包括言说行为(locutionary act)、意向行为(illocutionary act)和取效行为(perlocutionary act)三部分。

1967 年,奥斯汀的学生格莱斯(Paul Grice)提出的合作原则是对言语行为理论的补充。他认为交际双方为达到相互理解的目的必须进行合作,并遵守以下原则:质准则(Quantity Maxim)、量准则(Quality Maxim)、关系准则(Relevant Maxim)和方式准则(Manner Maxim)以及一些次准则。

1983 年,利奇(Geoffrey Leech)提出的礼貌原则是对合作原则的发展和“挽救”。他认为礼貌是交际的主要决定因素,具有一定的普遍性。礼貌原则分为六类:得体准则(Tact Maxim)、慷慨准则(Generosity Maxim)、赞誉准

---

① 这里的符号是符号学(Semiotics)概念,指具有社会功能并且可以表达意义的各种标记,如交通信号、旗语、公式、方程式等。当然,最重要的符号是语言,对语言的研究(语言学)是符号研究(符号学)的中心任务。

则(Approbation Maxim)、谦逊准则(Modesty Maxim)、一致准则(Agreement Maxim)和同情准则(Sympathy Maxim)。此外,每条准则之下还包括两条次准则。

1986年,斯珀伯和威尔森(Dan Sperber & Deirdre Wilson)提出的关联理论是对合作原则的全新发展。与以往侧重说话人话语生成研究的理论不同,关联理论从认知科学的角度出发,强调进行听话人话语理解的研究。该理论主要包括交际(Communicative)、明示－推理过程(Ostensive-referential process)、关联(Relevance)、认知原则(cognitive principle of relevance)和交际原则(communicative principle of relevance)等内容。

除上述理论外,维索尔伦(Jef Verschueren)的顺应论(Theory of Adaptation)等理论都对语用学的发展起到了积极的作用。

1. Definitions

1.1 Pragmatics

Pragmatics studies the use of language in human communication as determined by the conditions of society.

(Mey 1993: 6)

Pragmatics studies the factors that govern our choice of language in social interaction and the effects of our choice on others.

(Crystal 1987: 120)

Pragmatics can be usefully defined as the study of how utterances have meanings in situations.

(Leech 1983: x)

Pragmatics is the study of how more gets communicated than is said.

(Blakemore 1992: 39)

At the most elementary level, pragmatics can be defined as the study of language use, or, to employ a somewhat more complicated phrasing, the study of linguistic phenomena from the point of view of their ***usage properties*** and ***processes***.

(Verschuren 1999)

Pragmatics is the study of those principles that will account for why a certain set of sentences are anomalous, or not possible utterances.

(Levinson 1983: 6)

Pragmatics is the study of the ability of language users to pair sentences with the contexts in which they would be appropriate.

(Levinson 1983: 24)

Pragmatics is the study of all aspects of meaning not captured in a semantic theory. Pragmatics has as its topic those aspects of the meaning of utterances which cannot be accounted for by straightforward reference to the truth conditions of the sentences uttered. Put rudely: PRAGMATICS = MEANING-TRUTH CONDITIONS.

(Gazdar 1979: 2)

1.2 Context

Utterances and situation are bound up inextricably with each other and the CONTEXT OF SITUATION is indispensable for the understanding of the words. There is no way to characterize the meaning of utterances on the basis of internal considerations about the language alone. The meaning of spoken utterances could always be determined by the context of situation.

Three types of context of situation:

1. Situation in which speech interrelates with bodily activity.

2. Narrative situations

3. Situations in which speech is used to fill a speech vacuum — "PHATIC COMMNION"

(Malinowski 1923)

The context of situation as including the entire cultural setting of speech and the personal history of the participants rather than as simply the context of human activity going on at the moment.

(Firth 1950)

The linguistic features which are typically associated with a configuration of situational features-with particular values of the field, mode and tenor-constitute a REGISTER.

(Halliday 2001:22)

A context is a psychological construct.

(Sperber 1986)

Context is that which occurs before and/or after a word, a phrase or even a longer UTTERANCE or a TEXT. The context often helps in understanding the particular meaning of the word, phrase, etc.

(Richards 2005: 149)

"Context" refers to all elements of a communicative situation: the verbal and nonverbal context, the context of the given speech situation and the social context of the relationship between the speaker and hearer, their knowledge, and their attitudes.

(Bussmann 2000: 100 – 101)

1.3 Presupposition

Shared assumptions.

(Grundy 1995)

What a speaker or writer assumes that the receiver of the message already knows.

(Richards 2005: 536)

The concept of presupposition in logic: S_1 presupposes S_2 exactly if S_1 implies S_2 and if not-S_1 also entails S_2.

(Bussmann 2000: 379)

1.4 Deixis

(1) Act of pointing out or indicating elements of a situation by gesture or linguistic expressions.

(2) Characteristic function of linguistic expressions that relate to the personal, spatial, and temporal aspect of utterances depending upon the given utterance situation.

(Bussmann 2000:116 – 117)

Deixis is a central linguistic concept.

(Lyons 1977)

Deixis acts as a link between semantics and pragmatics to the extent that deictic expressions can only be determined within the context of the actual speech situation.

(Putnam 1975)

1.5 Implicature

In uttering a sentence *S*, a speaker implies that *p* is the case if, by having been uttered, *S* suggests as its conclusion *p*, without *p* having been literally said. If the conclusion rests exclusively on the conventional meaning of the words and grammatical construction that occur in *S*, then the conclusion is called a "conventional implicature."

(Grice 1975)

Most presuppositions are interpreted as conventional implicatures.

(Karttunen 1979)

2. Classical theories

2.1 Speech Act Theory

This is the first major theory in the study of language in use, which originated with the Oxford philosopher **John Austin** (1911 – 1960).

Speech act theory came from a series of lectures given by Austin at Harvard University in 1955, which were brought together in book form by J. O. Urmoson, based on Austin's own lecture notes and recordings of his lectures: ***How to do things with words***. In the latter part of *How to Do Things with Words*, Austin made a fresh start on the problem and considered it from the ground up again, i. e. in what sense to say something is to do something.

Austin says in *How to Do Things with Words*, 'We first distinguished a group of things we do in saying something, which together we summed up by saying we perform a *locutionary act*, which is roughly equivalent to "meaning" in the traditional sense.' Second, we said that we also perform *illocutionary acts* such as informing, ordering, warning, undertaking, &c., i. e. utterances which have a certain (conventional) force. Thirdly, we may also perform *perlocutionary acts*: what we bring about or achieve by saying something, such as convincing, persuading, deterring, and even, say, surprising or misleading. Here we have three, if not more, different senses or dimensions of the "use of a sentence" or of "the use of language" (and, of course, there are others also). All these three kinds of "actions" are, simply of course as actions, subject to the usual troubles and reservations about attempt as distinct from achievement, being intentional as distinct from being unintentional, and the like. We then said that we must consider these three kinds of act in greater detail.'

In order to further study illocutionary acts, Austin attempted a preliminary classification of them in the last chapter of *How to Do Things with Words*:

I distinguish five very general classes: but I am far from equally happy about all of them. I call then these classes of utterance, classified according to their illocutionary force, by the following more-or-less rebarbative names:

(1) Verdictives.

(2) Exercitives.

(3) Commissives.

(4) Behabitives (a shocker this).

(5) Expositives.

We shall take them in order, but first I will give a rough idea of each.

The first, verdictives, are typified by the giving of a verdict, as the name implies, by a jury, arbitrator, or umpire. But they need not be final; they may be, for example, an estimate, reckoning, or appraisal. It is essentially giving a finding as to something—fact, or value—which is for different reasons hard to be certain about.

The second, exercitives, are the exercising of powers, rights, or influence. Examples are appointing, voting, ordering, urging, advising, warning, &c.

The third, commissives, are typified by promising or otherwise undertaking; they *commit* you to doing something, but include also declarations or announcements of intention, which are not promises, and also rather vague things which we may call espousals, as for example, siding with. They have obvious connexions with verdictives and exercitives.

The fourth, behabitives, are a very miscellaneous group, and have to do with attitudes and *social behaviour*. Examples are apologizing, congratulating, commending, condoling, cursing, and challenging.

The fifith, expositives, are difficult to define. They make plain how our utterances fit into the course of an argument or conversation, how we are using words, or, in general, are expository. Examples are "I reply," "I argue," "I concede," "I illustrate," "I assume," "I postulate." We should be clear from the start that there are still wide possibilities of marginal or awkward cases, or of overlaps.

To sum up, we may say that the verdictive is an exercise of judgement, the exercitive is an assertion of influence or exercising of power, the commissive is an assuming of an obligation or declaring of an intention, the behabitive is the adopting of an attitude, and the expositive is the clarifying of reasons, arguments, and communications.

But there are problems with this classification. One of them is that the classes are not clear-cut. There are overlapping cases, as Austin himself concedes. In 1969, his student John Searle (1932 –), the American philosopher of language, has introduced some revisions to Austin's theory.

In "A Taxonomy of illocutionary Acts" published in 1975, he proposed a new classification of illocutionary acts. Searle thinks the metaphor of force in the expression "illocutionary force" is misleading since it suggests that different illocutionary forces occupy different positions on a single continuum of force. Therefore, he proposed a new criteria "*felicity conditions*". In his view, illocutionary acts may differ from each other in 12 dimensions, which therefore he uses as criteria for the classification. And the four important ones, most of which correlate to his felicity conditions, are the illocutionary point, the direction of fit between words and the world, the psychological state expressed and the propositional content. By these criteria, Searle establishes the five classes of assertives, directives, commissives, expressives and declarations.

And Searle also noticed the sentence like "Can you reach the salt?" The speaker utter this sentence not only mean it as a question, but also as a request to pass the salt. Such cases, in which the utterance has two illocutionary forces, are to be sharply distinguished from the cases in which, for example, the speaker tells the hearer that he wants him to do something; and then the hearer does it because the speaker wants him to, though no request at all has been made, meant, or understood. The cases we will be discussing are *indirect speech acts*, cases in which one illocutionary act is performed indirectly by way of performing another. The problem posed by indirect speech acts is the problem of how it is possible for the speaker to say one thing and mean that but also to mean something else.

Searle's classification is an improvement on that of Austin's in that there is a principled basis—the revised felicity conditions. But there are also problems here. In both their classifications, there are sub-classes also points to the need for more specific classes.

2.2 The Cooperative Principle

H. P. Grice (1913 - 1988), who worked with Austin at Oxford in the 1940s and 1950s, was also an ordinary language philosopher. His theory of implicature was outlined in 1967 and was published in a paper "logic and conversation" in 1975. He attempted at explaining how a hearer gets from what is said to what is meant, from the level of expressed meaning to the level of implied meaning. He thinks we seem to follow some principle like the following: "Make your conversational contribution such as is required, at the stage at which it occurs, by the accepted purpose or direction of the talk exchange in which you are engaged." (Grice 1975: 45) And this principle is known as THE

COOPERATIVE PRINCIPLE or CP for short.

To specify the CP further, Grice introduced four categories of maxims as follows:

Quantity

1. Make your contribution as informative as is required (for the current purposes of the exchange).
2. Do not make your contribution more informative than is required.

Quality

Try to make your contribution one that is true.

1. Do not say what you believe to be false.
2. Do not say that for which you lack adequate evidence.

Relation

Be relevant.

Manner

Be perspicuous.

1. Avoid obscurity of expression.
2. Avoid ambiguity.
3. Be brief.
4. Be orderly. (Grice 1975:45 -46)

The word IMPLICATURE was coined by Grice. And he tried to explore the question how people manage to convey implicature, which is not explicitly expressed. The fact that the CP and its component maxims are expressed in the imperative has misled many readers to regard them as prescriptive: telling speakers how they ought to behave; while the truth is that the CP is meant to describe what actually happens in conversation. Therefore it is also called the theory of CONVERSATIONAL IMPLICATURE, which is the second major theory in pragmatics.

2.3 The Politeness Principle

Austin's and Searle's speech act theory as well as Grice's work on conversational implicatures provided the first theoretical ground for the exploration of linguistic politeness in the 1960s and 70s. Some of the early models of politeness were thus expansions of Grice's Cooperative Principle (CP), or took CP as a starting point for a model of general pragmatics which would then include a Politeness Principle (PP).

Leech says in *Principles of Pragmatics*, "... no claim has been made that the CP applies in an identical manner to all societies.... However it must be admitted that the CP is in a weak position if apparent exceptions to it can not be satisfactorily explained..." It is for this reason that the PP can be seen not just as another principle to be added to the CP, but as a necessary complement, which rescues the CP from serious trouble.

The PP in Leech's terms is meant to regulate the "social equilibrium and the friendly relations which enable us to assume that our interlocutors are being cooperative in the first place." In its negative form, the PP might be formulated in a general way, "Minimize (other things being equal) the expression of impolite beliefs." In its corresponding positive form, the PP could be formulated as "Maximize (other things being equal) the expression of polite beliefs, which is somewhat less important."

The CP enables one participant in a conversation to communicate on the assumption that the other participant is being cooperative. In this the CP has the function of regulating what we say so that it contributes to some assumed illocutionary or discoursal goal(s). It could be argued, however, that PP has a higher regulative role than this: to maintain the social equilibrium and the friendly relations which enables us to assume that our interlocutors are being cooperative in the first place. To put matters at their most basic: unless you are polite to your neighbor, the channel of communication between you will break down, and you will no longer be able to borrow his mower.

Leech's maxims of the Politeness Principle includes as follows:

Tact Maxim

A. Minimize the cost to other.

B. Maximize the benefit to other.

Generosity Maxim

A: Minimize benefit to self.

B: Maximize cost to self.

The Approbation Maxim

A: Minimize dispraise of other.

B: Maximize praise of other.

The Modesty Maxim

A: Minimize praise of self.

B: Maximize dispraise of self.

Maxim of Agreement

A: Minimize disagreement between self and other.

B: Maximize agreement between self and other.

The Maxim of Sympathy

A: Minimize antipathy between self and other.

B: Maximize sympathy between self and other.

One of the central claims made in PP is that politeness is a universal feature of language usage. In other words, all of the world's languages possess the means to express politeness. Their claim for universality, however, is made in relation to their conceptualization of an idealised concept of politeness, not in relation to the ways in which groups of participants struggle over politeness (or whatever terms are available to them in their own languages) in social interaction. Those cultural norms, such as directness/indirectness, self-assertion, intimacy, which are reflected in speech acts, differ not only from one language to another, but also from one regional and social variety to another.

2.4 Relevance theory

Relevance theory, as a general theory of cognitive pragmatics, is first proposed in the book *Relevance: Communication and Cognition in* 1986. It introduces us its unique ideas about relevance, recommends its famous ostensive-inferential communication model, and establishes a general principle of interpreting the inner mechanism of human communication. Grice's account of conversation starts from a distinction between what is explicitly said and what is implicated. No explanation of explicit communication is given. The principle of relevance is intended to explain ostensive communication as a whole, both explicit and implicit.

Sperber and Wilson define **communication** as "**ostensive-inferential act**" (1995: 50 – 54). On the speaker's side, communication is an ostension, that is, communication is behavior which makes manifest an intention to make something manifest; on the hearer's side, communication is a process of inference. That is, the hearer infers the implied intention from the information provided by the speaker's ostension. The communicator produces a stimulus which makes it mutually manifest to communicator and audience that the communicator intends, by means of this stimulus, to make manifest or more manifest a set of assumptions I. (1995: 155) A communicator who produces an ostensive stimulus is trying to fulfill two intentions: first, the informative intention, to make manifest to her audience a set of assumptions I; and second, the communicative intention, to make her informative intention mutually manifest.

An assumption is relevant in a context if and only if it has some contextual effect in that context. (1995:122) According to Sperber & Wilson's theory, the notion of a contextual effect is essential to a description of the comprehension. Briefly speaking, **contextual effect** is the contextual implication that results from the interaction between newly-presented information and contextual assumptions (old information), along with which new context is constructed. Contextual effect is the necessary and sufficient condition for relevance. There are two factors relate to the degree of relevance. Contextual effect is the necessary and sufficient condition for relevance, and when other things being equal, the greater the contextual effects are, the greater the relevance is. But contextual effects are not the only factor to be taken into account in assessing the degree on relevance. Contextual effect is brought about in the mental processes that involve a certain effort, a certain expenditure of energy. So the processing effort involved in achieving contextual effects is the second factor to be taken into account in assessing degrees of relevance.

Sperber and Wilson claim in their book *Relevance*: *Communication and Cognition* that there are not one but **two principles of relevance**, so as to make it clear that there are differences between the maximum relevance and the optimal relevance. And the two principles of relevance are:

(1) Human cognition tends to be geared to the maximization of relevance.

(2) Every act of ostensive communication communicates a presumption of its own optimal relevance. (1995: 260)

Of these two principles, (1) is called Cognition Principle and (2) is Communicative Principle. In other words, human cognition often coincides with the maximum relevance while it is optimal relevance that is the very thing that communicators expect to achieve in communication.

Sperber and Wilson differentiate maximum relevance and optimal relevance as the following:

the maximum relevance is to obtain the greatest possible effects from the smallest possible effort when interpreting utterances in communication;

the optimal relevance is to obtain adequate effect for no unjustifiable effort. That is, the maximum relevance is aimed at the degree of relevance, and it is an objective reality; and the optimal relevance is aimed at the effect of relevance, it is related to the hearer's subjective desire.

3. Original selecting

Lecture VIII
Locutionary, Illocutionary, and Perlocutionary Acts

In embarking on a programme of finding a list of explicit performative verbs, it seemed that we were going to find it not always easy to distinguish performative utterances from constative, and it therefore seemed expedient to go farther back for a while to fundamentals-to consider from the ground up how many senses there are in which to say something *is* to do something, or *in* saying something we do something, and even by saying something we do something. And we began by distinguishing a whole group of senses of "doing something" which are all included together when we say, what is obvious, that to say something is in the full normal sense to do something-which includes the utterance of certain noises, the utterance of certain words in a certain construction, and the utterance of them with a certain "meaning" in the favourite philosophical sense of that word, i. e. with a certain sense and with a certain reference.

The act of "saying something" in this full normal sense I call, i. e. dub, the performance of a locutionary act, and the study of utterances thus far and in these respects the study of locutions, or of the full units of speech. Our interest in the locutionary act is, of course, principally to make quite plain what it is, in order to distinguish it from other acts with, which we are going to be primarily concerned. Let me add merely that, of course, a great many further refinements would be possible and necessary if we were to discuss it for its own sake refinements of very great importance not merely to philosophers but to, say, grammarians and phoneticians.

We had made three rough distinctions between the phonetic act, the phatic act, and the rhetic act. The phonetic act is merely the act of uttering certain noises. The phatic act is the uttering of certain vocables or words, i. e. noises of certain types, belonging to and as belonging to, a certain vocabulary, conforming to and as conforming to a certain grammar. The rhetic act is the performance of an act of using those vocables with a certain more-or-less definite sense and reference. Thus ' He said "The cat is on the mat" ', reports a phatic act, whereas "He said that the cat was on the mat" reports a rhetic act. A similar contrast is illustrated by the pairs:

' He said "I shall be there" ', "He said he would be there";

' He said "Get out" ', "He told me to get out";

' He said "Is it in Oxford or Cambridge?" '; "He asked whether it was in Oxford or Cambridge."

To pursue this for its own sake beyond our immediate requirements, I shall mention some general points worth remembering:

(1) Obviously, to perform a phatic I must perform a phonetic act, or, if you like, in performing one I am performing the other (not, however, that phatic acts are a sub-class of phonetic acts-as belonging to): but the converse is not true, for if a monkey makes a noise indistinguishable from "go" it is still not a phatic act.

(2) Obviously in the definition of the phatic act two things were lumped together: vocabulary and grammar. So we have not assigned a special name to the person who utters, for example, "cat thoroughly the if" or "the slithy toves did

gyre." Yet a further point arising is the intonation as well as grammar and vocabulary.

(3) The phatic act, however, like the phonetic, is essentially mimicable, reproducible (including intonation, winks, gestures, &c.). One can mimic not merely the statement in quotation marks "She has lovely hair," but also the more complex fact that he said it like this: "She has lovely *hair*" (shrugs).

This is the "inverted commas" use of "said" as we get it in novels: every utterance can be just reproduced in inverted commas, or in inverted commas with "said he" or, more often, "said she," &c., after it.

But the rhetic act is the one we report, in the case of assertions, by saying "He said that the cat was on the mat," "He said he would go," "He said I was to go" (his words were "You are to go"). This is the so-called "indirect speech." If the sense or reference is *not* being taken as clear, then the whole or part is to be in quotation marks. Thus I might say: 'He said I was to go to the "minister", but he did not say which minister' or 'I said that he was behaving badly and he replied that "the higher you get the fewer".' We cannot, however, always use "said that" easily: we would say "told to," "advise to," &c., if he used the imperative mood, or such equivalent phrases as "said I was to," "said I should," &c. Compare such phrases as "bade me welcome" and "extended his apologies."

I add one further point about the rhetic act: of course sense and reference (naming and referring) themselves are here ancillary acts performed in performing the rhetic act. Thus we may say 'I meant by "bank" ...' and we say 'by "he" I was referring to...'. Can we perform a rhetic act without referring or without naming? In general it would seem that the answer is that we cannot, but there are puzzling cases. What is the reference in "all triangles have three sides?" Correspondingly, it is clear that we can perform a phatic act which is not a rhetic act, though not conversely. Thus we may repeat someone else's remark or mumble over some sentence, or we may read a Latin sentence without knowing the meaning of the words.

The question when one pheme or one rheme is the *same* as another, whether in the "type" or "token" sense, and the question what is one single pheme or rheme, do not so much matter here. But, of course, it is important to remember that the same pheme (token of the same type) may be used on different occasions of utterance with a different sense or reference, and so be a different rheme. When different phemes are used with the same sense and reference, we might speak of rhetically equivalent acts ("the same statement" in one sense) but not of the same rheme or rhetic acts (which are the same statement in another sense which involves using the same words).

The pheme is a unit of *language*: its typical fault is to be nonsense-meaningless. But the rheme is a unit of *speech*; its typical fault is to be vague or void or obscure, &c. But though these matters are of much interest, they do not so far throw any light at all on our problem of the constative as opposed to the performative utterance. For example, it might be perfectly possible, with regard to an utterance, say "It is going to charge," to make entirely plain "what we were saying" in issuing the utterance, in all the senses so far distinguished, and yet not at all to have cleared up whether or not in issuing the utterance I was performing the act of *warning* or not. It may be perfectly clear what I mean by "It is going to charge" or "Shut the door," but not clear whether it is meant as a statement or warning, &c.

To perform a locutionary act is in general, we may say, also and *eo ipso* to perform an *illocutionary* act, as I propose to call it. To determine what illocutionary act is so performed we must determine in what way we are using the locution:

asking or answering a question,

giving some information or an assurance or a warning,

announcing a verdict or an intention,

pronouncing sentence,

making an appointment or an appeal or a criticism,

making an identification or giving a description,

and the numerous like. (I am not suggesting that this is a clearly defined class by any means.) There is nothing mysterious about our *eo ipso* here. The trouble rather is the number of different senses of so vague an expression as 'in what way are we using it'-this may refer even to a locutionary act, and further to perlocutionary acts to which we shall come in a minute. When we perform a locutionary act, we use speech: but in what way precisely are we using it on this occasion? For there are very numerous functions of or ways in which we use speech, and it makes a great difference to our act in some sens—esense(B)—in which way and which *sense* we were on this occasion "using" it. It makes a great difference whether we were advising, or merely suggesting, or actually ordering, whether we were strictly promising or only announcing a vague intention, and so forth. These issues penetrate a little but not without confusion into grammar (see above), but we constantly do debate them, in such terms as whether certain words (a certain locution) *had the force of* a question, or *ought to have heen taken as* an estimate and so on. I explained the performance of an act in this new and second sense as the performance of an "llocutionary" act, i. e. performance of an act *in* saying something as opposed to performance of an act *of* saying something; and I shall refer to the doctrine of the different types of function of language here in question as the doctrine of" illocutionary forces."

It may be said that for too long philosophers have neglected this study, treating all problems as problems of "locutionary usage," and indeed that the "descriptive fallacy" mentioned in Lecture I commonly arises through mistaking a problem of the former kind for a problem of the latter kind. True, we are now getting out of this; for some years we have been realizing more and more clearly that the occasion of an utterance matters seriously, and that the words used are to some extent to be "explained" by the "context" in which they are designed to be or have actually been spoken in a linguistic interchange. Yet still perhaps we are too prone to give these explanations in terms of "the meanings of words." Admittedly we can use "meaning" also with reference to illocutionary force—"He meant it as an order," &c. But I want to distinguish *force* and meaning in the sense in which meaning is equivalent to sense and reference, just as it has become essential to distinguish sense and reference within meaning.

Moreover, we have here an illustration of the different uses of the expression, "uses of language," or "use of a sentence," &c.—"use" is a hopelessly ambiguous or wide word, just as is the word "meaning," which it has become customary to deride. But "use," its supplanter, is not in much better case. We may entirely clear up the "use of a sentence" on a particular occasion, in the sense of the locutionary act, without yet touching upon its use in the sense of an *illocutionary* act.

Before refining any further on this notion of the illocutionary act, let us contrast both the locutionary *and* the illocutionary act with yet a third kind of act.

There is yet a further sense (C) in which to perform a locutionary act, and therein an illocutionary act, may also be to perform an act of another kind. Saying something will often, or even normally, produce certain consequential effects upon the feelings, thoughts, or actions of the audience, or of the speaker, or of other persons: and it may be done with the design, intention, or purpose of producing them; and we may then say, thinking of this, that the speaker has performed an act in the nomenclature of, which reference is made either (C. *a*), only obliquely, or even (C. *b*), not at all, to the performance of the locutionary or illocutionary act. We shall call the performance of an act of this kind the performance of a *perlocutionary* act or *perlocution*. Let us not yet define this idea any more carefully—of course it needs it—but simply give examples:

(E. 1)

Act (A) or Locution

He said to me "Shoot her!" meaning by "shoot" shoot and referring by "her" to *her*.

Act (B) or Illocution

He urged (or advised, ordered, &c.) me to shoot her.

Act (C. *a*) or Perlocution

He persuaded me to shoot her.

Act (C. *b*)

He got me to (or made me, &c.) shoot her.

(E. 2)

Act (A) or Locution

He said to me, "You can't do that."

Act (B) or Illocution

He protested against my doing it.

Act (C. *a*) or Perlocution

He pulled me up, checked me.

Act (C. *b*)

He stopped me, he brought me to my senses, &c.

He annoyed me.

We can similarly distinguish the locutionary act "he said that..." from the illocutionary act "he argued that..." and the perlocutionary act "he convinced me that...."

It will be seen that the consequential effects of perlocutions are really consequences, which do not include such conventional effects as, for example, the speaker's being committed by his promise (which comes into the illocutionary act). Perhaps distinctions need drawing, as there is clearly a difference between what we feel to be the real production of real effects and what we regard as mere conventional consequences; we shall in any case return later to this.

We have here then roughly distinguished three kinds of acts-the locutionary, the illocutionary, and the perlocutionary. ① Let us make some general comments on these three classes, leaving them still fairly rough. The first three points will be about "the use of language" again.

(1) Our interest in these lectures is essentially to fasten on the second, illocutionary act and contrast it with the other two. There is a constant tendency in philosophy to elide this in favour of one or other of the other two. Yet it is distinct from both. We have already seen how the expressions "meaning" and "use of sentence" can blur the distinction between locutionary and illocutionary acts. We now notice that to speak of the "use" of language can likewise blur the distinction between the illocutionary and perlocutionary act-so we will distinguish them more carefully in a minute. Speaking of the 'use of "language" for arguing or warning' looks just like speaking of 'the use of "language" for persuading, rousing, alarming'; yet the former may, for rough contrast, be said to be conventional, in the sense that at least it could be made explicit by the performative formula; but the latter could not. Thus we can say "I argue that" or "I warn you that" but we cannot say "I convince you that" or "I alarm you that." Further, we may entirely clear up whether someone was arguing or not without touching on the question whether he was convincing anyone or not.

(2) To take this farther, let us be quite clear that the expression ("use of language" can cover other matters even more diverse than the illocutionary and perlocutionary acts. For example, we may speak of the "use of language" *for* something, e.g. for joking; and we may use "in" in a way different from the

① Here occurs in the manuscript a note made in 1958 which says: "(1) All this is not clear (2) and in all senses relevant [(A) and (B) as distinct from (C)] won't all utterances be performative?"

illocutionary "in", as when we say 'in saying "p" I was joking' or "acting a part" or "writing poetry"; or again we may speak of "a poetical use of language" as distinct from "the use of language in poetry." These references to "use of language" have nothing to do with the illocutionary act. For example, if I say "Go and catch a falling star," it may be quite clear what both the meaning and the force of my utterance is, but still wholly unresolved which of these other kinds of things I may be doing. There are parasitic uses of language, which are "not serious," not the "full normal use." The normal conditions of reference may be suspended, or no attempt made at a standard perlocutionary act, no attempt to make you do anything, as Walt Whitman does not seriously incite the eagle of liberty to soar.

(3) Furthermore, there may be some things we "do" in some connexion with saying something which do not seem to fall, intuitively at least, exactly into any of "these roughly defined" classes, or else seem to fall vaguely into more than one; but any way we do not at the outset feel so clear that they are as remote from our three acts as would be joking or writing poetry. For example, *insinuating*, as when we insinuate something in or by issuing some utterance, seems to involve some convention, as in the illocutionary act; but we cannot say "I insinuate...," and it seems like implying to be a clever effect rather than a mere act. A further example is evincing emotion. We may evince emotion in or by issuing an utterance, as when we swear; but once again we have no use here for performative formulas and the other devices of illocutionary acts. We might say that we use swearing[①]I for relieving our feelings. We must notice that the illocutionary act is a conventional act: an act done as conforming to a convention.

(4) Acts of all our three kinds necessitate, since they are the performing of actions, allowance being made for the ills that all action is heir to. We must

① "Swearing" is ambiguous: "I swear by Our Lady" is to swear by Our Lady: but "Bloody" is not to swear by Our Lady.

systematically be prepared to distinguish between "the act of doing x," i. e., achieving x, and "the act of attempting to do x": for example, we must distinguish between warning and attempting to warn. We must expect infelicities here. The next three points that arise do so importantly because our acts are *acts*.

(5) Since our acts are acts, we must always remember the distinction between producing effects or consequences which are intended or unintended; and (i) when the speaker intends to produce an effect it may nevertheless not occur, and (ii) when he does not intend to produce it or intends not to produce it may nevertheless occur. To cope with complication (i) we invoke as before the distinction between attempt and achievement; to cope with complication (ii) we invoke the normal linguistic devices of disclaiming (adverbs like "unintentionally" and "so on") which we hold ready for personal use in all cases of doing actions.

(6) Furthermore, we must, of course, allow that as acts they may be things that we do not exactly *do*, in the sense that we did them, say, under duress or in any other such way. Other ways besides in which we may not fully do the action are given in (2) above.

(7) Finally we must meet the objection about our illocutionary and perlocutionary acts-namely that the notion of an act is unclear-by a general doctrine about action. We have the idea of an "act" as a fixed physical thing that we do, as distinguished from conventions and as distinguished from consequences. But

(*a*) the illocutionary act and even the locutionary act too may involve conventions: consider the example of doing obeisance. It is obeisance only because it is conventional and it is done only because it is conventional. Compare the distinction between kicking a wall and kicking a goal;

(*b*) the perlocutionary act may include what in a way are consequences, as when we say "By doing x I was doingy": we do bring in a greater or less stretch of "consequences" always, some of which may be "unintentional". There is no restriction to the minimum physical act at all. That we can import an indefinitely long stretch of what might also be called the "consequences" of our act into the act itself is, or should be, a fundamental commonplace of the theory of our language about all "action" in general. Thus if asked "What did he do?", we may reply either "He shot the donkey" or "He fired a gun" or "He pulled the trigger" or "He moved his trigger finger," and all may be correct. So, to shorten the nursery story of the endeavours of the old woman to drive her pig home in time to get her old man's supper, we may in the last resort say that the cat drove or got the pig, or made the pig get, over the stile. If in such cases we *mention* both a B act (illocution) and a C act (perlocution) we shall say "*by* B-ing he C-ed" rather than "*in* B-ing. . . ." This is the reason for calling C a perlocutionary act as distinct from an illocutionary act.

Next time we shall revert to the distinction between our three kinds of act, and to the expressions "in" and "by doing *x* I am doing *y*", with a view to getting the three classes and their members and non-members somewhat clearer. We shall see that just as the locutionary act embraces doing many things at once to be complete, so may the illocutionary and perlocutionary acts. ①

References

[1] Austin J. L. How to Do Things with Words [M]. Oxford: Oxford University Press, 1975.

[2] Grice H. Paul. Logic and Conversation [M]. In Cole P. & Morgan J. L. (eds.) Syntax and Semantics 3: Speech Acts. New York: Academic

① 摘自 Austin J. L. How to Do Things with Words [M]. Oxford: Oxford University Press, 1975.

Press, 1975.

[3]Grice H. Paul. Studies in the Way of Words[M]. Harvard: Harvard University Press, 1989.

[4]Leech G. N. Principle of Pragmatics[M]. London: Longman, 1983.

[5]Levinson S. C. Pragmatics[M]. Cambridge: Cambridge University Press, 1983.

[6] Mey J. L. Pragmatics: An Introduction [M]. Oxford: Blackwell, 1993.

[7]Searle J. R. Speech Acts: An Essay in the Philosophy of Language [M]. Cambridge: Cambridge University Press, 1969.

[8]Sperber D. & Wilson D. Relevance: Communication and Cognition [M]. Oxford: Blackwell's, 1986.

[9]Thomas J. Meaning in Interaction: An Introduction to Pragmatcs[M]. London: Routledge, 1995.

[10]布斯曼. 语言与语言学词典[M]. 北京:外语教学与研究出版社, 2000.

[11]理查兹. 朗文语言教学及应用语言学辞典[M]. 北京:外语教学与研究出版社, 2005.

[12]维索尔伦. 语用学新解[M]. 北京:外语教学与研究出版社, 2000.

第四章

社会语言学

导 读

社会语言学诞生于20世纪60年代,是一门研究语言的社会现象的学科。他关注的不是语言的核心部分——它的结构体系,而是语言的边缘部分——人在日常生活中的语言表现。语言与社会之间究竟存在什么样的关系呢？这是社会语言学所要解答的中心问题。

社会语言学作为一种跨学科研究,在理论模式和研究方法上存在着多样性的一面,不易在学科内部产生普遍的理论指导模式。由此,它的理论主要源于人类学、社会学、社会心理学、民族学和教育学等相关人文社会学科的各种理论学说。1935年英国语言学家J. R. Firth提出的“社会语言学”(sociological linguistics)概念类似今天社会语言学重要的分支之一“语言社会学”(sociology of language)。社会语言学的概念是1952年美国语言学家Haver C. Currie提出来的,但这门学科的兴盛并进而发展成为一个独立的学科领域还是20世纪60年代中期的事情,其代表人物是美国的W. Labov和D. Hymes。前者用定量研究的方法开城市方言研究的先河;后者则创建了“话语文化学”(the ethnography of speaking)。这些都是社会语言学中最具代表性的研究领域。

社会语言学运用语言学和社会学等学科的理论和方法,联系社会研究语言现象,主要研究语言的社会本质和差异。前者包括语言社会本质的特点和规律、语言内部规律和外部规律的相互关系和作用、民族语言和民族形成的关系、民族共同语的形成和社会发展的关系、语言演变和社会演变的关系等问题。后者包括语言的地域变体、社会变体、双语和多语现象、不同语言环境中的语言变体等问题,其目的是揭示社会结构变异和语言结构变异之间的系统对应关系及相互的因果关系。此外,社会语言学研究还为一个国家或民族的标准语的确定或选择、文字的制定和改革、语言政策的制定、语言计划的拟定与实施、语言教学及其研究提供依据和指导。

随着人类社会的不断进步,语言与社会之间的关系越来越受到人们的关注。社会语言学的理论也在解决人与人的世界之间的关系问题上发挥更大的作用。

1. Definitions

1.1 sociolinguistics

Sociolinguistics is the study of language in relation to social factors, that is social class, educational level and type of education, age, sex, ethnic origin, etc. Many linguists would include the detailed study of interpersonal communication, sometimes called **micro-sociolinguistics**. Such areas as the study of language choice in BILINGUAL or MULTILINGUAL communities, LANGUAGE PLANNING, LANGUAGE ATTITUDES, etc., may be included under sociolinguistics and are sometimes referred to as **macro-sociolinguistics**, or they are considered as being part of the SOCIOLOGY OF LANGUAGE or the SOCIAL PSYCHOLOGY OF LANGUAGE.

(Richards 2005: 635)

Sociolinguistics is the study of language in relation to society.

(Hudson 2000: 4)

1.2 variation

Variations are Differences in pronunciation, grammar, or word choice within a language. Variation in a language may be related to region, to social class and/or educational background or to the degree of formality of a situation in which language is used.

(Richards 2005: 739)

1.3 dialect

A linguistic system (in the sense of langue) that (a) shows a high degree of similarity to other systems so that at least partial mutual intelligibility is possible; (b) is tied to a specific region in such a way that the regional distribution of the system does not overlap with an area covered by another such system; (c) does not have a written or standard form, i. e. does not have officially standardized orthographic and grammatical rules.

(Bussmann 2000: 125)

1.4 pidgin

A language which develops as a **contact language** when groups of people who speak different languages try to communicate with one another on a regular basis. For example, this has occurred many times in the past when foreign traders had to communicate with the local population or groups of workers from different language backgrounds on plantations or in factories. A pidgin usually has a limited vocabulary and a reduced grammatical structure which may expand when a pidgin is used over a long period and for many purposes.

(Richards 2005: 516)

2. Classical theories

The relationship between language and society has long been recognized and examined. Evidence for this claim, discrete as it might be, can be conveniently gathered from the works by those great philosophers and grammarians either in the Graeco-Roman tradition or in the Indian history (Harris & Taylor 1997; Apte 1994).

Sociolinguistics, as an interdisciplinary study of language use, attempts to show the relationship between language and society.

2.1 The Whorf Hypothesis

The Whorf Hypothesis, also called linguistic relativity, a belief which was held by some scholars that the way people view the world is determined wholly or partly by the structure of their NATIVE LANGUAGE. As this hypothesis was strongly put forward by the American anthropological linguists Edward Sapir and Benjamin Whorf, it has often been called the **Sapir-Whorf hypothesis** or **Whorfian hypothesis**. In recent years, study of the relationships between cognition and linguistic expression has been revived in a more subtle form within COGNITIVE LINGUISTICS.

(J. Richards 2005:402)

Those quotes below are used most commonly to characterize the Sapir-Whorf hypothesis:

Human beings do not live in the objective world alone... but are very much at the mercy of the particular language which has become the medium of expression for their society. The worlds in which different societies live are distinct worlds, not merely the same world with different *labels* attached.

(Sapir in Mandelbaum 1963:162)

We dissect nature along lines laid down by our native languages. The categories and types that we isolate from the world of phenomena we do not find there because they stare every observer in the face...

(Whorf in Carroll 1956:213)

Both quotes emphasize the words or lexical resources of a language. That is, both stress that while nature is continuous human beings cut nature into discrete categories and each culture does this cutting somewhat differently. People make up words or concepts in order to talk about their world or cultural universe.

This version of the Sapir-Whorf hypothesis is one of two alternatives. It is called the lexical version in this article. While one could ascribe the "anomaly" that the hypothesis is usually characterized by the first, or Sapir's quote to some historical accident, there seem to exist deeper reasons that will soon become apparent.

The view expressed by Whorf in the second quote (above) is relatively unusual. He searched for the interface between language and culture beyond the vocabulary (or the lexicon) and sought to discover the roots of cultural regularities in a language's grammar. Finally, in the statements in which Whorf gives the Sapir-Whorf hypothesis its alternate name, he again sees the relationship of language and culture in grammar:

> ... the "linguistic relativity principle," which means, in informal terms, that users of markedly different grammars are pointed in different evaluations of externally similar acts of observations, and hence are not equivalent as observers but must arrive at somewhat different views of the world.
>
> (Whorf in Carroll 1956:221)

These quotes represent the second way of interpreting the Sapir-Whorf hypothesis—the grammatical version.

2.2 Gender

As a field of research, language and gender studies is interdisciplinary and relatively new. Until the late 1990s, most sociolinguistic studies of language and gender focused on language as the phenomenon to be explained, and did not recognize the complexity of gender (Cameron 1996).

As used here, the term "gender" does not refer to "grammatical gender" (the system to be found in some languages of organizing certain word classes into contrasting categories of "masculine," "feminine," "neuter"). Here gender refers to social categories based on sex but encompassing behavior, roles, and images that, although not biologically determined, are regarded by a society as appropriate to its male or female members. What is seen as appropriate to each gender thus differs in different societies and eras. Gender is distinguished from "sex" in that sex is taken to refer to biological characteristics of male and female whereas gender encompasses what is socially learned and acquired. Gender is also distinguished from "sexuality" and "sexual orientation" though much research on the latter does not make the distinction clear.

In the twentieth century, research in anthropology, sociology, psychology, sociolinguistics, and discourse analysis provided a wealth of interesting material about how various contemporary societies give verbal expression to their perceptions of boys and girls, men and women, about how they regard the language use of their male and female members, and about the factors that impinge upon these attitudes. Some of this work concentrated on describing ways in which aspects of linguistic form vary depending on sex of speaker or addressee. Other research sought to explain causes and effects of observed co-variation and also of patterns in the ways women and men are described.

In the late twentieth century, work on language use was drawn into a broader framework which examined silence and silencing as the other side of the coin of speech and writing. This framework is predicated upon the belief that societal power relationships manifest themselves in the granting or withholding of "speaking rights" in the broadest sense. In the humanities and social sciences there is an interest in discerning whose voice is heard and taken to be representative or truthful, and whose voice goes unheard in various contexts.

There are gender-related differences in the use of language by, to, and about males and females. In shaping them, gender may be neither the only nor the overriding factor. Where males and females are treated differently in language, it is seldom a case of separate but equal: the inequality is an extension of the prevailing power-relations between them in nonlinguistic fields.

2.3 Bilingualism

The reasons that bring languages into contact and hence foster bilingualism are many: migrations of various kinds (economic, educational, political, and religious), nationalism and federalism, education and culture, trade and commerce, intermarriage, etc. These factors create various linguistic needs in people who are in contact with two or more languages and who develop competencies in their languages to the extent required by these needs. In contact situations it is rare that all facets of life require the same language (people would not be bilingual if that were so) or that they always demand two languages (language A *and* B at work, at home, with friends, etc.).

The failure to understand that bilinguals normally use their languages for different purposes, with different people, and in different domains of life has been a major obstacle to obtaining a clear picture of bilinguals and has had many negative consequences: bilinguals have been described and evaluated in terms of the fluency and balance they have in their two languages; language skills in bilinguals have almost always been appraised in terms of monolingual standards; research on bilingualism has in large part been conducted in terms of the bilingual's individual and separate languages; and, finally, many bilinguals evaluate their language competencies as inadequate. Some criticize their mastery of language skills, others strive their hardest to reach monolingual norms, others hide their knowledge of their "weaker" language, and most simply do not perceive themselves as being bilingual even though they use two (or more) languages in their everyday lives.

Researchers are now starting to view the bilingual not so much as the sum of two (or more) complete or incomplete monolinguals but rather as a specific and fully competent speaker-hearer who has developed a communicative competence that is equal, but different in nature, to that of the monolingual. This competence makes use of one language, of the other, or of the two together (in the form of mixed speech; see below) depending on the situation, the topic, the interlocutor, etc. This in turn has led to a redefinition of the procedure used to evaluate the bilingual's competencies. Bilinguals are now being studied in terms of their total language repertoire, and the domains of use and the functions of the bilingual's various languages are being taken into account.

It should be noted finally that as the environment changes and the needs for particular language skills also change, so will the bilingual's competence in his or her various language skills. New situations, new interlocutors, and new language functions will involve new linguistic needs and will therefore change the language configuration of the person involved. Extreme cases of restructuring are language forgetting and a return to functional monolingualism, be it in the person's first, second, or third language.

3. Original selecting

I conceive of two sorts of inequality in the human species; one, which I call natural or physical, because it is established by nature and consists in the difference of ages, health, bodily strengths, and qualities of mind or soul; the other, which may be called moral or political inequality, because it depends upon a sort of convention and is established, or at least authorized, by the consent of men. The latter consists in the different privileges that some men enjoy to the prejudice of others, such as to be richer, more honored, more powerful than they, or even to make themselves obeyed by them.

Rousseau (1964)

I use the second paragraph of Rousseau's second *Discourse* as an epigraph, and adapt its title, because I want to call attention to a link between his concerns and ours. Like him, we think knowledge of human nature essential and pursue it; like him, we think the present condition of mankind unjust, and seek to transform it. These two concerns, for example, provide the frame for Noam Chomsky's recent Russell lectures. Unlike Chomsky, but like Rousseau, moreover, some linguists are beginning to attend to a conception of linguistic structure as interdependent with social circumstances, and as subject to human needs and evolutionary adaptation. And like Rousseau, our image of the linguistic world, the standard by which we judge the present situation, harks back to an earlier stage of human society. Here Rosseau has the advantage over us. He knew he did this, and specified the limitations of it (see the end of note *h* to the *Discourse*). Many of us do it implicitly, falling back on a "Herderian" conception of a world composed of traditional units of languageand-culture, for lack of another way of seeing the resources of language as an aspect of human groups, because we have not thought through new ways of seeing how linguistic resources do, in fact, come organized in the world. We have no accepted way of joining our understanding of inequality with our understanding of the nature of language.

Chomsky's Russell lectures (1971) are a case in point The first lecture, "On Interpreting the World," presents implications of a certain conception of the nature of language and of the goals of linguistic research, leading to a humanistic, libertarian conception of man. The second lecture, "On Changing the World," is about injustice, its roots in inequality of power, and the failure of scholars and governments to deal with the true issues in these respects.

There is little or no linguistics in the second lecture, just as there is little or nothing of social reality in the first. Such principled schizophrenia besets linguistics today; the scientific and social goals of many practitioners are compartmentalized. Edward Sapir warned years ago against such an alienation from experience and social reality on the part of "the many kinds of segmental scientists of man" [1939, cited from Mandelbaum (1949): 578]. It mirrors neither the true nature of language nor its relation to social life; it reflects, rather, a certain ideological conception of that nature and that relation, one which diverts and divorces linguistics from the contribution, desperately needed, that it might make to the understanding of language as a human problem.

The heart of the matter is this. A dominant conception of the goals of "linguistic theory"1 encourages one to think of language exclusively in terms of the vast potentiality of formal grammar, and to think of that potentiality exclusively in terms of its universality. A perspective which treats language only as an attribute of man leaves language as an attribute of *men* unintelligible. In actuality language is in large part what users have made of it. Navajo is what it is partly because it is a human language, partly because it is the language of the Navajo. The generic potentiality of the human faculty for language is realized differently, as to direction and as to degree, in different human communities, and is useless except insofar as it is so realized. The thrust of Chomskian linguistics has been to depreciate the actuality of language under the guise of rejecting an outmoded philosophy of science. We must see beyond the ideological effect of such a thrust and recognize that one cannot change a world on which one's theory permits no purchase. One of the problems to be overcome with regard to language is a widespread linguist's conception of it. A conception of how we encounter and use language in the world, a notion which I call that of *ways of speaking*, is needed.

Let me consider now four broad dimensions of language and of sources of inequality with regard to them. Throughout I shall try to indicate the place of a conception of ways of speaking. Linguistics as part of the problem will be addressed again at the end of the chapter, and as well in the chapter that follows, and in the final chapter of the book.

3.1 Some Dimensions of Language as a Human Problem

It is striking that we have no general perspective on language as a human problem, not even an integrated body of works in search of one. Salient problems, such as translation, multilingual ism, literacy and language development, have long attracted attention, but mostly as practical matters, constituting applications of linguistics, rather than as proper, theoretically pertinent parts of it. There have been notable exceptions, as in the work of Einar Haugen and Uriel Weinreich, but for about a generation most linguistic thought in the United States has seen the role of language in human life only as something to praise, not as something to question and study. Perhaps this situation reflects a phase in the alternation of "high" and "low" evaluations of language to which the philosopher Urban (1939:23) called attention. The skeptical period after the First World War did see leading American theorists of language devote themselves to language problems, such as those involving new vehicles for international communication (Jespersen, Sapir), the teaching of reading (Bloomfield), literacy (Swadesh), language as an instrument and hence a shaper of thought (Sapir, Whorf), and linguistic aspects of psychiatric and other interpersonal communication (Trager, Hockett, in the early 1950s). Perhaps this issue of *Daedalus* is a sign that the climate of opinion is shifting once again toward a balanced recognition of language as "at one and the same time helping and retarding us," as Sapir put it in one context (1933), cited from Mandelbaum (1949:11). In any case, it is unusual today to think of language as something to overcome, yet four broad dimensions of language can usefully be considered in just that way: *diversity* of language, *medium* of language (spoken, written), *structure* of language, and *functioning* of language. Of each we can ask,

- when, where, and how it came to be seen as a problem;
- from what vantage point it is seen as a problem (in relation to other vantage points from which it may not be so seen);
- in what ways the problem has been approached or overcome as a practical task and also as an intellectual, conceptual task;

- what its consequences for the study of language itself have been;
- what kinds of study, to which linguists might contribute, are now needed.

I cannot do more than raise such questions; limitations of knowledge would prevent my doing more, if limitations of space did not. To raise such questions may help, I hope, to stimulate development of a general perspective.

3.2 Overcoming Diversity of Language

This problem may be the most familiar, and the historical solutions to it form an important part of the subject matter of linguistics itself: lingua francas, koines, pidgins and Creoles, standardized languages, diffusion and areal as in India convergence, multilingual repertoires, and constructed auxiliary languages. The myths and lexicons of many cultures show a widespread and presumably ancient recognition of diversity of language, although not uniformly in the mold of the Tower of Babel. The Busama of New Guinea and the Quileute of the State of Washington believed that originally each person had a separate language, and that community of language was a subsequent development created by a culture hero or transformer. Thus it is an interesting question whether it is unity or diversity, within or between speech communities, that has seemed the thing requiring an explanation.

In Western civilization the dominant intellectual response to the existence of diversity has been to seek an original unity, either of historical or of psychological origin (sometimes of both). The dominant practical response has been to impose unity in the form of the hegemony of one language or standard. The presence of the Tower of Babel story in the civilization's sacred book legitimated, and perhaps stimulated, efforts to relate languages in terms of an original unity and played a great part in the development of linguistic research. Indeed, some rather sophisticated work and criticism on the subject can be found from the Renaissance onward. The dating of the origin of linguistic science with the comparative-historical work of the early nineteenth century reflects institutionalization as much as or more than intellectual originality (Diderichsen, 1974; Metcalf, 1974). Christian and humanitarian concern to establish the monogenesis of man through the monogenesis of language was felt strongly well through the nineteenth century, from the dominance of the "ethnological question" in the first part through controversies involving Max Müller, Darwin, Broca, and others (discussed in Hymes, 1971a). The special interest of Europeans in Indo-European origins became increasingly important in the century, the idea of a common linguistic origin stimulating and legitimating studies of common cultural origins and developments. Humanitarian motives played a part as well—Matthew Arnold appealed to Indo-European brotherhood as a reason for the English to respect Celtic (Irish) culture and perhaps the Irish, and Sir Henry Maine made a similar appeal on behalf of the peoples of India. Sheer intellectual curiosity and satisfaction must also always be assigned a part in motivating work in comparative—historical linguistics, and humanistic concern probably played a part in a major contemporary effort to establish a common historical origin for all languages, that of the late Morris Swadesh (1971). (For other aspects of the history of linguistic anthropology see Hymes, 1983a).

The most salient effort toward a conceptual unity of human languages today is linked, of course, with the views of Noam Chomsky. Concern for such a unity is itself old and continuous—the appearance of disinterest among part of a generation of US linguists before and after the Second World War was a local aberration whose importance is primarily due to Chomsky's reaction against it. He has reached back to the seventeenth and eighteenth centuries for an ancestral tradition (1966), when he had only to take up the tradition in this country of Boas and Sapir, or the European tradition, partially transplanted to this country, of Trubetzkoy and Jakobson. In both of these traditions some significant things were being said about universals of language in the 1930s and early 1940s. It is true, however, that the history of the tradition of general linguistics stretching back through the nineteenth century (and, Jakobson would argue, continuing through the Enlightenment to origins in medieval speculative grammar), had been lost from sight in American linguistics, and a sense of it is only now being recovered. It is true, too, that the tradition since Herder and von Humboldt did not much appeal to Chomsky, since its universalism is combined with an intense interest in typology, understood as characterizing the configurations of specific languages as well as characterizing general features of language.

Here we touch on the inescapable limitation of either kind of effort to conceive the unity of human language. Although one used to speak of the discovery of a genetic relationship as *reducing* the number of linguistic groups, the word and the thought were both badly misleading. Languages may disappear through the destruction of their speakers, but not through the publication of linguistic papers and maps. Related languages remain to be accounted for as to their differences and developments as well as to the portion (often quite small) of their makeup that shows a common origin. Likewise, the discovery of putative universals in linguistic structure does not erase the differences. Indeed, the more one emphasizes universals, in association with a powerful, self-developing faculty of language, the more mysterious actual languages become. Why are there more than one, or two or three? And if the internal faculty of language is so constraining, must not social, historical, adaptive forces have been even *more* constraining, in order to produce the plenitude of languages actually found? For Chinookan is not Sahaptin is not Klamath is not Takelma is not Coos is not Siuslaw is not Tsimshian is not Wintu is not Maidu is not Miwok is not Yokuts is not Costanoan... (is not Tonkawa, is not Zuni, is not Mixe, is not Zoque, is not any of the numerous Mayan languages, or affiliates of Mayan, if one extends the horizon). The differences do not disappear, and the likenesses, indeed, are far from all Chomskian universals. Some likenesses exist because of a genetic common origin (Penutian), some because of areal adaptations (Northwest Coast for some, California for others), some because of diffusion, some because of limited possibilities and implications (à la Greenberg's typology). Franz Boas once argued (1920) against exclusive concentration on genetic classification, calling the true historical problem the development of languages in all their aspects. A similar point can be made today as against concentration on putative universals. Most of language begins where universals leave off. In the tradition from Herder and von Humboldt through Boas and Sapir, languages are "concrete universals," and most of language as a human problem is bound up with the adjective of that term.

As modes of overcoming diversity of language intellectually, both genetic classification and putative universals locate their solutions in time. There is a past reference, a historical origin of languages or an evolutionary origin of the faculty of language, and there is a present and future reference, one which draws the moral of the unity that is found. Neither speaks to the present and future in terms of processes actually shaping the place of language in human life, for the faculty of language presumably is a constant and genetic diversification of languages is mostly a thing of the past. For the present and foreseeable future the major process is the adaptation of languages and varieties to one another, and their integration into special roles and complex speech communities. Understanding this process is the true problem that diversity of language poses, both to humankind and to those who study humankind's languages.

The essence of the problem appears as communication, intelligibility. Some are concerned with the problem at the level of the world as a whole, and efforts to choose or shape a world language continue. Some project this concern on to the past, speaking of a "stubborn mystery" in the '"profoundly startling," "anti-economic" multiplicity of languages spoken on this crowded planet' (Steiner,

1971: 70). Such a view is anachronistic, for the diversity was not "antieconomic" when it came into being; it was just as much a "naturally selected, maximalized efficiency of adjustment to local need and ecology" as the great variety of fauna and flora to which Steiner refers in the passage just quoted. Universal processes of change inherent in language, its transmission and use, together with separation and separate adaptation of communities over the course of many centuries, suffice to explain the diversity. Simply the accumulation of unshared changes would in time make the languages of separate groups mutually unintelligible. There is of course more to it than physical and temporal distance (as Steiner insightfully suggests); there is social distance as well. Boundaries are deliberately created and maintained, as well as given by default. Some aspects of the structures of languages are likely due to this. If the surface form of a means of communication is simplified greatly when there is need to overcome barriers, as it is in the formation of pidgin languages, then the surface form of means of communication may be complicated when there is a desire to raise or maintain barriers (Hymes, 1971b:73). This latter process may have something to do with the fact that the surface structures of languages spoken in small, cheek-by-jowl communities so often are markedly complex, and the surface structures of languages spoken over wide ranges less so. (The observation would seem to apply at least to North American Indian languages and Oceania).

3.3 Speech Communities

In any case, the problem is one of more than languages. It is one of speech communities. Here the inadequacy of concepts and methods is most painfully apparent. The great triumph of linguistic science in the nineteenth century, the comparative-historical method, deals with speech communities as the source and result of genetic diversification. The great triumph of linguistic science in the twentieth century, structural method, deals with speech communities as equivalent to language. 3 Genetic diversification can seldom be said to occur any longer, and a speech community comprising a single language hardly exists. The study of complex speech communities must benefit mightily from the tools and results both of historical linguistics, for the unraveling and interpretation of change, and of structural linguistics, for the explicit analysis of linguistic form. But it cannot simply apply them, it must extend them and develop new tools.

The needs can be expressed in terms of what is between speech communities and what is within them. Despite their well-known differences as to psychology, both Bloomfield and Chomsky reduce the concept of speech community to that of a language (Bloomfield, 1933, Ch. 3; Chomsky, 1965:3). This will not do. The boundaries between speech communities are thought of first of all as boundaries of communication, but communication, or mutual intelligibility as it is often phrased, is not solely a function of a certain objective degree of difference between two languages or some series of related languages. One and the same degree of objective linguistic differentiation may be taken to demarcate boundaries in one case, and be depreciated in another, depending on the social and political circumstances. 4 And intelligibility itself is a function not only of features of linguistic form (phonological, lexical, syntactic), but also of norms of interaction and conduct in conversation, and of attitudes towards differences in all these respects. In Nigeria one linguist found that as soon as members of a certain community recognized a related hinterland dialect, they refused to understand it (Wolff, 1959). Other communities are noted for the effort they make to understand despite great difference.

Such considerations cut across language boundaries. One may be at a loss to understand fellow speakers of his own language if his assumptions as to appropriate topics, what follows what, and the functions of speech are different (as happens often enough in classrooms between teachers of one background and students of another), while many of us have had the experience of following a discussion in a language of which we have little grasp, when the topics, technical terminology, and norms of conduct are professionally shared.

To repeat, communication cannot be equated with a *common* language. A term such as *the English language* comprises all linguistic varieties that owe their basic resources to the historical tradition known as English. That language is no longer an exclusive possession of the English, or even of the English and the Americans—there are perhaps more users of English in the Third World (just as there are more Christians), and they have their own rights to its resources and future. Many varieties of "English" are not mutually intelligible within Great Britain and the United States as well as elsewhere. In fact, it is an important clarification if we can agree to restrict the term *language* (and the term *dialect*) to just this sort of meaning: identification of a historically derived set of resources whose social functioning—organization into used varieties, mutual intelligibility etc.—is not given by the fact of historical derivation itself, but is problematic, needing to be determined, and calling for other concepts and terms.

We are in poorly explored territory here. Even with consideration restricted to groups which can communicate, there is a gamut from "I can make myself understood" at one end, to "she talks the same language" at the other. Probably it is best to employ terms such as *field* and *network* for the larger spheres within which a person operates communicatively. One's *language field* would be the sphere within which one has knowledge (or command) of languages as such; one's *speech field* would be the sphere within which one has knowledge (or command) of patterns of use (implicating competence in speaking, hearing, writing, reading); one's *network* would be the sphere of relationships in which the two kinds of knowledge (or command) are joined. The term *community* is best reserved for units with some degree of self-reproduction and support.

Clearly the boundary (and the internal organization) of a speech community is not a question solely of degree of interaction among persons (as Bloomfield said, and others have continued to say), but a question equally of attributed and achieved membership, of identity and identification. If interaction were enough, school children would speak the TV and teacher English they constantly hear. Some indeed can so speak, but do not necessarily choose to do so. Some years ago I was asked by teachers then at Columbia Point (Boston) why the children in the school did not show the influence of TV, or, more pointedly, of daily exposure to the talk of the teachers. A mother present made a telling observation: she had indeed heard children talk that way, but on the playground, playing school. When playing school stopped, that way of talking stopped, too.

Community, in this sense, is a dynamic, complex, and sometimes subtle thing. There are latent or obsolescent speech communities on some Indian reservations in this country, brought into being principally by the visit of a linguist or anthropologist who also can use the language and shows respect for uses to which it can be put. There are emergent communities, such as New York City would appear to be, in the sense that they share norms for the evaluation of certain variables (such as post-vocalic *r*), that have developed in this century. There are other communities whose stigmata are variable and signs of severe insecurity, like those of New York, or the community of *porteños* in Buenos Aires, composed principally of immigrants concerned to maintain their distance and prestige *vis-à-vis* speakers from the provinces (who, ironically enough, have lived in the country much longer). There can be multiple membership, and there is much scope for false perception; authorities, both governmental and educational, are often ignorant of the existence of varieties of language and communication under their noses. An unsuspected variety of creolized English was discovered recently on an island off Australia by the chance of a tape recorder being left on in a room where two children were playing. When the linguist heard the tape and could not understand it, he came to realize what it was. That such a language was known by the children was entirely unknown to the school. Indians who have been beaten as children for using their Indian tongue or blacks who have been shamed for using deep Creole will not necessarily trot the language out for an idle enquirer.

In general, when we recognize that this diversity of speech communities involves social as well as linguistic realities, we must face the fact that there are different vantage points from which diversity may be viewed. One person's obstacle may be someone else's source of identity. In the United States and Canada today one can find Indians seeking to learn the Indian language they did not acquire as children. Leveling of language seems neither inevitable nor desirable in the world today. It is common to mock efforts at preservation and revitalization of languages as outmoded romanticism, but the mockery may express a view of human nature and human needs whose shallowness bodes ill.

What is within a speech community in linguistic terms has begun to be understood better through recent work in sociolinguistics. Empirical and theoretical work has begun to provide a way of seeing the subject steadily as a whole. It suggests that one think of a community (or any group, or person) in terms, not of a single language, but of a *repertoire*. A repertoire comprises a set of ways of speaking. Ways of speaking, in turn, comprise *speech styles*, on the one hand, and *contexts of discourse*, on the other, together with *relations of appropriateness* obtaining between styles and contexts.

Membership in a speech community consists in sharing one or more of its ways of speaking—that is, not in knowledge of a speech style (or any other purely linguistic entity, such as a language) alone, but in terms of knowledge of appropriate use as well. There are rules of use without which rules of syntax are useless. Moreover, the linguistic features that enter into speech styles are not only the "referentially-based" features usually dealt with in linguistics today, but also the "stylistic" features that are complementary to them, and inseparable from them in communication. Just as social meaning is an integral part of the definition and demarcation of speech communities, so it is an integral part of the organization of linguistic features within them. (Cf. Bernstein's concept of "restricted" and "elaborated" code, classical diglossia, liturgy.) The sphere adequate to the description of speech communities, of linguistic diversity as a human problem, can be said to be: *means of speech*, *and their meanings to those who use them*. (This concept is dealt with in more detail in Hymes (1972b; 1973a)).

No one has ever denied the facts of multilingualism and heterogeneity of speech community in the world, but little has been done to enable us to comprehend and deal with them. Until now a "Herderian" conception of a world of independent one language-one culture units, a conception appropriate enough, perhaps, to a world pristinely peopled by hunters and gatherers and small-scale horticulturalists, has been tacitly fallen back upon. There has begun to be work to characterize complex linguistic communities and to describe speech communities adequately. Such description must extend to the value of speech itself in the life of a community: whether it is a resource to be hoarded or something freely expended, whether it is essential or not to public roles, whether it is conceived as intrinsically good or dangerous, what its proper role in socialization and demonstration of competence is conceived to be, and so forth. Through such work one can hope to provide adequate foundations for assessing diversity of language as both a human problem and a human resource.

Diversity could stand as the heading for all of the problems connected with speech and language, once our focus is enlarged from languages as such to speech communities—existing diversity as an obstacle, and sometimes diversity that it is desired to maintain or achieve. Nevertheless, it is worthwhile to comment separately on three topics that have been singled out for attention in their own right. These are problems connected with the media, the structures, and the functions of language. ①

References

[1] Gee J. P. The Social Mind: Language, Ideology and Social Practice [A]. in D. Macedo (Eds), Series in Language and Ideology [C]. New York: Bergin and Garvey, 1992.

[2] Gumperz J. J. Language and Social Identity [M]. Cambridge: Cambridge University Press, 1982.

[3] Hymes D. Introduction: Toward Ethnographies of Communication [A]. in Gumperz J. (Eds), The Ethnography of Communication [C]. Washington, DC.: American Anthropological Association, 1964.

[4] Hymes D. Foundations in Sociolinguistics [M]. London: Routledge, 1974.

[5] Hymes D. Ethnography, Linguistics, Narrative Inequality: Toward an Understanding of Voice [M]. Bristol: Taylor & Francis, 1996.

[6] Labov W. A. The Social Stratification of English in New York City [M]. Washington, DC: Center for Applied Linguistics, 1966.

[7] Sapir E. Language [M]. New York: Henry Holt, 1921.

[8] Spolsky B. Sociolinguistics [M]. Oxford: Oxford University Press, 1998.

[9] 赫德森. 社会语言学教程[M]. 北京:外语教学与研究出版社,2000.

[10] 沃德霍. 社会语言学引论[M]. 北京:外语教学与研究出版社,2000.

---

① 摘自 Hymes D. *Ethnography, Linguistics, Narrative Inequality: Toward an Understanding of Voice* [M]. Bristol: Taylor & Francis, 1996.

第五章

第二语言习得

导读

第二语言习得研究作为一门独立的学科形成于20世纪60年代末70年代初，发展到今天已经有快40年的历史。其中，Corde的《学习者言语错误的意义》是二语习得研究的开山之作，Selinker的《中介语的功能》推动了二语习得研究的理论框架的形成。这两篇论文的发表标志着对第二语言习得的系统研究的开始。此后，《第二语言习得研究》《第二语言研究》《语言学习》等国际性期刊，专门刊登第二语言习得方面的研究论文，推动了研究的发展，产生了一批重要的研究者，如：Corder、Selinker、Krashen、Gardner、Gregg、Lightbown、McLaughlin、Ellis等，也诞生了一些重要的第二语言习得理论和假说，如内部大纲假说、输入假说、普遍语法假说及文化适应假说等。

第二语言习得研究的基本问题可以归纳为四个方面：

（一）学习者在第二语言习得过程中获得了什么？即关于学习者语言的研究。

（二）学习者是怎样获得第二语言的？即关于习得过程的研究。

（三）学习者的个体差异，即关于第二语言学习者自身的研究。

（四）语言教学对第二语言习得的影响，即关于语言教学与语言习得关系的研究。

Ellis（1994:18）总结出第二语言习得研究的四个研究领域：

研究领域1：第二语言学习者语言特征研究

（1）偏误分析

（2）习得顺序与发展过程研究

（3）语言变异性研究

(4)语言的语用特征研究

研究领域2:学习者外部因素研究

(1)社会环境

(2)语言输入与互动的研究

研究领域3:学习者内部习得机制研究

(1)母语迁移

(2)认知过程

(3)交际策略

(4)语言普遍性的研究

研究领域4:第二语言学习者研究

(1)一般个体差异因素

(2)学习者策略的研究

第二语言习得研究所取得的诸多成果,既丰富和发展了第二语言习得理论,也为改进第二语言教学、外语教学提供了新的科学理论指导。

1. Definitions

1.1 Second Language Acquisition (SLA)

Term used with varying meanings: (a) the acquisition of a (first) foreign language; (b) the (essentially) non-directed acquisition of a foreign language in an environment in which that language is used as a trade language; (c) in an even narrower sense, the (essentially) non-directed acquisition of a second language before the acquisition of the first language has been completed.

(Baussmann 1996: 1034)

1. Refers in general to all types of learning of one or more languages additional to the first language or mother tongue. This sense of the term is all encompassing. including both formal and informal types of language learning as well as foreign language learning.

2. In a more restricted sense, second language acquisition (SLA) refers to the academic field of research into the learning of second languages.

(Davies 2002: 176)

This is the common term used for the name of the discipline. In general, SLA refers to the process of learning another language after the native language has been learned.

(Gass 2008: 2)

1.2 Interlanguage (IL)

Interlanguage refers to the separateness of a second language learner system, a system that has a structurally intermediate status between the native and target language.

(Selinker 1972: 209 – 231)

The relatively systematic transition from initial knowledge of a language (near-) native proficiency during the process of language acquisition. Often manifested as an unstable set of productive characteristics, interlanguage includes the rules of both the native language and the target language as well as a set of rules that belongs to neither, but rather manifests universal principles inherent in the language learner's competence.

(Bussmann 1996: 582)

The term INTERLANGUAGE (IL) is now used widely to refer to learners' developing L2 system that gradually approximates the target language or the language being learned.

(胡壮麟 2002: 572)

1.3 Native Language (NL)

This refers to the first language that a child learns. It is also known as the primary language, the mother tongue, or the first language.

(Gass 2008: 2)

1.4 Target Language (TL)

This refers to the language being learned.

(Gass 2008: 2)

1.5 Heritage language speakers

Heritage language speakers are, broadly speaking, those who have been exposed to a language of personal connection.

(Fishman, 2001)

1.6 Bilingualism

The investigation of bilingualism is a broad and complex field, including the study of the nature of the individual bilingual's knowledge and use of two (*or more*) languages (emphasis ours).

(Bhatia 2006: 5)

2. Classical theories

Generally speaking, SLA established itself as an independent discipline around 1970, particularly after the publication of Selinker's seminal paper "Interlanguage" in 1972.

What is the scope of SLA? What does the study of SLA consist of? It is the study of how second languages are learned. In other words, it is the study of the acquisition of a non-primary language; that is, the acquisition of a language beyond the native language. It is the study of how learners create a new language system with only limited exposure to a second language. It is the study of what is learned of a second language and what is not learned; it is the study of why most second language learners do not achieve the same degree of knowledge and proficiency in a second language as they do in their native language; it is also the study of why only some learners appear to achieve native-like proficiency in more than one language. Additionally, second language acquisition is concerned with the nature of the hypotheses (whether conscious or unconscious) that learners come up with regarding the rules of the second language. (Gass, S. M. &

Selinker, L. 2008: 1)

Over the years, the study of second language acquisition has become inextricably intertwined with language pedagogy; in the current text, one goal is to disentangle the two fields. Second language acquisition is not about pedagogy unless the pedagogy affects the course of acquisition.

In sum, second language acquisition is a complex field whose focus is the attempt to understand the processes underlying the learning of a second language. It is important to reemphasize that the study of second language acquisition is separate from the study of language pedagogy, although this does not imply that there are not implications that can be drawn from second language acquisition to the related discipline of language teaching.

2.1 Behaviorism

Early research into language learning (both first and second) was heavily dependent on the dominant linguistic and psychological paradigms. In this chapter we present some of the background as it relates more generally to language learning, in particular first language learning.

2.1.1 Linguistic background

The typical behaviorist position is that language is speech rather than writing. Furthermore, speech is a precondition for writing. The justification for this position came from the facts that (a) children without cognitive impairment learn to speak before they learn to write and (b) many societies have no written language, although all societies have oral language; there are no societies with only written but no spoken language systems.

Within the behaviorist framework speaking consists of mimicking and analogizing. We say or hear something and analogize from it. Basic to this view is the concept of habits. We establish a set of habits as children and continue our linguistic growth by analogizing from what we already know or by mimicking the speech of others. But what makes us talk and carry on conversation.

To understand the answer to this question within the behaviorist framework, consider the following information:

> Suppose that Jack and Jill are walking down a lane. Jill is hungry. She sees an apple in a tree. She makes a sound with her larynx, tongue and lips. Jack vaults the fence, climbs the tree, takes the apple, brings it to Jill and places it in her hand. Jill eats the apple.
>
> (Bloomfield, 1933, pp. 22 - 23)

To sum up, from a theoretical perspective, the child learns to make the stimulus—response connection. One such connection is the uttering of the word *doll* (response) when the child sees the object (stimulus). Another connection is the reverse: the child gets the doll (response) when he or she hears the word (stimulus). Thus, learning involves the establishment of a habit by means of which these stimulus—response sets become associated.

2.1.2 Psychological background

One of the key concepts in behaviorist theory was the notion of transfer. The main claim with regard to transfer is that the learning of task A will affect the subsequent learning of task B. What is of interest is how fast and how well you learn something after having learned something else. Some examples will help clarify this notion.

From a physical perspective, if someone knows how to play tennis and then picks up a table tennis racket for the first time, she or he will use the knowledge/skills that have been gained from playing tennis in this new, but related, situation. Thus, old knowledge/skills are transferred to a new situation.

In a transfer experiment related to verbal learning, consider a study by Sleight (1911) in which he was concerned with the ability to memorize prose more easily if one has had "prior experience" in memorizing poetry. He compared four groups of 12-year-old children on their ability to memorize prose. Three groups had prior training on the memorization of (a) poetry, (b) tables of measures, or (c) content of prose passages. A fourth group had no prior training in any type of memorization.

Following training, the groups were given tests that tested their ability to memorize prose. The question was: "To what extent does poetry memorization, or more precisely, the skills used in poetry memorization, transfer to memorization of prose?" (The results were nonsignificant.)

From this framework emerged contrastive analysis, because if one is to talk about replacing a set of habits (let's say, the habits of English) with another set of habits (let's say, those of Italian), valid descriptions are needed comparing the "rules" of the two languages. It would be misleading, however, to consider contrastive analysis in a monolithic fashion.

In fact, there are two distinct traditions of contrastive analysis that emerged. In the North American tradition, the emphasis was on language teaching and, by implication, language learning. Contrastive analyses were conducted with the ultimate goal of improving classroom materials. As Fisiak (1991) noted, this is more appropriately considered "applied contrastive analysis." In the European tradition, the goal of contrastive analysis was not pedagogical. Rather, the goal of language comparison was to gain a greater understanding of language. In fact, within the European tradition, it is maintained that contrastive analysis is a subdiscipline of linguistics. Its goal, like the goal of linguistics, is to understand the nature of language.

2.2 Universal Grammar (UG)

UG is postulated as an explanation of how it is that learners come to know properties of grammar that go far beyond the input, how they know that certain things are not possible, why grammars are of one sort rather than another. The claim is that such properties do not have to be learned. Proposals for an innate UG are motivated by the observation that, at least in the case of L1 acquisition, there is a mismatch between the primary linguistic data (PLD), namely the utterances a child is exposed to, and the abstract, subtle, and complex knowledge that the child acquires. In other words, the input (the PLD) underdetermines the output (the grammar). (Handbook p20)

The distinction between performance and competence is most closely associated with Chomsky's work on the universal features of language that Chomsky claims are shared by all languages. Chomsky argues that we need to distinguish between people's language performance, what they say at any given moment (which may be influenced and explained by an enormous number of factors), and their competence, what they know about language. Chomsky concentrates exclusively on linguistic competence, which, in Bachman's model, is just one part of one component. We will examine Chomsky's arguments, and their relevance to SLA, in some detail later, so suffice it to say for now that Chomsky's approach to language assumes that language is a restricted psychological phenomenon. Chomsky takes language to be a complex, abstract system of rules, and Chomsky supposes that the job of a theory of language acquisition is to describe that system of knowledge and to explain how it is acquired. The question of language use, of what Chomsky has referred to as "the creative aspect of language... the ability of normal persons to produce speech that is appropriate to situations, though perhaps quite novel, and to understand when others do so" (Chomsky 1980), lies completely outside the domain of Chomskian linguistics. To Chomsky, this question, and many others included in the Bachman model, are "mysteries" which simply lie beyond the reach of our minds, structured and organised as they are, either absolutely beyond those limits, or at so far a remove from anything we can comprehend with requisite facility that they will never be incorporated within explanatory theories intelligible to humans. (Chomsky, 1980: 136)

The issue of what sort of knowledge and abilities are involved in SLA, and the extent to which they can be adequately described and explained, is one of the most vexed issues in SLA research and theory construction.

2.3 Interlanguage Theory

To more completely understand SLA, it is necessary to go beyond the NL and the TL. In this section we focus on interlanguage. The basic assumption in SLA research is that learners create a language system, known as an interlanguage (IL). This concept validates learners' speech, not as a deficit system, that is, a language filled with random errors, but as a system of its own with its own structure. This system is composed of numerous elements, not the least of which are elements from the NL and the TL. There are also elements in the IL that do not have their origin in either the NL or the TL. These latter are called new forms and are the empirical essence of interlanguage. What is important is that the learners themselves impose structure on the available linguistic data and formulate an internalized system (IL). Central to the concept of interlanguage is the concept of fossilization, which generally refers to the cessation of learning. *The Random House Dictionary of the English Language* (Flexner and Hanck, 1988, p. 755) defines fossilization of a linguistic form, feature, rule, and so forth in the following way: "to become permanently established in the interlanguage of a second language learner in a form that is deviant from the target-language norm and that continues to appear in performance regardless of further exposure to the target language."

Because of the difficulty in determining when learning has ceased, some hold that it is more appropriate to refer to stabilization of linguistic forms, rather than to fossilization or permanent cessation of learning. In SLA, one often notes that learners reach plateaus that are far from the TL norms. Furthermore, it appears to be the case that fossilized or stabilized interlanguages exist no matter what learners do in terms of further exposure to the TL. Unfortunately, a solid explanation of permanent or temporary learning plateaus is lacking at present due, in part, to the lack of longitudinal studies that would be necessary to create databases necessary to come to conclusions regarding "getting stuck" in another language.

Selinker's (1974) interlanguage concludes:

1) the "language of the learner," a system in development and not yet a totally accurate approximation of native speaker language.

2) an approximative system

3) The type of language produced by second- and foreign language learners who are in the process of learning a language. In language learning, learners' errors are caused by several different processes, which include:

a) borrowing patterns from the mother tongue (language transfer: I am here since Monday)

b) extending patterns from the target language, e. g. by analogy. (overgeneralization: mans for man, gooder, etc.)

c) expressing meaning using the words and grammar which are already known. (Communication strategy: This place, cannot park.)

4) An individual linguistic system created by second language learners as a result of five cognitive processes:

d) effect of instruction (approach, rules provided by the teacher, classroom activities, etc.);

e) overgeneralization of target language rules (application of rules to contexts where they do not apply)

f) strategies involved in second language learning, such as rote memorization, use of formal rules, and guessing in context; and g) strategies involved in second language communication, such as circumlocution, use of gestures, appeal for assistance from a conversational partner.

Learners modify their own interlanguage only when they integrate into their long-term memories the input to which they attend, that is, construct new hypotheses in order to incorporate the noticed features into the interlanguage system (Ellis, 1997; Gass, 1988)

2.4 Monitor Model

Monitor hypothesis, also monitor model of second language development a theory proposed by **Krashen(1982)** which distinguishes two distinct processes in second and foreign language development and use. One, called "acquisition," is said to be a subconscious process which leads to the development of "competence" and is not dependent on the teaching of grammatical rules. The second process, called "learning" refers to the conscious study and knowledge of grammatical rules. In producing utterances, learners initially use their acquired system of rules. Learning and learned rules have only one function: to serve as a monitor or editor of utterances initiated by the acquired system, and learning cannot lead to acquisition.

Monitor Model, the most widely known and controversial theory, posits five hypotheses:

1) ***the acquisition-learning hypothesis***:

a. Acquisition

a) a subconscious "picking up" of rules characteristic of the L1 acquisition process that leads to spontaneous, unplanned communication.

b) a subconscious process which leads to the development of "competence" and is not dependent on the teaching of grammatical rules.

c) the natural assimilation of language rules through using language for communication

d) an unconscious process that involves the naturalistic development of language proficiency through understanding language and through using language for meaningful communication.

e) a subconscious process that results from informal, natural communication between people where language is a means and not a focus or an end it itself.

b. **Learning**:

a) the conscious study and knowledge of grammatical rules

b) a conscious focus on knowing and applying rules

c) second language learners utilize primarily "acquired, subconscious" knowledge rather than "learned, conscious" knowledge in real communication and that two types of knowledge are stored separately and are unrelated.

d) the formal study of language rules and a conscious process

e) a process in which conscious rules about the forms of a language and the ability to verbalize this knowledge.

f) formal teaching is necessary for "learning" to occur, and correction of errors helps with the development of learned rules.

2) ***the monitor hypothesis***:

a. the Monitor is an editing device that may operate before language performance.

b. The conscious knowledge of rules prompts the action of an "editor" or "monitor" that checks, edits, and polishes language output and is used only when the language user has sufficient time, attends to linguistic form, and knows the rule being applied.

c. The monitor is the repository of conscious grammatical knowledge about a language that is learned through formal instruction and that is called upon in the editing of utterances produced through the acquired system.

d. Acquisition is more "important" than learning. The main role of learning is a secondary one: to monitor what we say and write in the foreign language.

e. Learning and learned rules have only one function: to serve as a monitor or editor of utterances initiated by the acquired system, and learning cannot lead to acquisition.

f. Conscious language learning can only ast as a monitor that checks and corrects the utterances of the acquired system.

g. Conscious learning can function only as a monitor or editor that checks and repairs the output of the acquired system.

h. Monitoring occurs when there is sufficient time, when there is pressure to communicate correctly and not just convey meaning, and when the appropriate rules of speech are known.

i. We may call upon learned knowledge to correct ourselves when we communicate, but that conscious learning (i. e., the *learned* system) has only this function. Three conditions limit the successful use of the monitor:

— *Time*. There must be sufficient time for a learner to choose and apply a learned rule.

— *Focus on form*. The language user must be focused on correctness or on the form of the output.

— *Knowledge of rules*. The performer must know the rules. The monitor does best with rules that are simple in two ways. They must be simple to describe and they must not require complex movements and rearrangements.

3) ***the natural order hypothesis***:

a. grammatical structures are acquired in a predictable order for both children and adults, irrespective of the language being learnt.

b. Learners acquire the rules of a language in a predictable sequence, in a way that is independent of the order in which rules may have been taught.

c. Studies have shown that learners experience similar stages in development of linguistic structures in spite of their first languages.

d. There is a natural order of morpheme acquisition that applies to foreign language acquisition.

4) ***the input hypothesis***:

a. comprehensible input refers to utterances that the learner understands based on the context in which they are used as well as the language in which they are phrased.

b. "An acquirer can "move" from a stage *i* (where *i* is the acquirer's level of competence) to a stage *i* + **1** (where *i* + 1 is the stage immediately following I along some natural order) by understanding language containing *i* + 1." (Krashen & Terrel, 1983

c. Acquisition occurs only when learners receive optimal comprehensible input that is interesting, a little beyond their current level of competence (*i* + **1**), and not grammatically sequenced, but understandable through their background knowledge, their use of context, and other extralinguistic cues such as gestures and intonation.

d. Input must be comprehensible, slightly above the learner's present level of competence, interesting or relevant, not grammatically sequenced, in sufficient quantity, and experienced in low-anxiety contexts.

e. The ability speak fluently cannot be taught directly; rather, it "emerges" independently in time, after the acquirer has built up linguistic competence by understanding input.

f. If there is a sufficient quantity of comprehensible input, *i* + **1** will be provided automatically.

g. Learning will occur when unknown items are only just beyond the learner's present level.

h. Learners progress by understanding language containing $i+\mathbf{1}$; language just above present competence.

5) ***the affective filter hypothesis***:

a. The learner's emotional state or attitudes are an adjustable filter that freely passes, impedes, or blocks input necessary to acquisition. A low affective filter is desirable, since it impedes or blocks less of this necessary input.

b. The hypothesis identifies three kinds of affective or attitudinal variables related to SLA:

— *Motivation*. Learners with high motivation generally do better.

— *Self-confidence*. Learners with self-confidence and a good self-image tend to be more successful.

— *Anxiety*. Low personal anxiety and low classroom anxiety are more conducive to SLA

c. Language learning must take place in an environment where learners are "off the defensive" and the affective filter (anxiety) is low in order for the input to be noticed and gain access to the learners' thinking.

d. Affective factors can have a strong influence on foreign language learning. A helpful way of conceptualizing that influence is to regard affect as a "filter"' through which foreign language input has to pass before it is acquired.

— where the feelings of the learner are "positive", s/he is more "open" to input;

— where the feelings of the learner are "negative", s/he is "closed" to input.

2.5 Sociocultural Theory

As noted earlier, in recent years there has been an increased emphasis on language use. One consequence of this new emphasis is that the field has begun to incorporate approaches that go beyond the purely linguistic and psycholinguistic orientations that had focused on "in the head" phenomena of acquisition and that had been prevalent.

Sociocultural theory is based on work by the Russian psychologist Vygotsky, and represents a fundamentally different way of looking at language and learning than has been discussed in other parts of this book. Sociocultural theory is grounded in the ontology of the social individual. This does not mean a divorce from psychological processes, for a sociocultural approach considers language and, by extension, second language acquisition as contextually situated and is concerned with situated language as it relates to internal processes.

Sociocultural Theory focuses on the social nature of language learning and development and the role of learners' interaction in the classroom setting:

1) linguistic, cognitive, and social development as members of a community is socioculturally constructed (Vygotsky, 1978, Wertsch, 1991)
2) Our development "is inherently linked to the cultural, institutional and historical settings in which it occurs." (Wertsch, 1994)
3) Learning and development are as much social processes as cognitive processes, and occasions for instruction and learning are situated in the discursive interactions between experts and novices. (Appel & Lantolf, 1994; Brooks, 1990)

Piaget (1979) thinks: learning and mental development are independent processes; learning does not affect the course of development since maturation precedes learning. Vygotsky says learning precedes and contributes maturation, and the learner's language performance with others exceeds what the learner is able to do with the language without assistance

Vygotsky's Zone of Proximal Development:

1) "the distance between the actual develop0mental level as determined by independent problem solving and the level of potential development as

determined through problem solving under adult guidance or in collaboration with more capable peers" (Vygotsky, 1978)

2) the learner brings two levels of development to the learning task:

h) an actual developmental level : representing what the learner can do

i) a potential developmental level: representing what the learner should be able to do in the future.

Through interaction with others, the learner progresses from the "actual developmental level" to the "potential developmental level."

1) the potential development level of the learner becomes the next actual developmental level as a result of the learner's interaction with others and the expansion of cognitive abilities.

2) Today's potential development level becomes tomorrow's actual developmental level.

3) Language learning occurs when the learner receives appropriate types of assistance from the expert (i. e., teacher).

4) While learners need a great deal of contextualized input, acquisition may be contingent on cooperative, meaningful interaction.

3. Original Selecting

3.1 The study of second language acquisition

Second language acquisition (SLA) is a relatively young field. We would be hard-pressed to state a "beginning" date, but it is probably fair to say that the study of SLA has expanded and developed significantly in the past 40 - 45 years. This is not to say that there wasn't interest in the fields of language teaching and learning before then, for surely there was. It is to say, however, that since that time the body of knowledge of the field has seen increased sophistication.

We are far from a complete theory of SLA, but there is progress. By approaching SLA from a variety of disciplinary perspectives, as we will see in this chapter and in the remainder of this book, we have come a long way from pure descriptive studies to research that connects with other disciplines.

What is the scope of SLA? What does the study of SLA consist of? It is the study of how second languages are learned. In other words, it is the study of the acquisition of a non-primary language; that is, the acquisition of a language beyond the native language. It is the study of how learners create a new language system with only limited exposure to a second language. It is the study of what is learned of a second language and what is not learned; it is the study of why most second language learners do not achieve the same degree of knowledge and proficiency in a second language as they do in their native language; it is also the study of why only some learners appear to achieve native-like proficiency in more than one language. Additionally, second language acquisition is concerned with the nature of the hypotheses (whether conscious or unconscious) that learners come up with regarding the rules of the second language. Are the rules like those of the native language? Are they like the rules of the language being learned? Are there new rules, like neither language, being formed? Are there patterns that are common to all learners regardless of the native language and regardless of the language being learned? Do the rules created by second language learners vary according to the context of use? Do these rules and patterns vary more in individuals in a second language than they vary in the native language? Given these varied questions, the study of second language acquisition draws from and impacts many other areas of study, among them linguistics, psychology, psycholinguistics, sociology, sociolinguistics, discourse analysis, conversational analysis, and education, to name a few.

Given the close relationship between second language acquisition and other areas of inquiry, there are numerous approaches from which to examine second language data, each one of which brings to the study of second language acquisition its own goals, its own data-collection methods, and its own analytic tools. Thus, second language acquisition is truly an interdisciplinary field. This introductory text attempts to shed light on the nature of second language acquisition from multiple perspectives.

One way to define second language acquisition is to state what it is not. Over the years, the study of second language acquisition has become inextricably intertwined with language pedagogy; in the current text, one goal is to disentangle the two fields. Second language acquisition is not about pedagogy unless the pedagogy affects the course of acquisition. Although it may be the case that those who are interested in learning about how second languages are learned are ultimately interested in doing so for the light this knowledge sheds on the field of language teaching, this is not the only reason second language acquisition is of interest, nor is it the major reason scholars in the field of second language acquisition conduct their research.

Let us briefly consider some of the reasons why it might be important for us to understand how second languages are learned and what is not learned.

Linguistics

> When we study human language, we are approaching what some might call the human essence, the distinctive qualities of mind that are, so far as we know, unique to [humans].
>
> (Chomsky, 1968, p. 100)

The study of how second languages are learned is part of the broader study of language and language behavior. It is not more central or peripheral than any other part of linguistic study, which in turn has as its larger goal the study of the nature of the human mind. In fact, a major goal of second language acquisition research is the determination of linguistic constraints on the formation of second language grammars. Because theories of language are concerned with human language knowledge, one can reasonably assume that this knowledge is not limited to first language knowledge, and that linguistic principles reflect the possibilities of human language creation and the limits of human language variation. This scope of inquiry includes second languages.

Language pedagogy

Most graduate programs whose goal is to train students in language teaching now have required course work in second language acquisition, unlike a generation ago. Why should this be the case? People have come to realize that if one is to develop language-teaching methodologies, there has to be a firm basis for those methodologies in language learning. It would be counterproductive to base language teaching methodologies on something other than an understanding of how language learning does and does not take place. To give an example, some language-teaching methodologies are based exclusively on rule memorization and translation exercises. That is, a student in a language class is expected to memorize rules and then translate sentences from the native language to the language being learned and vice versa. However, studies in second language acquisition have made language teachers and curriculum designers aware that language learning consists of more than rule memorization. More important, perhaps, it involves learning to express communicative needs. The details of this new conceptualization of language learning have resulted in methodologies that emphasize communication. In other words, pedagogical decision-making must reflect what is known about the process of learning, which is the domain of second language acquisition.

A second, perhaps equally important but less assuming, rationale related to language pedagogy has to do with the expectations that teachers have of their students. Let's assume that a teacher spends a class hour drilling students on a particular grammatical structure. Let's further assume that the students are all producing the structure correctly and even in an appropriate context. If, after the class is over and the drill is finished, a student comes up to the teacher and uses the incorrect form in spontaneous speech, what should the teacher think? Has the lesson been a waste of time? Or is this type of linguistic behavior to be expected? If a student produces a correct form, does that necessarily mean that the student has learned the correct rule? These sorts of issues are part of what teachers need to be aware of when assessing the success or failure of their teaching. Or, to take an example from a mystery novel, *Speaker of Mandarin* by Ruth Rendell, Inspector Wexford is in a museum and accompanied by Mr. Sung who is showing him the well-preserved body of a woman who had lived 2000 years earlier. Mr. Sung says "Let's go" and Inspector Wexford takes the opportunity to provide an English lesson .

Wexford: I wish you wouldn't keep saying that. If I may suggest it, you should say, "Shall we go? Or "Are you ready?"

Sung: You may suggest. Thank you. I am anxious to speak good. Shall we go? Are you leady?

Wexford: Oh, yes, certainly.

Sung: Don't reply, please. I practice. Shall we go? Are you leady? Good, I have got it. Come, let's go. Are you leady to go to the site? Reply now, please.

Thus, after practicing "Shall we go?", Sung, when it is time to make a spontaneous utterance, reverts back to "Let's go." Further, when Sung believes that he is repeating, and therefore, practicing, his repetition of "Are you ready?", his utterance is no different than his original faulty utterance.

Cross-cultural communication and language use

We have noted some expectations that teachers have about students. Similarly, in interactions with speakers of another language/culture, we have certain expectations and we often produce stereotyped reactions. For example, we may find ourselves making judgments about other people based on their language. It turns out that many stereotypes of people from other cultures (e. g., rudeness, unassertiveness) are based on patterns of nonnative speech. These judgments in many instances are not justified, because many of the speech patterns that nonnative speakers use reflect their nonnativeness rather than characteristics of their personality. As an example, consider the following exchange between a teacher and a former student (NNS = nonnative speaker; NS = native speaker):

(1-1) From Goldschmidt (1996, p. 255)

NNS: I have a favor to ask you.

NS: Sure, what can I do for you?

NNS: You need to write a recommendation for me.

Many teachers would, of course, react negatively to the seeming gall of this "request," perhaps initially thinking to themselves, "What do you mean I *need* to write a letter?" when most likely the only problem is this nonnative speaker's lack of understanding of the forceful meaning of *need*. A second example occurred in the life of one of the authors. An international student whom the professor did not know emailed to ask the professor for an appointment, stating that she was interested in the discipline of SLA. The professor wrote back with a suggestion of a time that they finally agreed on. The student arrived at the appointed time and said:

(1-2) NNS: You wanted to see me?

Many would, of course, also react negatively to the seeming strangeness of the introduction, probably initially thinking, "What do you mean I *wanted* to see you; it's you who wanted to see me." So, understanding second language acquisition and, in this case, how nonnative speakers use language, allows us to separate issues of cross-cultural communication from issues of stereotyped behavior or personal idiosyncrasies.

But it is not only cross-cultural questions that are at issue. In the following example, understanding L2 phonology could have helped in the recent but brief horse-racing scandal when a Chilean jockey, after winning the Kentucky Derby, was accused of carrying something in his hand other than his whip. Apparently, he had told a reporter that he wore a Q-Ray, which is a therapeutic bracelet used for arthritic conditions. What had been understood was a "Q-ring," which apparently the reporter had never heard of, probably because it doesn't exist. So, despite the fact that he didn't know what it was, the reporter assumed it to be something illegal. Had the reporter minimally recognized that perception of nonnative speech often occurs through the filter of our native language phonological system and that that perception is not always accurate, the problem might have been avoided. That coupled with the fact that he had never heard of a Q-ring might have suggested the need to seek greater clarification and the two or three day scandal could have been avoided.

Language policy and language planning

Many issues of language policy are dependent on a knowledge of how second languages are learned. For example, issues surrounding bilingualism, such as the English Only Movement in the United States, or the many different types of bilingual education (including immersion programs) can only be debated if one is properly informed about the realities and constraints of learning a second language. National language programs often involve decision making that is dependent on (a) information about second language learning, (b) the kinds of instruction that can be brought to bear on issues of acquisition, and (c) the realities and expectations one can have of such programs. All too often, these issues are debated without a clear understanding of the object of debate; that is, the nature of how second languages are learned.

In sum, second language acquisition is a complex field whose focus is the attempt to understand the processes underlying the learning of a second language. It is important to reemphasize that the study of second language acquisition is separate from the study of language pedagogy, although this does not imply that there are not implications that can be drawn from second language acquisition to the related discipline of language teaching.

Many disciplines quite clearly find themselves as part of the humanities (e.g., literature) or part of the sciences (e.g., biology). Second language acquisition, because of its complexity and its reliance on and import for other disciplines, is not placed so easily. SLA is part of the humanities, in the sense that it is part of the branch of "learning (as philosophy, arts, or languages) that investigate[s] human constructs and concerns as opposed to natural processes (as in physics or chemistry) and social relations (as in anthropology or economics)" (from Merriam-Webster online dictionary), although clearly there are areas of the field that do consider social relations as an integral part of learning. Given that the humanities are concerned with human constructs and concerns, language acquisition is relevant, for one way of understanding the human condition is through an understanding of language. While this is probably uncontroversial, unfortunately this central area of humanistic study is often confined to general issues of language and the human capacity for language as referring to studies of primary language knowledge and the acquisition of primary language. But this book assumes that we cannot adequately examine the nature of language knowledge if we confine ourselves to only a small portion of the world's population; that is, monolingual native speakers.

Second language acquisition, while rightfully part of the humanities, is also part of the social sciences, defined (Merriam-Webster online) as "a branch of science that deals with the institutions and functioning of human society and with the interpersonal relationships of individuals as members of society." Given that second language acquisition deals with interpersonal relations as it does when studying many issues of language use, it is definitely part of the social sciences. Interactions involving nonnative speakers of a language are undoubtedly highly frequent in the broader context of the world's interactions, and, thus, the study of these interactions has a central place in the social sciences and cognitive science. Finally, since some SLA research focuses on the biology of the brain, and what SLA neurophysiology can show about neural workings, SLA itself can be considered a part of the developing cognitive neurosciences.①

References

[1] Adjemian C. On the Nature of Interlanguage Systems [J]. Language Learning, 1976, 26(2).

[2] Bley-Vroman R. The Comparative Fallacy in Interlanguage Studies: the Case of Systematicity [J]. Language Learning, 1983, 33(1).

[3] Corder S. P. The Significance of the Learner's Errors [J]. International Review of Applied Linguistics, 1967 (5).

[4] Corder S. P. Idiosyncratic Dialects and Error Analysis [J]. International Review of Applied Linguistics in Language Teaching, 1971, 9(2).

[5] Ellis R. The Study of Second Language Acquisition [M]. Oxford: Oxford University Press, 1994.

[6] Gass S. M. & Selinker L. Second Language Acquisition [M]. New York: Routledge, 2008.

① 摘自 S. Gass S. *Second Language Acquisition*[M]. New York: Routledge, 2008.

[7]Lado R. Linguistics across Cultures: Applied Linguistics for Language Teachers[M]. Ann Arbor, Michigan: University of Michigan Press, 1957.

[8]Nemser W. Approximative Systems of Foreign Language Learners[J]. International Review of Applied Linguistics, 1971(9).

[9]Oxford R. L. Individual Differences among Your ESL Students: Why a Single Method Can't Work[J]. Journal of Intensive English Studies, 1993(7).

[10]Schachter J. An Error in Error Analysis[J]. Language Learning, 1974(27).

[11] Selinker L. Interlanguage [J]. International Review of Applied Linguistics, 1972(10).

[12] Selinker L. Rediscovering Interlanguage [M]. London: Longman, 1992.

[13]Weinreich U. Language in Contact[M]. The Hague: Mouton, 1953.

[14] Williams M. and Robert L. Burden. Psychology for Language Teachers: A Social Constructivist Approach[M]. Cambridge: CUP, 1997.

[15]理查兹.朗文语言教学及应用语言学辞典[M]. 北京:外语教学与研究出版社,2005.

[16]胡壮麟,姜望琪. 语言学高级教程[M]. 北京:北京大学出版社,2002.

第六章

外语教学

导　读

外语教学法是一门交叉性极强的科学。它是在语言科学和教育科学交叉点上成长起来的科学,既可算作语言学,也可算作教育学。在外语教学法的历史上,任何一个教学法新思想、新流派的产生都有其语言学、教育学和心理学的依据,是当时流行的各学科新学说的综合应用。但外语教学法至今未有一个为所有人所公认的统一的理论模式,而是以一定的流派的形式存在。一部外语教学法的历史,在某种意义上可说是一部外语教学法流派的竞争史。目前为止,外语教学法流派大大小小数以百计,但曾经影响到全世界的只有十几个。我们只挑选其中几个影响面相对大的做以介绍。

截至目前,主要的教学法有以下几种:

· 语法 - 翻译教学法

· 直接教学法

· 听说教学法

· 交际教学法

· 认知教学法

需要强调的是,任何一个流派都不是万能的。一方面,它既有其"强项",适用于一定条件,在一定条件下能充分发挥自己的优势,较好地完成自己所胜任的任务,在某个方面达到别的流派达不到的效果;另一方面,它又有自己的弱点,而这又恰恰是原有流派的"强项"。所以说,各主要流派都有自己的用武之地,而同时有都有自己的弱点。任何一个学派都不能最终取代别的主要流派,大家"各有千秋",这也是它们能长期共存的原因之一。

1. Definitions

1.1 teacher-directed instruction

It is also called **teacher-fronted instruction**, a teaching style in which instruction is closely managed and controlled by the teacher, where students often respond in unison to teacher questions, and where whole-class instruction is preferred to other methods. Many current teaching approaches try to encourage less teacher-directed interaction through the use of individualized activities or group work.

(Richards 2005: 696)

1.2 Pedagogy

The term "pedagogy" refers to culture-specific ways of organizing formal teaching and learning in institutional sites such as the school. In educational theory, pedagogy is typically is divided into curriculum, instruction, and evaluation, referring respectively to cultural knowledge and content, classroom interaction, and the evaluation of student performance.

(Spolsky 1999: 332)

The term *pedagogy* in a broad sense to include not only issues pertaining to classroom strategies, instructional materials, curricular objectives, and evaluation measures but also a wide range of historiopolitical and sociocultural experiences that directly or indirectly influence L2 education.

(Kumaravadivelu 2003: 34)

1.3 Approach

A set of correlative assumptions dealing with the nature of language teaching and learning. An approach is axiomatic. It describes the nature of the subject matter to be taught.

(Anthony 1963)

An approach to language teaching is something that reflects a certain model or research paradigm — a theory, if you like.

(Celce-Murcia 2006)

1.4 Method

Method is an overall plan for the orderly presentation of language materials, no part of which contradicts, and all of which is based upon, the selected approach. An approach is axiomatic, a method is procedural.

(Anthony 1963)

A methods, is a set of procedures, i. e., a system that spells out rather precisely how to teach a second or foreign language. It is more specific than an *approach* but less specific than a technique. Methods are typically compatible with one (or sometimes two) approaches.

(Celce-Murcia 2006)

1.5 Affective-Humanistic Approach

It is a reaction to the general lack of affective considerations in both Audio-lingual approach and the Cognitive approach.

1.6 Comprehension-Based Approach

An outgrowth of research in first language acquisition that led some language methodologists to assume that second or foreign language learning is very similar to first language acquisition.

1.7 Cognitive Academic Language Learning Approach (CALLA)

An instructional model that was developed to meet the academic needs of students learning English as a second language in American schools.

1.8 Natural Approach

An approach proposed by Tracy Terrell and Stephen Krashen in the late 1970s as a method of teaching second language that emphasizes the centrality of the acquisition process.

1.9 The Silent Way

A method introduced by Caleb Gattegno in 1976, based on the premise that the teacher should be silent as much as possible in the classroom and the learner should encouraged to produce as much target language as possible.

1.10 Total Physical Response (TPR)

Developed by James Asher, and based on the theory that second language acquisition is similar to a child's first language acquisition. That is, as a baby, our first involvement in language is through responding to commands out parents give us.

2. Classical theories

The formation and development of schools of foreign language teaching methodology is closely related to linguistics. With the profound study of linguistics, there appeared schools of grammar-translation method, direct method, audio-lingual method, cognitive approach, communicative approach and otherwise one after another. In the course of their self-readjustment and reform, they have made a noticeable change respectively in their teaching concepts, basic tenets and teaching procedures and have shown great prospects for a wider application to ELT.

Now we have **an overview of the approaches and methods**:

1) Traditional Behaviorist Methods:

a. Grammar-translation Method

b. Direct Method

c. Audiolingual Method (ALM)

2) Rationalist and Mentalist Methods

a. Cognitive Anti-Method

b. Cognitive-Code Method

3) Functional Approaches

a. Cognitive Academic Language Learning Approach

b. Total Physical Response

c. Total Physical Response Storytelling

d. Natural Approach

4) Humanistic Approaches

a. Community Language Learning

b. The Silent Way

c. Suggestopedia

d. Rassias Method

2.1 Grammar-translation Approach

The Grammar-translation method was used for centuries in teaching the reading of Latin and classical Greek — "dead languages" —and the method was very appropriate for this purpose. This method of teaching focus on grammar and words.

Hadley(1993) take this approach as an extension of the approach used to teach classical languages to the teaching of modern languages; a "mental disciple," wherein the teacher seeks to strengthen students' minds through the exploration of literary works and extensive grammatical analysis of the structure of the target language.

There are seven main ideas of this approach:

1) Instruction is given in the native language of the students.

2) There is little use of the target language for communication.

3) Focus on grammatical parsing, i. e. , the form and inflection of words.

4) There is early reading of difficult texts.

5) A typical exercise is to translate sentences from the target language into the mother tongue (or vice versa).

6) The result of this approach is usually an inability on the part of the student to use the language for communication.

7) The teacher does not have to be able to speak the target language.

2.2 Direct method

The label that has survived today from the nineteenth century is the Direct Method. In content it seems to go back to J. S. Blackie, a Scottish classics teacher who in the 1850s was advocating (one might say re-advocating) the avoidance of the mother tongue, the direct association of word with object, and the relegation of grammar to a subordinate position. The new method attempted to legitimate itself by reference to the way a child learns its first language, but it was phonetics which appeared to give both a scientific respectability and also a way round the doubtful and difficult orthography of the printed word and the attendant stress on reading and writing. Above all it seemed to provide easy classroom access to communication in society rather than to literature in the study.

At first the reform methods made slow progress. From the central place that language learning had had in the medieval and Renaissance curricula, it had by the nineteenth century been pushed to the periphery, partly because its aims had remained unchanged from those of the eighteenth century, as had its methods, largely grammar-translation. Thus nothing obviously relevant was being taught, and the "mental discipline" aspect of the work, central to the approach and method originally, was felt to be far better catered for by classics and mathematics. Those modern language teachers who were concerned to transform their discipline in the direction of language for communication came together for the first time in a national conference in 1890 and two years later formed the Modern Languages Association. This was something of a turning-point for the new methods in Britain. The teachers were inspired by the German debate surrounding Vi? tor's pamphlet (Vi? tor himself addressed the 1890 conference) and passed resolutions supporting oral work, direct method and the use of phonetics.

However, the man whose name is most closely associated with the Direct Method is Otto Jespersen, Professor of English at the University of Copenhagen, whose book *Sprogundervisning* (translated into English in 1904 as *How to Teach a Foreign Language*) had tremendous success. The *Academy* magazine wrote of a later edition of it "The Reform method of teaching has prevailed and to no one is more honour due for the victory than the distinguished Danish linguist and teacher, Dr Otto Jespersen." And in fact its successes included the adoption of this method as the sole one to be used in schools by France, Belgium and Germany. This book is an easily read, common-sense, practical work that assumes communication as an end and suggests a range of means, most of which would be acceptable to the modern comprehensive school teacher with the same end in view (the notable exception is the stress on phonetics). Like Comenius's work, Jespersen's book seems surprisingly modern only because similar aims tend to produce similar methods. He advocates natural, useful language material, careful listening, direct association of word with object or idea, grammar derived from language known, and the foreign language as the principal if not only means of communication in the classroom.

Direct Approach is a reaction to the Grammar-Translation Approach and its failure to produce learners who could communicate in the foreign language they had been studying; modeled after the way in which children acquire their first language, by listening to it in large quantities.

1) No use of the mother tongue is permitted (i. e., the teacher does not need to know the students' native language).

2) Lessons begin with dialogues and anecdotes in modern conversational style.

3) Actions and pictures are used to make meanings clear.

4) Grammar is learned inductively.

5) Literary texts are read for pleasure and are not analyzed grammatically.

6) The target culture is also taught inductively.

7) The teacher must be a native speaker or have nativlei8ke proficiency in the target language.

2.3 Audio-Lingual Method(ALM)

The new approach was based on behaviourist ideas of learning. These saw language—spoken language—as a collection of habits, and language teaching as habit formation. The amount of language to which the learner was exposed was to be strictly limited but unsimplified; real language with real intonation at real speed. It was to be "overlearned" by repetition so that it became automatic, and was not to be analysed grammatically (there was no grammar progression in the early courses) but manipulated by the substitution of items in "open" slots in the utterance. The tape-recorder was essential to provide the repeated models for pupil repetition. With only a tape-recorder the method was termed "audio-lingual"; with the addition of film-strip still-pictures to give instant recognition of the "meaning" of the utterance (i. e. the context in which it could be effectively uttered) the method became "audio-visual."

Audio-lingual Method is also named the Aural-Oral, Functional Skills, New Key, or American Methods. Evolved from the school of structural, or descriptive linguistics.

Based on structural linguistics and behavioristic psychology and places heavy emphasis on spoken rather than written language, stressing habit formation as a mode of learning. A reaction to the Reading Approach and its lack of emphasis on oral-aural skills: this approach became dominant in the US during the 1940s, 1950s, and 1960s; it draws from the Reform Movement and the Direct Approach but adds features from structural linguistics and behavioral psychology.

C. C. Fries and W. F. Twaddell divided five steps in this method:

Recognition—Imitation—Repetition—Variation—Selection.

Their main ideas can be summarized as follow:

1) Lessons begin with dialogues.

2) Mimicry and memorization are used, based on the assumption that language is habit formation.

3) Grammatical structures are sequenced and rules are taught inductively.

4) Skills are sequenced: listening, speaking — reading, writing postponed.

5) Pronunciation is stressed from the beginning.

6) Vocabulary is severely limited in initial stages.

7) A great effort is made to prevent learner errors.

8) Language is often manipulated without regard to meaning or context.

9) The teacher must be proficient only in the structures, vocabulary, etc. that he or she is teaching since learning activities and materials are

carefully controlled.

2.4 The Cognitive Approach

Its demise was hastened by criticisms of the behaviourist learning theory that underpinned it. The central figure of behaviourist psychology in terms of its application to language learning was B. F. Skinner. From 1959 criticism of his work and theory by Noam Chomsky and his followers produced an alternative approach that stressed language as rule-governed behaviour and suggested that the mechanism for formulation of these rules to generate "new" language was a good deal more subtle than mere habit-formation. In teaching terms this meant exposure to a great deal more of the language than the behaviourists were prepared to admit, much more opportunity for use by pupils of their own acquired store of the foreign language for purposes that they perceived as their own, and a view of error that saw it not as something to be avoided at all costs but as something to be learnt from, with fluency a higher good than accuracy.

Directly opposed to the Audio-lingual Approach, Carrol(1966) proposed the COGNITIVE APPROACH in L2 teaching, which was further explained and elaborated by Chastain(1969:79 – 106) and Diller(1971). Theoretically, this approach was related to TG grammar and cognitive psychology. Diller(1971:23 – 37) summarized four principles of the Cognitive Approach as follows:

1. A living language is characterized by rule-governed creativity.
2. The rules of grammar are psychologically real.
3. Man is specifically equipped to learn languages.
4. A living language is a language in which we can think.

The first principle emphasizes that language learning is rule-governed rather than the result of habitformation. A language learner, working like a linguist, forms provisional rules based on the initial input and then cheeks them against the additional incoming input. Gradually, the rules will approximate the norms of a target language by a repetitive cycle of hypothesis-forming and hypothesis-testing. The second principle advocates the explicit leaching of grammatical rules and students' conscious learning of these rules. The third principle argues that human beings are born language learners so that they can learn a language at any time in their life. Therefore, L2 adult learners are not necessarily less advantageous than Children. The last principle lays emphasis on meaning-driven learning but discourages repetitive pattern drills.

Although the principles were well constructed and clearly explained, there were not any constructive procedures available that could be applied to L2 leaching. Therefore, the Cognitive Approach could hardly be regarded as a qualified competitor against the Audio-lingual Approach.

2.5 The Communicative Approach

The "communicative approach" to foreign language teaching is by now around twenty years old. It is not a tightly structured "method" of teaching, like the French audio-visual movement of the 1960s, for example, or some commercially marketed language teaching methods of today, such as "Suggestopedia" or the "Silent Way." Rather it is a broad assembly of ideas, from a range of sources (some linguistic, others more broadly educational), which have together come to be accepted as "good practice" by many contemporary teachers.

In the decades following World War II, broad changes in the world economy and in society, as well as changes in the educational systems of the developed world, led to the creation of large new publics interested in foreign language learning. The number of adults wanting to learn foreign languages for a variety of purposes—business, vocational, access to higher education—increased very greatly. At secondary school level, foreign language learning had traditionally been reserved in many countries for an elite minority, attending academically oriented schools (such as the grammar schools of Britain). But in the 1960s and 1970s, foreign language learning was extended much more widely, as part of a general movement to broaden and upgrade the content of secondary education for the population overall. In Britain, the widespread establishment of comprehensive schools led for the first time to the teaching of a foreign language to virtually all children, at least in the early years of secondary school.

This broadening of the "market" for foreign languages created pressure for change in teaching methods and curricula, to suit the needs of non-traditional groups of learners. At the same time, changes in general educational thinking were leading to requirements that learning outcomes in all subjects be specified much more clearly, often in the form of behavioral objectives—much more precise statements of what it was expected that the learners would be able to do with the knowledge and skills they had acquired during any given course of study. Similarly, more active and experiential modes of learning (such as the use of group work) were coming into favour across the curriculum as a whole. These general educational themes again created new expectations and pressures for those concerned more specifically with the teaching and learning of foreign languages.

The rise of the communicative approach can thus be seen as the response of the language teaching profession to their new situation, and a recognition of the inadequacy of traditional "grammar/translation" methods, and also of the "structural" methods of the 1950s (which stressed speaking and listening but relied heavily on meaningless pattern drills and repetition), to meet the needs of their new publics. Fortunately, at the time when there was a will for change, a range of new ideas in different branches of linguistics began to offer a range of possible new solutions.

3. Original selecting

Basic Principles

The preceding chapter, in discussing several aspects of language has suggested the complexity of this essentially human activity; whilst the detailed questions posed at the end of Chapter 2 imply a professional dimension no less complicated.

Clearly there are people who teach the English language successfully without professional training or rigorous language study, succeeding by virtue of those sensitive and sympathetic qualities which mark the natural teacher. There are also those whose training for and experience of other kinds of teaching is successfully transferred to language teaching. There are students of linguistics whose studies have provided such insights into English that they are better teachers thereby. Ideally, however, the professional English language teacher should have not only the required personal qualities, but also training in the disciplines and fields of study appropriate to the language teaching process. Training of this kind can be stated in terms of what the teacher should know and what he should do.

Even with the very wide range of educational settings in the world today, from kindergarten groups of twelve in Argentina to strictly audio-visual classes in Senegal, or traditionally taught university seminars in Japan, there are certain basic principles common to all good language teaching, principles derived from the interaction of aspects of those fields of study which contribute to the theory and practice of EFL teaching. The contributory areas of knowledge may be represented in Figure 3.

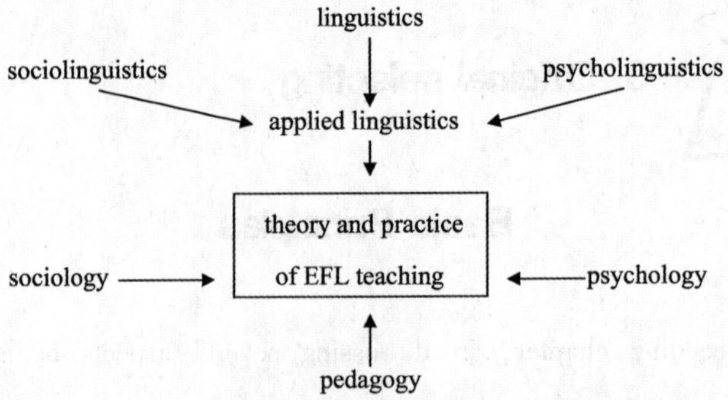

Figure 3

Linguistics, the study of language itself, has drawn on ideas from sociology to establish the place and role of language in the sociology of human behaviour, and from *psychology* to investigate among other things how language is learned. The result is two new disciplines, *sociolinguistics and psycholinguistics*, which, together with linguistics proper, form the central area of *applied linguistics*. This last field is concerned with many activities involving language—for example, speech pathology, machine translation, mother tongue acquisition, literary analysis. But for the present purpose its chief relevance is to language teaching.

The conjunction of sociology and psychology with the theory and practice box is a reminder that teaching of any kind draws upon knowledge from these fields quite apart from language considerations: group interaction, the status of the teacher and the school in the local culture, the social role of education as a whole—from sociology; and facts about memory span, motivation, cognitive development from psychology. The often forgotten field of *pedagogy* is concerned with class management, questioning techniques, lesson planning and teaching strategies and the numerous daily tricks of the trade that separate the professional teacher from the amateur.

Whether the teacher is well read or not in all the above disciplines, he inevitably makes decisions about the problems involved. Consciously or unconsciously, he reflects in his teaching the beliefs he holds about the needs of the learners, their ways of learning, the best method of motivating them, etc. The more knowledge he can glean from the wealth of writing in the field, the better he will be able to combine this knowledge with practical experience to produce a suitable teaching methodology for his own purposes. In the light of his knowledge, he can then decide what English to teach, how to give practice in a meaningful way, and how to prepare and execute a progression of enjoyable, well-organised lessons.

3.1 Selection and grading

In common with every other subject of the curriculum, English language teaching requires that decisions are made about what is to be taught: the process of selection; and about the breaking down of that body of knowledge or skills into teachable units: the process of grading. Whilst decisions of this kind are usually made for the teacher by textbook writers and syllabus designers, his teaching is inevitably structured and controlled by the underlying theories.

Language teaching presupposes a theory of language, and this is supplied by applied linguistics. The traditional view that the English language consisted of a battery of grammatical rules and a vocabulary book produced a teaching method which selected the major grammar rules with their exceptions and taught them in a certain sequence. This was the grammar-translation method whose rules with examples, its paradigms and related exercises have for so many years produced generations of non-communicators. The later structural theory of language described the syntax of English as a limited number of patterns into which the lexis or vocabulary could be fitted. Selection and grading them consisted of identifying the major structural patterns and teaching them in a suitable sequence. In its extreme form, the structural approach enabled many learners to use "language like behaviour," reflecting a one-dimensional, and essentially non-communicative, view of the nature of language.

Such approaches to language teaching are about as practical as driving lessons in an immobilised car. Language, as a form of human social behaviour, functions within a context of situation. Recognition of this second dimension, and the fact that it is difficult to divorce linguistic forms from their setting, gave rise to situationalised language teaching, or the situational approach. Here, the processes of selection and grading are applied not only to syntax and lexis, but identify a series of appropriate settings: in the classroom, at home, in the shop, at the railway station and so on. Clearly, however, whilst selection from a finite set of rules or structures is possible, it is more difficult to select from an infinite range of situations.

The third dimension of language, which has most recently received the attention of linguists, is that of linguistic functions and notions. The argument is that linguistic forms—sounds, words and structures—are used in situations to express functions and notions.

It is possible to identify a wide range of notions: of time, number, length and quantity; of agreement and disagreement, of seeking and giving information, suasion, and concession, to name a few; and thereafter select and grade them into a teaching sequence of communicative goals. The sociolinguistic developments which have in recent years made language teachers more conscious of the functional dimension of language usage have had a number of other effects. At one level, they have given the death-blow to the naive assumption that a particular linguistic form is identifiable with a particular function. As Widdowson (1971) points out:

> One might imagine, for example, that the imperative mood is an unequivocal indicator of the act of commanding. Butconsider these instances of the imperative: "Bake the pie in a slow oven," "Come for dinner tomorrow," "Take up his offer," "Forgive us our trespasses". An instruction, an

invitation, advice and prayer are all different acts, yet the imperative serves them all.

At another level, acknowledgment of the functional dimension has given greater complexity to the basic principle of grading and selection. If these processes are equally applicable to all the three dimensions of Figure 4, which is to have primacy? All must be represented in language courses, but in our present state of knowledge it is the language dimension that is the most completely understood system. The result is that for most non-specialised English teaching in the world today, the principle of grading and selection are applied to the prime dimension of linguistic structure, before those of situation and function.

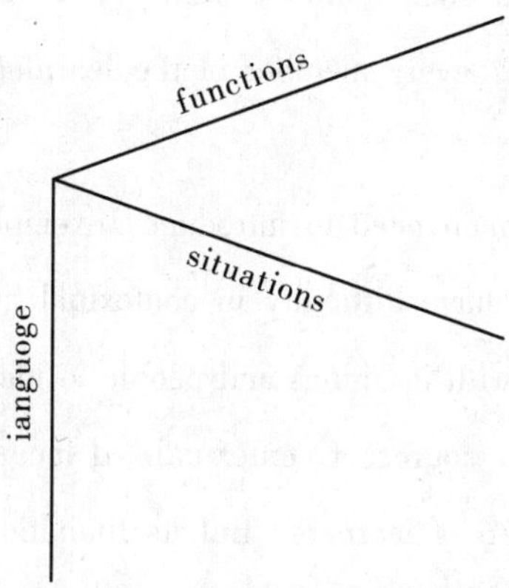

Figure 4

3.2 Contextualisation

Sounds, words and structures, then, are to language what steel, glass, plastic and rubber are to motor cars and the language teacher is no more concerned with teaching philology or transformational grammar than the driving instructor is with teaching car technology. We have seen in Chapter 3 how language is a communicative system representative of reality and thought. Every utterance, to be language, has a meaning, relating to and part of its context.

This is why the first two lessons in Chapter 2 were illustrations of English language teaching in a way that the third was not. A sentence like "My aunt's pen is in the garden" only has meaning when we know who is speaking, and when we can identify the other references and implications. The phrase book for Portuguese learners of English which included the often-quoted and bizarre sentence "Pardon me, but your postillion has been struck by lightning" demonstrates a total lack of sense of context: who can have said this, to whom, when and in what circumstances?

We know that words and phrases are easier to learn and remember if they are meaningful and in context: it follows that the foreign language should always be taught and practised in a contextualised form. And when the learning is being done in a class situation, every member of the learning group should recognise the context.

Faced with the common need to introduce, exemplify and practise items of language, teachers often have difficulty in contextualising them. The immediate classroom environment, with its things and people to identify, count and relate to each other, is an obvious source of contextualised language which is common to the experiences of a group of learners. But its limitations are soon felt after the most elementary lessons. Supplementation of the classroom's physical resources is possible and many enthusiastic teachers enliven their lessons by bringing appropriate realities (called *realia*) into their classrooms. Actual fruit and a knife may be used to ensure that *apple*, *orange* and *to cut* are contextualised: but again there are limits to professional resources and ingenuity.

However, there are no limitations to the introduction of the physical world at one remove, namely by its pictorial representation. Visual aids are an invaluable contextual resource, whether completely teacher-produced like blackboard or over-head projector drawings, or more professional representations: cut out pictures, maps, wall charts, film strips, flannelgraphs and film. Of these, it is the former group over which the teacher has most control in terms of restricting the context and every language teacher should be able to produce recognisable blackboard sketches as part of his professional skill.

Visual identification of the physical world, however, is not the only form of contextualisation available in a given teaching situation. To illustrate one meaning of *to grow*, a teacher may use the sentence "Apples grow on trees," verification of which is not needed from a picture since at least in temperate climates the fact is part of the common stock of knowledge of the learners. This contextual source, drawing upon common experience, is clearly culture-bound, and dependent upon the learners' ages. But even for a class of students drawn from the most widely differing backgrounds, there are many areas of common knowledge. In every culture, the sun rises in the east and sets in the west, water is wet, people get hungry and tired, babies cry, metal is stronger than wood and fire will destroy things: the eternal verities are the basis of any common stock of knowledge. An important second layer is a common cultural background, providing a wealth of events, institutions, people and attitudes, both past and present as a contextual frame of reference.

Clearly, the longer a group of learners continues to work together, the more they build their shared stock of experience. Every happening in that classroom, natural or contrived, is a contextual source of language for as long as the group continues together.

The physical world, however, is of less potential than the world of the imagination. Every shared anecdote or dream, every item of literature becomes part of the class's common experience and therefore the contextual raw material for communicative language work. Given Coleridge's "willing suspension of disbelief," the world of the imagination is as acceptable as the tangible physical world. Indeed the whole process of foreign language learning is a willing suspension of this kind, where the learners are pretending to be at home in another language. To this end, role play is a useful activity, whereby learners simulate attitudes and roles, which—however briefly and superficially—they adopt as acceptable. The Spanish adolescents in the first lesson described in Chapter 2, by identifying with a manifestly imaginary girl making a telephone call, were role-playing and their resulting dialogues were no less in context than if they had been making an inventory in Spanish of their classroom furniture.

We have argued, then, that the nature of contextualized language for our professional purposes is that the items of language are acceptable or verifiable by all members of the learning group as representing actual or imagined reality. It is clear that a language item which is contextualised in this way is part of a larger body of language (whether realised or not) which the same context may generate. In this way the imaginary dialogues of Lesson 1 and the comprehension discussion of Lesson 2 of Chapter 2 are contextualised in a way that utterances like "Do we not walk?" in Lesson 3 are not.

3.3 Presentation and practice

Just as the processes of language teaching presuppose a theory of the nature of language, they equally need to be based upon a theory of language learning. The one is derived from applied linguistics and sociolinguistics, the other from educational psychology and psycholinguistics.

There is now a considerable body of research on the acquisition of the first language, though much less on the learning of a foreign or second language. The two competing theories about how a language is acquired have had great influence on teaching through methodology books and courses and through textbooks themselves. Whether a teacher has studied the theories, or not, his methods necessarily reflect presuppositions about how language is learned.

The argument is between the behaviourists and the mentalists, in psychological terms, or in linguistics terms, between the structuralists and the generative grammarians. The view on one hand is that language is learned by habitformation by imitating utterances and then producing new ones by analogy. On the other hand, it is believed that people learn language by utilising certain innate capacities. This view is based on the idea that every human being possesses a subconscious language acquisition device (the LAD) which takes in the language encountered, works out the rules that govern it, and then after some trial and error, manages to apply them.

The behaviourist view applied to foreign language learning emphasises the importance of conditioning and reinforcement through the repetition of correct (and only correct) responses to a controlled stimulus. "Knowing the meaning" is equated with "giving the correct response." Learning a foreign language is said to be learning a skill, like riding a bicycle or playing the piano, and these are held to be best learned through automatic and frequent imitation, being positively hindered by conscious awareness on the part of the learner.

The mentalists, or rationalists, reply to this that when a person produces an original sentence of a language he is not repeating something he has learned through imitation—and many of the sentences we produce are original. They may be similar to other sentences in the language, but the actual choice of words and their arrangement is new virtually every time we produce an utterance. (Set phrases, ritual speech as in greetings and farewells, idioms, etc., make a very small list of exceptions.) When the behaviourists answer to this that we make new sentences by *analogy* with those we've learned already, they are, claim the rationalists, contradicting their own stimulus-response theory. For the only way to explain the process of making new sentences by analogy involves the notion of observing the regularities (rules, patterns, structure) underlying them and working out how to operate them to generate new sentences. Language is, thus, rule-governed behaviour. This does not mean that the language-learner indulges in any conscious formulation of rules. The argument is that rules are "internalised" and their application is quite unconscious. It is not a matter of deliberate problem solving.

But the split between the two schools of thought is not really as fundamental as its proponents may imply. It is extremely difficult to give a water-tight definition of "habit" or "rule," and for the practising teacher it seems quite reasonable to say that the oral skill aspects of language (articulation and discrimination of sounds) are acquired as habits which are as hard to change after childhood as other motor habits are hard to change or acquire (learning to play the violin, to skate). But at the same time one can also say that other aspects of language need a knowledge (conscious or unconscious) of rules, but that these are eventually applied habitually, i. e. without conscious attention.

Whether a particular methodology is stricly behaviourist or mentalist, or eclectic, items of language still need to be presented and practised. Presentation consists of introducing each new item of language to the learners in such a way that it can be absorbed efficiently into the corpus of language already mastered.

Whether the new language is lexical or structural, its central meaning must be clear from the context in which it is introduced, but the presentation needs to take place in such a way that the learners' attention is focused upon it. Therefore presentation calls for simple contexts which are at once adequate to demonstrate meaning, but at the same time not so interesting that they distract attention away from the important item of the moment.

Another variable in the presentation process is the teaching mode. One cornerstone of behaviourist theory was the insistence on the primacy of the spoken word. Nothing was to be written before it had been said: nothing was to be said before it had been heard. This principle probably continues to hold good for many young learners and for all whose goal is primarily a mastery of the spoken language, but provided that spelling pronunciations are guarded against (and English is not a particularly phonic language) many students find it helpful not only to hear and say new items of language, but also to read and write them during the presentation process. As in any teaching situation, theoretical considerations must give way to considerations of how the learners involved can benefit most.

Basically, during English language lessons the teacher is only involved with three processes: presenting new material, practising familiar material and testing it. And up to 90 per cent of his time is taken up by practice of one kind or another. Ways of practising listening and speaking, reading and writing are dealt with in subsequent chapters, but the way in which this practice is related to presentation and woven into the fabric of each lesson is of the very essence of a teacher's professional expertise. Lessons should be planned and executed so that new language material is soundly integrated with the old. This calls for a sensitive shift from a presentation stage during which the learner's focus of attention is on the new material through early practice where the attention is gradually diverted, into a later practice stage during which the new material is being handled without conscious attention. The shift of attention can be achieved by a gradual increasing of the contextual depth and interest, also by the teacher's sensitive adjustment of the pace of the teaching. Like a stream, a good lesson flows more rapidly over the shallower sections and more slowly over the deeper.

The question of student errors during practice is often hotly debated. A behaviourist would argue that by making mistakes the learner is practising the wrong things and developing undesirable habits: therefore learners should never be put into the position of making errors. A mentalist view assumes that errors are inevitable, that learners at any given point of their growing competence have command of an interim grammar which is by definition imperfect, that we actually learn from our mistakes. There is truth in both arguments. Certainly repeated errors become confirmed and unless the learner is made aware of them he cannot learn from them. On the other hand, that very strict kind of control on a class's language practice which makes error almost impossible is rarely of interest, is rarely motivating. The skilled teacher is able to ensure that during presentation no incorrect language is heard or used and that his gradual relaxation of complete control during the subsequent practice maintains interest and enables him to make the learners conscious of any mistakes as they arise.

Motivation is a basic principle of all kinds of teaching. It is true that there is a certain superficial satisfaction in getting things right. But the student who is satisfied by doing mechanical language exercises correctly has the same superficial motivation as the needlewoman working on samplers, the learner driver operating a simulator or the tyro nurse giving injections to sandbags. The language student is best motivated by practice in which he senses the language is truly communicative, that it is appropriate to its context, that his teacher's skills are moving him forward to a fuller competence in the foreign language.

Ultimately, however, it is the teacher's professional judgment which must count. Every human being is a potential foreign language learner, no less than he is a potential patient; and just as no doctor accepts a patient's own diagnosis and prescription, no professional language teacher can take the view that the customer is always right. Professionalism consists of the operation of a complex of judgment and skills which are soundly based on basic principles of which the layman is usually unaware. It is against the background knowledge of the principles discussed above that the three lessons of Chapter 2 are best evaluated and the procedures and techniques of subsequent chapters are best exercised. ①

① 摘自 Broughton G. et al. Teaching English as a Foreign Language (2nd edition) [M]. London: Routledge, 1980.

References

[1] Broughton G. et al. Teaching English as a Foreign Language (2nd edition)[M]. London: Routledge., 1980.

[2] Brown H. D. Teaching by Principles[M]. Englewood: Prentice Hall Regent, 1994.

[3] Carrol J. B. The Contributions of Psychological Theory and Educational Research to the Teaching of Foreign Languages[J]. The Modern Language Journal, 1965, 49(5).

[4] Chastain K. The Audio-lingual Habit Theory Versus the Cognitive Code-learning Theory: Some Theoretical Considerations[J]. International Review of Applied Linguistics in Language Teaching, 1969, 7(2).

[5] Diller K. C. The Language Teaching Controversy[M]. Mass: Newbury House Publishers, 1978.

[6] 理查兹. 朗文语言学及应用语言学辞典[M]. 北京:外语教学与研究出版社, 2005.

[7] 胡壮麟,姜望琪. 语言学高级教程[M]. 北京:北京大学出版社,2002.

第七章

语言测试

导　读

测试是语言教学中的一个主要评估手段。通过测试可以了解我们语言学习的程度以及存在的问题，对于后续的教学与学习具有重要的指导作用。目前的主要测试理论有以下四种：

1. 写作－翻译法(the essay-translation approach)。该方法对测试技能没有专门的要求，主要依靠教师的主观判断力。试卷题型主要包括写作、翻译和语法分析等，试卷内容带有明显的文学和文化特征。试题通常采用书面回答形式，试卷需要人工阅卷。

2. 结构主义－心理测量法(the structuralist-psychometic approach)。该方法以结构主义语言学为理论基础，主张对不同语言成分和语言技能进行分项测试。同时，它采用了心理测量学的某些方法，强调测量的客观性和可靠性。该方法的典型试题是多项选择题。

3. 综合法(the integrative approach)。这种方法主张测试必须在某种语境下进行，不刻意追求某种单项语言技能的测试，而是强调对两种以上技能综合评测。能体现综合法的题型有完形填空、听写、翻译和写作等。

4. 交际法(the communicative approach)。同综合法类似，交际法同样强调对意义的测试，但是更注重语言在交际过程中的使用。该方法包括对语言形式和成分的测试，但是更强调评价学生在特定语言使用环境中的交际能力。

近年来，语言测试又出现了一些新的特点，主要体现在以下几个方面：

- 研究测试方法对测试成绩的影响
- 定量测试与定性测试分离

· 重新认识语言能力

· 进行对受试人特征的研究

总之,语言测试旨在全面评测受试人的语言水平,既需要对听、说、读、写、译等分项技能的考核,又必须考察在实际语言交际环境中的语言使用情况。因此对语言技能、测试的信度和效度都需要全面关注。

1. Definitions

1.1 test

A psychological or educational test is a procedure designed to elicit certain behavior form which one can make inferences about certain characteristics of an individual.

(Carroll 1968: 46)

A language test which seeks to find out what candidates can do with language provides a focus for purposeful, everyday communication activities.

(Heaton 1988: 5)

A test is a measurement instrument designed to elicit a specific sample of an individual's behavior. As one type of measurement, a test necessarily quantifies characteristics of individuals according to explicit procedures.

(Bachman 1990: 20)

Test is any procedure for measuring ability, knowledge, or performance.

(Richards 2002: 546)

1.2 reliability

Certain stringent conditions which were thought to be necessary if an examination was provide a qualification which might affect the career of a candidate.

(UCLES 1976: 8)

Reliability refers to the consistency of the scores obtainable form a test. It is usually an estimate on a scale of zero to one of the likelihood that the test would rank testees in the same order from one administration to another proximate one.

(Henning 1987: 196)

Reliability is a necessary characteristic of any good test: for it to be valid at all, a test must first be reliable as a measuring instrument.

(Heaton 1988: 162)

Reliability is the extent to which test scores are consistent.

(Alderson 1995: 6)

(in testing) a measure of the degree to which a test gives consistent results. A test is said to be reliable if it gives the same results when it is given on different occasions or when it is used by different people.

(Richards 2002: 454)

1.3 validity

Validity is the extent to which a test measures the ability or knowledge that is purported to measure.

(Henning 1987: 198)

Briefly, the validity of a test is the extent to which it measures what it is supposed to measure and nothing else.

(Heaton 1988: 159)

An integrated evaluative judgment of the degree to which empirical evidence and theoretical rationales support the adequacy and appropriateness of inferences and actions based on test scores or other modes of assessment

(Messick 1989 :13)

The most important quality of test interpretation or use is validity, or the extent to which the inferences or decisions we make on the basis of test scores are meaningful, appropriate, and useful.

(Bachman 1997: 25)

(in testing) the degree to which a test measures what it is supposed to measure, or can be used successfully for the purposes for which it is intended.

(Richards 2002: 575)

1.4 assessment

A term often used interchangeably with testing; but also used more broadly to encompass the gathering of language data, including test data, for the purpose of evaluation and making use of such instruments as interview , case study, questionnaire, observation techniques. More narrowly the term is used to indicate assessment procedures which do not involve tests.

(Davies 1999: 11)

A systematic approach to collecting information and making inferences about the ability of a student or the quality or success of a teaching course on the basis of various sources of evidence. Assessment may be done by test, interview, questionnaire, observation, etc. The term "testing" is often associated with large-scale standardized tests, whereas the term "assessment" is used in a much wider sense to mean a variety of approaches in testing and assessment.

(Richards 2002: 35)

An assessment is a machine for reasoning about what students know, can do, or have accomplished, based on a handful of things they say, do, or make in particular settings.

(Mislevy 2003: 4)

1.5 task

A task is any activity in which a person engages, given an appropriate setting, in order to achieve a specifiable of objectives.

(Carroll 1992: 8)

What a test taker is required to do during a test or part of a test, such as note-taking from a spoken text, participating in an interview or role play, reading a text and answering comprehension questions. This general sense of the term thus includes the input and the instructions as well the task itself.

(Davies 2002: 196)

(in teaching) an activity which is designed to help achieve a particular learning goal. A number of dimensions of tasks influence their use in language teaching.

(Richards 2002: 539)

2. Classical Theories

2.1 Objective vs. Subjective Tests

Usually these types of tests are distinguished on the basis of the manner in which they are scored. An objective test is said to be one that may be scored by comparing examinee responses with an established set of acceptable responses or scoring key. No particular knowledge or training in the examined content area is required on the part of the scorer. A common example would be a multiple-choice recognition test. Conversely a subjective test is said to require scoring by opinionated judgment, hopefully based on insight and expertise on the part of the scorer. An example might be the scoring of free written compositions for the presence of creativity in a situation where no operational definitions of creativity are provided and where there is only one rater. Many tests, such as doze tests permitting all grammatically acceptable responses to systematic deletions from a context, lie somewhere between the extremes of objectivity and subjectivity (Oller, 1979). So-called subjective tests such as free compositions are frequently objectified in scoring through the use of precise rating schedules dearly specifying the kinds of errors to be quantified, or through the use of multiple independent raters.

Objectivity-subjectivity labels, however, are not always confined in their application to the manner in which tests are scored. These descriptions may be applied to the mode of item or distractor selection by the test developer, to the nature of me response: elicited from the examinee, and to the use that is made of the results for any given individual. Often the term subjective is used to denote unreliable or undependable. The possibility of misunderstanding due to ambiguity suggests that objective-subjective labels for tests are of very limited utility.

2.2 Direct vs. Indirect Tests

It has been said that certain tests, such as ratings of language use in real and uncontrived communication situations, are testing language performance directly; whereas other tests, such as multiple-choice recognition tests, are obliquely or indirectly tapping true language performance and therefore are less val id for measuring language proficiency. Whether or not this observation is true, many language tests can be viewed as lying somewhere on a continuum from narural-situarional to unnatural-conceived. Thus an interview may be thought of as more direct than a close test for measuring overall language proficiency. A contextualized vocabulary test may be thought more natural and direct than a synonym-matching rest.

The issue of test validity is treated in greater detail in chapter seven. It should be noted here that the usefulness of tests should be decided on the basis of other criteria in addition to whether they are direct or natural. Sometimes cost-efficiency, and statistical measures of reliability or predictive validity, are more reflective of test utility than the naturalness or directness of the testing situation. Sometimes tests are explicitly designed to elicit and measure language behaviors that occur only rarely if at all in more direct situations. Sometimes most of the value of direct language data is lost through reductionism in the manner of scoring.

2.3 Discrete-point vs. Integrative Tests

Another way of slicing the resting pie is to view test as lying along a continuum from discrete-point to integrative. This distinction was originated by John B. Carroll (1961). Discrete-point tests, as a variety of diagnostic tests, are designed to measure knowledge or performance in very restricted areas of the target language. Thus a test of ability to use correctly the perfect tenses of English verbs or co supply correct prepositions in a doze passage may be termed a discrete-point test. Integrative tests, on the other hand, are said to tap a greater variety of language abilities concurrently and therefore may have less diagnostic and remedial-guidance value and greater value in measuring overall language proficiency. Examples of integrative tests are random close, dictation, oral interviews, and oral imitation tasks.

Frequently an attempt is made to achieve the best of all possible worlds through the construction and use of *ten test batteries* comprised of discrete-point *subtests* for diagnostic purposes, but which provide a total score that is considered to reflect overall language proficiency. The comparative success or failure of such attempts can be determined empirically by reference to data from test administrations. Farhady (1979) presents evidence that "there are no statistically revealing differences" between discrete-point and integrative tests.

Here again, some tests defy such ready-made labels and may place the label advocates on the defensive. A test of listening comprehension may tap one of the four general language skills (i. e., listening, speaking, reading, and writing) in a discrete manner and thus have limited value as a measure of overall language proficiency. On the other hand, such a test may examine a broad range of lexis and diverse grammatical structures and in this way be said to be integrative.

2.4 Communicative Approach

Communicative approach also used the term "communicative language teaching." It is an approach to foreign or second language teaching which emphasizes that the goal of language learning is communicative competence and which seeks to make meaningful communication and language use a focus of all classroom activities. The communicative approach was developed particularly by British applied linguists in the 1980s as a reaction away from grammar-based approaches such as Situational Language Teaching and the audio-lingual method.

The major principles of Communicative Language Teaching are:

- learners use a language through using it to communicate
- authentic and meaningful communication should be the goal of classroom activities
- fluency and accuracy are both important goals in language learning
- communication involves the integration of different language skills

- learning is a process of creative construction and involves trial and error

Communicative language teaching led to a re-examination of language teaching goals, syllabuses, materials, and classroom activities and has had a major impact on changes in language teaching world wide. Some of its principles have been incorporated into other communicative approaches, such as Task-Based Language Teaching, Cooperative Language Learning, and Content-Based Instruction.

2.5 Communicative Language Ability (CLA)

In the quest to understand the nature of CLA and how second or foreign (L2) language knowledge can be used successfully to communicate a variety of meanings in different social and academic contexts, language testing researchers have proposed an array of theoretical models of L2 ability as a basis for assessment. Some of these models explicitly represent the components of the L2 ability construct along with their presumed interrelationships. Examples of knowledge components specified in these models include, among others, grammatical knowledge, lexical knowledge, discourse knowledge, sociolinguistic knowledge, and pragmatic knowledge. These models aim to reflect the most scientifically credible ways in which learners represent L2 knowledge and the ability to use this knowledge for communication. These models also aim to provide a broad theoretical basis for the definition of CLA in creating and interpreting language tests in a variety of language use settings. Rather than providing a prescription for test development, they represent potential targets of assessment that can be adapted to a range of test purposes and contexts-while at the same time, sharing certain common principles with a unifying framework.

In another approach to assessing CLA, the components of language ability are derived not so much from empirical research or a theoretical model of language ability, but from the opinions of experts with firsthand experience teaching the local curricula and assessing student performance. These experts are believed to have clear ideas about the knowledge and skills needed for successful communication in the target language. In this approach, curriculum and assessment standards are often developed to describe levels of student achievement without explicit guidance of learning theories or models of language proficiency, or the systematic empirical inquiry needed to verify these standards and their use.

In yet another approach to assessing CLA, the components of language ability are not so much defined in terms of the formal elements of language knowledge (e. g., grammatical or pragmatic), but rather in terms of how language is used in the context of a language skill (listening, reading, writing, speaking). This test measures these components through both independent and integrated tasks. In other words, listening ability is measured separately in some tasks and in others it is assessed together with speaking and/or writing ability.

In each approach to characterizing CLA, separate components of the L2 construct have been identified, either explicitly or implicitly, with the assumption that each component can to some degree be isolated, taught, and assessed independent of the other components, if needed, or each component can be measured in combination with other components. The notion of 'separate' and 'integrated' reflects the beliefs that a student's L2 knowledge and ability in one component can be expected to change as a function of deliberate study (Carroll, 1993) or other learning conditions (e. g., exposure) (Kunnan, 1995), while her knowledge and ability in another component may remain stable. It also suggests that her knowledge and ability in one component (e. g., grammatical form) can develop at a different rate and to a different extent from her knowledge and ability in another (e. g., semantic meaning) (Purpura, 2004), and that her L2 knowledge and ability in one component may vary as a function of their interaction with her knowledge and ability of another. Finally, it implies that her

L2 knowledge and ability in one component may fluctuate across the contextual attributes of test or language use tasks (Chapelle, 1998).

Currently, most researchers (e. g., Chalhoub-Deville, 1997, 2003; Kunnan, 1998) generally endorse the claim that CLA is multicomponential. This has framed how assessment is organized in both classroom and large-scale assessment contexts. Researchers have not, however, reached a consensus on the specific components that constitute CLA. Some define them in terms of the formal elements of the language, others in terms of standards, and still others in terms of the language skills. Researchers also do not agree on how knowledge of these components is organized in the mind, how the components interact, how learners develop conceptual understanding of these components over time, or how knowledge might develop differentially with diverse learners under different conditions. A related question for assessment researchers concerns whether these discrete components of CLA should be assessed independently or together in the context of performing meaningful social and academic activities.

3. Original selecting

Psychometric Approaches to Fairness:Bias and DIF

In this and the following chapter, we explore the way in which the social dimension of language testing has been explored within the psychometric tradition. In this chapter, we consider the fairness of tests for particular social groups, an area known as bias. Investigations of bias are part of general work on test fairness. Test fairness is a broad area, encompassing quality management in test design, administration and scoring, adequate coverage of relevant content, sufficient construct validation work, equal learning opportunities and access to testing, and items measuring only the skill or ability under investigation without being unduly influenced by construct-irrelevant variance introduced through test-taker background factors (Kunnan, 2000; Saville, 2003, 2005; Shohamy, 2000). In this chapter we focus on the last point, the functioning of test items in ways that advantage or disadvantage groups of test takers. The potential social consequences of a systematic preference for one group of test takers over another are easy to imagine: The dispreferred group's representation in coveted college programs and jobs might be disproportionately small, whereas their representation in stigmatized "remedial" programs might be disproportionately large. Test-inherent bias distorts measurement of the construct of interest by allowing other test-taker characteristics to influence scores systematically, thereby introducing multidimensionality into the measurement. Characteristics that are commonly investigated include race, gender, socioeconomic status, and first language (L1) background, but, theoretically, any background characteristic that some test takers possess and others do not (or not to the same degree) can introduce systematic construct-irrelevant variance and lead to bias.

In this chapter we first summarize the history of bias research in assessment and follow with a discussion of various ways to detect bias, problems with bias research, and approaches to preempt bias.

3.1 Bias and Differential Item Functioning: Definition and History

3.1.1 Bias

The use of the term "bias" in assessment research fundamentally follows its popular usage, which conveys a skewed and unfair inclination toward one side (group, population) to the detriment of another. The notion of bias is directly tied to fairness, in popular usage as well as assessment: A biased judgment unduly takes into account factors other than those that should be informing it.

For assessment, bias can be seen in traditional validity terms as construct-irrelevant variance that distorts the test results and therefore makes conclusions based on scores less valid. Specifically, a test or an item is biased if test takers of equal ability but from different groups score differently on the item depending on their group membership (Angoff, 1993). In this case, group membership introduces systematic construct-irrelevant variance, which has a consistent effect on scores. Another way to look at this is to consider bias a factor that makes a unidimensional test multidimensional: The test measures something in addition to what it is intended to measure, and the result is a confound of two measurements.

Whereas any construct-irrelevant variance is harmful to valid interpretations, bias systematically harms one group (Shepard, Camilli, & Averill, 1981) by inflating one group's scores and depressing the other group's scores. In a broader sense, biased tests harm all stakeholders because students might get exempted from language programs although they would benefit from them, others do not get admitted to a program in which they would excel, universities or employers reject perfectly qualified applicants and accept less qualified ones, and society is deprived of potentially excellent doctors, lawyers, language teachers, or electricians and must make do with mediocre ones.

3.1.2 Differential Item Functioning

Bias is a general description of a situation in which construct-irrelevant group characteristics influence scores, but because of its semantic association with societal issues like discrimination, another term was coined for more technical analyses of test items: differential item functioning (DIF). DIF identifies test items that function differently for two groups of test takers, without the discriminatory overtones of the term *bias*. Angoff (1993) admitted that there is the temptation to use the term *bias* because it is shorter and less cumbersome than the somewhat unwieldy term *differential item functioning*, but he argued for keeping the two separate and using DIF for nonjudgmental analyses of score differences between groups and using bias to discuss the larger social issues caused by DIF.

Differential item functioning is a necessary but not sufficient condition for bias because a test item that functions differently for two groups might do so because it advantages one group in a construct-irrelevant way, but there might also be legitimate reasons for differential functioning. For example, cognates of target language vocabulary in the L1 of some test takers might make an item easier for that group, but the content tested might still be completely legitimate and construct-relevant, and their L1 knowledge would confer an advantage on these test takers in the exact same way in real-world language use situations. Thus, test makers could well decide to retain such an item, arguing that it measures a necessary part of the construct and that group differences are real ability differences in terms of the construct.

Another case in which DIF does not constitute bias is where items function differently for two groups of test takers simply because the two groups differ in their ability (e. g. , low-proficiency and high-proficiency English as a second language [ESL] students). These groups would be expected to score differently on most items of an ESL test. In fact, if they do not, something is wrong with the test! Thus, although items will function differently depending on whether a test taker is in the low-proficiency or high-proficiency group, it would not make sense to say that the test is biased toward the high-proficiency group.

However, the situation is usually more complicated because test-taker ability is not known in advance. What if the low-proficiency test takers are mostly international students from Europe and the high-proficiency test takers are mostly international students from Asia? A DIF analysis would then seem to show that the test is biased toward test takers of Asian background. Indeed, a native-country effect is a nondesirable source of variance in an ESL proficiency test, but in this case native country is simply confounded with proficiency. This example already highlights one of the greater challenges of DIF and bias analysis: In practice, it can be very difficult to determine the source of DIF, and only if that determination is made, can we consider an item or a whole test biased.

The above examples show how DIF analysis is usually a first step in a larger bias analysis. An item that does not show DIF is not biased, whereas an item that shows DIF needs to be investigated further to uncover the reasons for its differential functioning. Most DIF analyses compute DIF for a potentially disadvantaged group (also known as the *focal* group) compared to the potentially advantaged group (also known as the *reference* group). DIF analyses outside language testing often investigate DIF for minority groups (Blacks vs. Whites) or gender (women vs. men), whereas in language testing, group membership tends to be determined by native language and there is less a priori hypothesizing about likely disadvantages.

Although it is desirable that illegitimate DIF be minimized to ensure precise measurement, a single differentially functioning item on a multi-item test is not likely to make the entire test unfair. Only when the effect of a number of DIF items accumulates can this lead to a biased test. However, if an individual test taker's score is right at the cut score level, illegitimate DIF on a small number of items can unfairly advantage or disadvantage that test taker. It is important to note that DIF can work in both directions, so, in practice, DIF favoring the reference group is often balanced out by DIF favoring the focal group, but, of course, there is no guarantee that this will happen and an individual test form might be strongly biased toward one or the other group.

3.1.3 History

Researchers have been investigating the impact of construct external test-taker characteristics on scores for a century. From 1905 to 1911, Binet and his associates published five studies on the effect of socioeconomic status on students' performance on intelligence tests. Originally, Binet considered "intellectual capacity" a singular innate, invariant trait (Binet & Simon, 1916), but he became increasingly aware of the complexity of this construct and the effects of schooling and environment. He tried to counter the effect of extraneous factors by eliminating items that were based too much on schooling, but, even so, he found that children from a higher socioeconomic background outperformed children from lower socioeconomic levels. The original claim that the intelligence test measured raw intellectual capacity was obviously not tenable. Stern (1914) conducted the first analysis of differences in item functioning, when he considered which items were easier and more difficult for test takers of lower and higher socioeconomic status. Weintrob and Weintrob (1912) were the first to use race as an explanatory variable in their findings, which would later become a central issue in bias analyses in the United States. Eells, Davis, Havighurst, Herrick, and Tyler (1951) provide a summary of the research from the first part of the century and report their own study with 650 high-school students, whose answers on an IQ test were used to identify and eliminate items that measured opportunity to learn rather than intellectual ability. This early work on bias and group-related differences followed a general notion of fairness, had the goal of avoiding construct-irrelevant variance, and was quite optimistic in its outlook; that is, sources of item bias could be identified, systematically eliminated, and the result would be a fair, precise, unbiased test.

In the second half of the 20th century, work on bias was informed by larger concerns of social equity and began to shift away from IQ tests to tests that provided access to educational or job opportunity. It went hand in hand with the development of more formal concepts of validity and the use of powerful statistical tools to identify biased items. Interestingly, concern also shifted from socioeconomic influences on test scores to test-taker background variables such as race and gender and, to some extent, native-speaker (NS) status. Studies that included effects of NS status often framed findings in terms of the effects of cultural differences on test scores.

The relevance of producing fair tests with little DIF was highlighted by the Golden Rule Settlement. In 1976, the Golden Rule Insurance Company sued the Illinois Department of Insurance and Educational Testing Service (ETS) for alleged racial bias in the licensing test for insurance agents. The licensing exam had caused furor in the Illinois insurance industry because the general passing rate was only 31% and it appeared that the test was "for all practical purposes excluding Blacks entirely from the occupation of insurance agent" (Rooney, 1987, p. 5). ETS modified the test and the passing rate rose to 70% – 75%, but when no specific steps were taken to address the allegedly disastrous impact of the test on minority test takers, Golden Rule filed suit in July 1976. The court issued an injunction stopping the test temporarily, but only based on fee issues, not on the substantive grounds that it violated the equal protection clause of the U.S. constitution. After the Illinois legislature dealt with the fee problem and ETS revised the test, the case was dismissed, but Golden Rule refiled, alleging discrimination in both the old test and the new test. The case was dismissed again, but Golden Rule appealed and the circuit court unanimously reinstated it. Whereas the subordinate court had considered ETS not liable because the company was only under contract of the insurance licensing board, the circuit court found that ETS by virtue of making the test was responsible for its effect—a finding that raised the stakes for the testing industry considerably and a practical endorsement of Messick's position on test consequences as part of validity (see chapter 2). The circuit court also argued that the defendants could be held liable for intentional racial discrimination if they had knowledge that the test was disadvantaging Black test takers but failed to remedy the situation. In other words, the court demanded that test makers monitor the effect of their test on minority test takers, and if they found deleterious effects, they needed to alleviate these effects.

The case was settled out of court in 1984, with the defendants agreeing to consider any item biased for which correct answer rates for White and African American test takers differed by more than 15%. Also, items that fewer than 40% of African American test takers answered correctly were flagged as too difficult. The test makers agreed that items would be pretested and that future test forms would be constructed to the largest extent possible from unbiased and nondifficult items. This possibility was constrained by the test's content specifications, which required that certain areas needed to be tested. For this reason, biased or difficult items sometimes needed to be included because otherwise an aspect of the construct would be underrepresented in the operational test. Allowing a difficulty difference of up to 15% indicated that the parties recognized that there could be some random measurement error as well as some true underlying difference between the groups, which was most likely related to their previous training. The agreed procedure only applied to two insurance specializations: life insurance and accident and health insurance.

The Golden Rule settlement had consequences beyond Illinois. A similar suit was settled in Alabama, imposing an even stricter standard of only 5% difference between scores of Black and White test takers. Legislatures in California, New York, and Texas discussed imposing test construction and bias-monitoring requirements (Faggen, 1987). ETS had not anticipated this wide impact, and in January 1987, then-president of ETS, Gregory Anrig, called the settlement an "error of judgment" on his part (Anrig, 1987). Richard Jaeger, the president of the National Council on Measurement in Education, sent letters to legislators, urging them not to pass any similar provision into law (Jaeger, 1987).

A whole issue of the Journal of Educational Measurement: Issues and Practice was devoted to the Golden Rule settlement in 1987, and the discussion showed an interesting contrast in opinions and concerns. Whereas psychometricians were scornful of the settlement and claimed that it would harm test quality, other contributors hailed the focus on minority performance in tests that the settlement forced test makers to adopt.

From the psychometric perspective, Linn and Drasgow (1987) showed that a test following the Golden Rule settlement would be reduced in quality because it would be more likely for items with weak discriminating power to be included, lowering the test's overall reliability. For example, if all test takers were answering a certain item randomly, this item would seem perfectly unbiased, as all groups would have very similar scores. Depending on the number of distracters, it might be too difficult (four answer choices would mean that about 25% of test takers would answer correctly, three answer choices would lead to 33.3% correctness, etc.), but from a bias point of view, it would be just fine. Of course, such an item would do nothing to help discriminate between high- and low-ability test takers, as both groups would have an equal likelihood of answering it correctly.

Linn and Drasgow (1987) also pointed out that some group differences are actually real and simply reflections of different educational experiences, so tests should not be faulted for detecting such differences. In fact, they see a need for remedial action at a larger, societal scale, because an "artificial reduction of differences in average test scores might conceal this situation, but it would not rectify it" (p. 15). It is probably this position more than anything else that sets them apart from the proponents of the settlement, as psychometricians tend to take the stance that DIF (or even differential test functioning) is not in itself evidence of bias. Only if test takers of the same ability level perform differently is there bias involved. Although this is true, the Achilles' heel of this argument is that the ability level is determined by the overall test score or the score of a criterion measure; so if the whole test or the criterion measure is biased, it will never appear that there is item-level bias because the reference and the focal group will simply seem to have a radically different ability levels.

The second weakness of this argument is that it must be possible to pinpoint reasons for the differential functioning of these items. In other words, test makers must be able to "explain away" the appearance of bias by constructing a theory about construct relevant causes for group differences such as different educational opportunities, a higher propensity of one group to take relevant college courses, or more interest in the subject matter by one group than the other. This has never been done rigorously and has never been tested as theory. Explanations for DIF tend to be based on speculative ad hoc hypotheses, and as long as that is the case, simple bias can also function as a valid explanation.

These different arguments reflect two different stances toward test makers' responsibility: Proponents of the Golden Rule Settlement saw the score difference on the test between Blacks and Whites as evidence of the test's bias, following the underlying assumption that there is no good reason that the test scores should differ by race. In a sense, they accepted the (unproven) premise that true ability would not differ by race, and if test scores did not reflect this invariance, the test was wrong (i.e., biased).

Opponents of the settlement, on the other hand, could suggest several good reasons why test scores might differ by race: first and foremost, different educational background and opportunity. They saw the test as a faithful operationalization of a construct, and if the test found differences between the races, then that was not the test's fault but a true finding. In a sense, they accepted the (unproven) premise that the test was inherently neutral with regard to racial background, and, therefore, if test scores showed differences between racial groups, this meant that these groups actually differed in their abilities.

In fact, both can be the case. It is certainly possible for a test to be biased against a group of test takers but at the same time be a faithful operationalization of the construct. However, in fact, it is only one possible operationalization;

others that might be less biased would be conceivable. At the same time, groups can differ in their ability for real-world reasons, extraneous to the test, and the test might simply detect this. Obviously, there is nothing that test makers can do about real-world differences, other than measure them. However, there is something that they can do about a test that is biased: They can search for sources of bias in the test items.

Of course, the substantive issues raised by the Golden Rule case were far-reaching and went much beyond simply finding better techniques for detecting DIF. It established that test makers are not only responsible but also legally liable for their products and that they need to take all reasonable precautions to avoid disadvantaging groups of test takers. However, the settlement did not address issues for test users: Should they take test scores as the only criterion for decision-making? What prevents them from taking other factors into account, as is commonly done in university admission in the United States? For example, a test user might decide that having a diverse population of students or insurance agents or police officers is as valuable as having this population made up of high-ability individuals. Test users can ensure this diversity in a variety of ways: by using quotas or giving extra weight to nontest factors, for example. Of course, if they were to do so, they would be making a value judgment, but by not doing so, they are also making a value judgment, namely that ability (as defined by the test) is the only issue that matters. Adducing additional criteria to make decisions is probably more defensible in situations in which the predictive validity of the test is low or in which only a minimum threshold of performance is required and other skills are learned on the job. Nevertheless, biased test items distort results and a great deal of work has been undertaken to identify such items. ①

① 摘自 McNamara T. Language Testing: The Social Dimension [M]. Oxford: Oxford University Press, 2000.

References

[1]Carroll J. B. The Modern Language Aptitude Test[M]. New York: The Psychological Corporation, 1966.

[2]McNamara T. Language Testing: The Social Dimension[M]. Oxford: Oxford University Press, 2000.

[3]Richards J. C. Longman Dictionary of Language Teaching and Applied Linguistics[M]. London: Pearson Education Ltd, 2002.

[4]Lyle F. Bachman. 语言测试要略[M]. 上海:上海外语教育出版社,1999.

[5]奥尔德森等. 语法测试的设计与评估[M]. 北京:外语教学与研究出版社,2000.

[6]戴维斯. 语言测试词典[M]. 北京:外语教学与研究出版社,2002.

[7]希顿. 英语测试[M]. 北京:外语教学与研究出版社,2000.

[8]亨宁. 语言测试指南:发展、评估与研究[M]. 北京:外语教学与研究出版社,2001.

[9]李筱菊. 语言测试科学与艺术[M]. 长沙:湖南教育出版社,1997.

[10]邹申,杨任明. 简明英语测试教程[M]. 北京:高等教育出版社,2000.

第八章

话语分析

导　读

话语分析就是对话语的分析与研究。话语分析常常被称为一门既古老又年轻的学科。说它古老,它的历史可以追溯到古希腊和古罗马时期,那时的修辞学可以说是话语分析的前身。说它年轻是因为从20世纪开始人们才真正将话语分析作为一个术语提出,并进行专门的研究。

古典修辞学主要是对古希腊时期的雄辩术的研究。1952年,语言学家哈里斯(Z. Harris)第一次使用了"话语分析"(discourse analysis)这一术语。他在文中明确指出:"语言不是在零散的词或句子中发生的,而是在连贯的话语中。"(Harris 1952:351)

1975年,英国学者库尔撒德(M. Coulthard)通过对课堂话语的研究构建出话语分析的基本模式:课文(Lesson)——交换(exchange)——步骤(move)——行为(act)。这样一种由上至下逐级细化的话语分析单位,奠定了伯明翰学派会话分析的基础。

1983年,布朗(G. Brown)出版《话语分析》(*Discourse Analysis*)一书。她认为,语篇分析的目的是说明语言形式如何用于交际;对语言使用的研究,不能局限于语言形式的描写而脱离语言形式在人类活动中所要表现的意图或功能(Brown 1983:ix)。

1981年,荷兰语言学家范戴克(van Dijk)主编的《语篇》(*Text*)杂志在欧洲创刊。它包括全球主要国家和地区以及各个研究领域学者的最新话语分析成果。1985年,他邀请世界各地研究话语的有关专家撰稿,编辑出版了四卷本的《话语分析手册》(*Handbook of Discourse Analysis*)。该手册"可以看作是这门新的跨学科独立和自我体系形成的标志"(van Dijk 1985:ix)。

20世纪90年代以来，话语分析的重要分支——批评性话语分析(Critical Discourse Analysis，简称CDA)开始兴起。1995年，CDA的领军人物费尔克劳(N. Fairclough)提出了该理论的三维框架：(1)对语篇的语言学描述(Description)；(2)对语篇与语篇过程之间的关系做出阐释(Interpretation)；(3)对语篇过程与社会过程之间的关系做出解释(Explanation)(Fairclough 1995)。

总之，话语分析是一门富有趣味并且具有良好前景的学科。

1. Definitions

1.1 Discourse

The term discourse analysis was introduced by Zellig Harris in 1952. In an effort to analyze connected speech and writing, Harris took language description beyond the sentence, examining what language elements might occur next to each other, or in the same linguistic environment. There are other terms such as "text" or "conversation" that express similar meaning with "discourse". In this book, we use them as the same one. The main definitions for this term are following:

The sentence, an undefined creation of limitless variety, is the very life of human speech in action. We conclude from this that with the sentence we leave the domain of language as a system of signs and enter into another universe, that of language as an instrument of communication, whose expression is discourse.

(Benveniste 1971: 110)

Instead of gradually reducing the rather fluctuating meaning of the word discourse, I believe I have in fact added to its meanings: treating it sometimes as the general domain of all statements, sometimes as an individualizable group of statements, and sometimes as a regulated practice that accounts for a number of statements.

(Foucault 1972: 80)

Discourse is a domain of language use, structured as a unity by common assumptions. There may be competing discourses, and discourses will change over time.

(Abercrombie 1984: 70)

The word "discourse," means language-in-use or stretches of language (like conversations or stories).

(Gee 1999: 17)

I see discourses as ways of representing aspects of the world — the processes, relations and structures of the material world, the "mental world" of thoughts, feelings, beliefs and so forth, and the social world.

(Fairclough 2003: 125)

Discourse will be treated as a general mode of semiosis, i. e. meaningful symbolic behavior.

(Blommaert 2005: 2)

1.2 Discourse Analysis

The analysis of discourse is, necessarily, the analysis of language in use. As such, it cannot be restricted to the description of linguistic forms independent of the purposes or functions which those forms are designed to serve in human affairs.

(Brown 1983: 1)

The term *discourse analysis* is very ambiguous. Roughly speaking, it refers to attempts to study the organization of language above the sentence or above the clause, and therefore to study larger linguistic units, such as conversational exchanges or written texts. It follows that discourse analysis is also concerned with language in use in social contexts, and in particular with interaction or dialogue between speakers.

(Stubbs 1983: 1)

We shall use the term *discourse analysis* to cover the study of spoken and written interaction. Our overall aim is to come to a much better understanding of exactly how natural spoken and written discourse looks and sounds.

(McCarthy 1991: 14)

Discourse analysis prioritizes the interactive nature of language. In relation to the spoken language, this means that the co-operation of more than one individual is essential to its performance.

(Coulthard 1992: 83)

1.3 Critical Discourse Analysis

By "critical" discourse analysis I mean discourse analysis which aims to systematically explore often opaque relationships of causality and determination between (a) discursive practices, events and texts, and (b) wider social and cultural structures, relations and processes; to investigate how such practices, events and texts arise out of and are ideologically shaped by relations of power and struggles over power; and to explore how the opacity of these relationships between discourse and society is itself a factor securing power and hegemony.

(Fairclough 1995: 130)

The term CDA is used nowadays to refer more specially to the critical linguistic approach of scholars who find the larger discursive unit of text to be the basic unit of communication. This research specially considers institutional, political, gender and media discourses (in the broadest sense) which testify to more or less overt relations of struggle and conflict.

(Wodak 2001: 2)

2. Main Schools

2.1 Malcolm Coulthard

As a leading member of the Birmingham Group, Malcolm Coulthard set out a developmental approach to spoken language analysis that changed prevailing notions of linguistic description (Coulthard, 1992).

He uses a *rank scale* for our descriptive model because of its flexibility. The basic assumption of a rank scale is that a unit at a given rank. The unit at the lowest rank has no structure. However, if one moves from the level of grammar to the level of phonology, morphemes can be shown to be composed of a series of phonemes. Similarly, the smallest unit at the level of discourse will have no structure, although it is composed of words, groups or clauses at the level of grammar. Each rank above the lowest has a structure which can be expressed in terms of the units next below. Thus, the structure of a clause can be expressed in terms of nominal, verbal, adverbial and prepositional groups.

The unit at the highest rank is one which has a structure that can be expressed in terms of lower units, but does not itself form part of the structure of any higher unit. It is for this reason that "sentence" is regarded as the highest unit of grammar. Paragraphs have no grammatical structure; they consist of a series of sentences of any type in any order. Where there are no grammatical constraints on what an individual can do, variations are usually regarded as "stylistic."

We assumed that when, from a linguistic point of view, classroom discourse became an unconstrained string of units, the organization would be fundamentally pedagogic. The highest unit of classroom discourse, consisting of one or more transactions, we call *lesson*. This unit may frequently be coextensive with the pedagogical unit *period*, but need not be.

We then realized that moves too can have a structure and so we needed another rank with which we could describe this structure. This we labeled *act*. Moves and acts in discourse are very similar to words and morphemes in grammar. By definition, move is the smallest free unit although it has a structure in terms of acts. Just as there are bound morphemes which cannot alone realize words, so there are bound acts which cannot alone realize moves.

We needed to distinguish discourse acts from grammatical structures, or there would be no point in proposing a new level of language description we would simply be analyzing the higher ranks of grammar. Of course if acts did turn out to be arrangements of clauses in a consistent and hierarchical fashion, then they would replace (in speech) our confusing notions of 'sentence' and the higher ranks of what we now call discourse would arrange themselves on top.

The lowest rank of the discourse scale overlaps with the top of the grammar scale (see table below). Discourse acts are typically one free clause, plus any subordinate clauses, but there are certain closed classes where we can specify almost all the possible realizations which consist of single words or groups.

Levels and ranks

Non-linguistic organization	Discourse	Grammar
course		
period	LESSON	
topic	TRANSACTION	

续表

Non-linguistic organization	Discourse	Grammar
	EXHANGE	
	MOVE	sentence
	ACT	clause
	group	
	word	
	morpheme	

There is a similar overlap at the top of the discourse scale with pedagogical structures and we have been constantly aware of the danger of creating a rank for which there is only pedagogical evidence. We have deliberately chosen *lesson*, a word specific to the particular language situation we are investigating, as the label for the top rank. We feel fairly certain that the four lower ranks will be present in other discourses; the fifth may also be, in which case, once we have studied comparative data, we will use the more general label *interaction*.

We see the level of discourse as lying between the levels of *grammar* and *non-linguistic organization*. There is no need to suppose a one-to-one correspondence of units between levels; the levels of phonology and grammar overlap considerably, but have only broad general correspondence. We see the top of our discourse scale, lesson, corresponding roughly to the rank *period* in the non-linguistic level, and the bottom of our scale, act, corresponding roughly to the clause complex in grammar.

2.2 Gillian Brown

Gillian Brown combined linguistics, cognitive psychology, and the study of discourse structure to create a book that helped define the field of discourse analysis for many linguists.

She has insisted on the view which puts the speaker/writer at the centre of the process of communication. It is people who communicate and people who interpret. It is speakers/writers who have topics, presuppositions, who assign information structure and who make reference. It is hearers/readers who interpret and who draw inferences. This view is opposed to the study of these issues in terms of sentences considered in isolation from communicative contexts.

The analysis of discourse is, necessarily, the analysis of language in use. As such, it cannot be restricted to the description of linguistic forms independent of the purposes or functions which those forms are designed to serve in human affairs. We will adopt only two terms to describe the major functions of language and emphasize that this division is an analytic convenience. It would be unlikely that, on any occasion, a natural language utterance would be used to fulfill only one function, to the total elusion of the other. That function which language serves in the expression of "content" we will describe as transactional, and that function involved in expressing social relations and personal attitudes we will describe as interactional. Our distinction, "transactional/interactional," stands in general correspondence to the functional dichotomies — "representative/expressive," found in Bühler (1934), "referential/emotive" (Jakobson, 1960), "ideational/interpersonal" (Halliday, 1970b) and "descriptive/ social-expressive" (Lyons, 1977).

There are, however, other ways in which the discourse analyst's approach to linguistic data differs from that of the formal linguist and leads to a specialized use of certain terms. Because the analyst is investigating the use of language in context by a speaker/writer, he is more concerned with the relationship between the speaker and the utterance, on the particular occasion of use, than with the potential relationship of one sentence to another, regardless of their use. The discourse analyst is describing what speakers and hearers are doing, and not the relationship which exists between one sentence or proposition and another.

Any analytic approach in linguistics which involves contextual considerations, necessarily belongs to that area of language study called **pragmatics**. "Doing discourse analysis" certainly involves "doing syntax and semantics," but it primarily consists of "doing pragmatics." In discourse analysis, as in pragmatics, we are concerned with what people using language are doing, and accounting for the linguistic features in the discourse as the means employed in what they are doing.

In summary, the discourse analyst treats his data as the record (text) of a dynamic process in which language was used as an instrument of communication in a context by a speaker / writer to express meanings and achieve intentions (discourse). Working from this data, the analyst seeks to describe regularities in the linguistic realizations used by people to communicate those meanings and intentions.

2.3 van Dijk

Tune A. van Dijk regard critical discourse analysis (CDA) as a type of discourse analytical research that primarily studies the way social power abuse, dominance, and inequality are enacted, reproduced, and resisted by text and talk in the social and political context. With such dissident research, critical discourse analysts take explicit position, and thus want to understand, expose, and ultimately resist social inequality.

CDA is not so much a direction, school, or specialization next to the many other "approaches" in discourse studies. Rather, it aims to offer a different "mode" or "perspective" of theorizing, analysis, and application throughout the whole field. We may find a more or less critical perspective in such diverse areas as pragmatics, conversation analysis, narrative analysis, rhetoric, stylistics, sociolinguistics, ethnography, or media analysis, among others.

Crucial for critical discourse analysts is the explicit awareness of their role in society. Continuing a tradition that rejects the possibility of a "value-free" science, they argue that science, and especially scholarly discourse, are inherently part of and influenced by social structure, and produced in social interaction. Instead of denying or ignoring such a relation between scholarship and society, they plead that such relations be studied and accounted for in their own right, and that scholarly practices be based on such insights. Theory formation, description, and explanation, also in discourse analysis, are sociopolitically "situated," whether we like it or not. Reflection on the role of scholars in society and the polity thus becomes an inherent part of the discourse analytical enterprise. This may mean, among other things, that discourse analysts conduct research in solidarity and cooperation with dominated groups. Critical research on discourse needs to satisfy a number of requirements in order to effectively realize its aims:

* As is often the case for more marginal research traditions, CDA research has to be "better" than other research in order to be accepted,
* It focuses primarily on *social problems* and political issues, rather than on current paradigms and fashions.
* Empirically adequate critical analysis of social problems is usually *multidisciplinay*. Rather than merely *describe* discourse structures, it tries to *explain* them in terms of properties of social interaction and especially social structure,
* More specifically, CDA focuses on the ways discourse structures enact, confirm, legitimate, reproduce, or challenge relations of *power and dominance* in society.

CDA also focuses on how discourse structures influence mental representations. At the global level of discourse, topics may influence what people see as the most important information of text or talk, and thus correspond to the top levels of their mental models. For example, expressing such a topic in a headline in news may powerfully influence how an event is defined in terms of a "preferred" mental model. Similarly, argumentation may be persuasive because of the social opinions that are "hidden" in its implicit premises and thus taken for granted by the recipients, e. g. immigration may thus be restricted if it is presupposed in a parliamentary debate that all refugees are "illegal." Likewise, at the local level, in order to understand discourse meaning and coherence, people may need models featuring beliefs that remain implicit (presupposed) in discourse. Thus, a typical feature of manipulation is to communicate beliefs implicitly, that is, without actually asserting them, and with less chance that they will be challenged.

2.4 Norman Fairclough

There are many versions of discourse analysis. One major division is between approaches which include detailed analysis of texts, and approaches which don't. I have used the term "textually oriented discourse analysis" to distinguish the former from the latter (Fairclough 1992). Discourse analysis in social sciences is often strongly influenced by the work of Foucault (Foucault 1972, Fairclough 1992). Social scientists working in this tradition generally pay little close attention to the linguistic features of texts. My own approach to discourse analysis has been to try to transcend the division between work inspired by social theory which tends not to analyze texts, and work which focuses upon the language of texts but tends not to engage with social theoretical issues. This is not, or should not be, an "either/or."

On the one hand, any analysis of texts which aims to be significant in social scientific terms has to connect with theoretical questions about discourse. On the other hand, no real understanding of the social effects of discourse is possible without looking closely at what happens when people talk or write. So, text analysis is an essential part of discourse analysis, but discourse analysis is not merely the linguistic analysis of texts. I see discourse analysis as "oscillating" between a focus on specific texts and a focus on what I call the "order of discourse," the relatively durable social structuring of language which is itself one element of the relatively durable structuring and networking of social practices. Critical discourse analysis is concerned with continuity and change at this more abstract, more structural, level, as well as with what happens in particular texts. The link between these two concerns is made through the way in which texts are analyzed in critical discourse analysis. Text analysis is seen as not only linguistic analysis; it also includes what I have called "interdiscursive analysis," that is, seeing texts in terms of the different discourses, genres and styles they draw upon and articulate together.

Fairclough summarize the main tenets of CDA as follows:

1. CDA addresses social problems
2. Power relations are discursive
3. Discourse constitutes society and culture
4. Discourse does ideological work
5. Discourse is historical
6. The link between text and society is mediated
7. Discourse analysis is interpretative and explanatory
8. Discourse is a form of social action.

Critical discourse analysis is viewed as integrating (a) analysis of text, (b) analysis of processes of text production, consumption and distribution, and (c) sociocultural analysis of the discursive event (be it an interview, a scientific paper, or a conversation) as a whole. My attempt at drawing together language analysis and social theory centers upon a combination of this more social-theoretical sense of "discourse" with the "text-and-interaction" sense in linguistically-oriented discourse analysis. This concept of discourse and discourse analysis is three-dimensional. Any discursive "event" (i. e. any instance of discourse) is seen as being simultaneously a piece of text, an instance of discursive practice, and an instance of social practice. The "text" dimension attends to language analysis of texts. The "discursive practice" dimension, like "interaction" in the "text-and-interaction" view of discourse, specifies the nature of the processes of text production and interpretation, for example which types of discourse (including "discourses" in the more social-theoretical sense) are drawn upon and how they are combined. The "social practice" dimension attends to issues of concern in social analysis such as the institutional and organizational circumstances of the discursive event and how that shapes the nature of the discursive practice, and the constitutive/constructive effects of discourse referred to above.

3. Original selecting

Building tasks

3.1 Building things through language

Language has a magical property: when we speak or write, we design what we have to say to fit the situation in which we are communicating. But, at the same time, how we speak or write creates that very situation. It seems, then, that we fit our language to a situation that our language, in turn, helps to create in the first place.

This is rather like the "chicken and egg" question: which comes first—the situation we're in, e.g., a committee meeting, or the language we use, e.g., our committee ways of talking and interacting? Is this a "committee meeting" because we are speaking and acting this way, or are we speaking and acting this way because this is a committee meeting? After all, if we did not speak and act in certain ways, committees could not exist; but, then, if institutions, committees, and committee meetings didn't already exist, speaking and acting this way would be nonsense. The answer here is that this magical property is real and language and institutions "bootstrap" each other into existence in a reciprocal process through time.

Another way to look at the matter is this: we always actively use spoken and written language to create or build the world of activities (e.g., committee meetings), identities (e.g., committee chairs, members, facilitators and obstructionists), and institutions (committees) around us. However, thanks to the workings of history and culture, we often do this in more or less routine ways. These routines make activities, identities, and institutions, like committees, committee members (of various types) and committee meetings, seem to exist apart from language and action in the here-and-now: Nonetheless, these activities, identities, and institutions have to be continuously and actively rebuilt in the here-and-now: This is what accounts for change and transformation.

We continually and actively build and rebuild our worlds not just through language but through language used in tandem with actions, interactions, non-linguistic symbol systems, objects, tools, technologies, and distinctive ways of thinking, valuing, feeling, and believing. Sometimes what we build is quite similar to what we have built before; sometimes it is not. But language-in-action is always and everywhere an active building process.

So language-in-use is a tool, used alongside other tools, to design or build things. Whenever we speak or write, we always and simultaneously construct or build seven things or seven areas of "reality." Let's call these seven things the "seven building tasks" of language. In turn, since we use language to build these seven things, a discourse analyst can ask seven different questions about any piece of language-in-use. Below, I list the seven building tasks and the discourse analysis question to which each gives rise.

Significance

We use language to make things significant (to give them meaning or value) in certain ways, to build significance. As the saying goes, we make "mountains out of molehills." For example, I enter a plain, square room. There is no clear "front" or "back" to the room. But I speak and act in a certain way (e.g., like someone about to run a meeting), and, low and behold, where I sit becomes the "front" of the room. I have used language in such a way as to make where I am sitting have the significance of being the "front of the room" for the time being.

***Discourse analysis question*: How is this piece of language being used to make certain things significant or not and in what ways?**

Activities

We use language to get recognized as engaging in a certain sort of activity, that is, to build an activity here-and-now: For example, I talk and act in one way and I am engaged in formally opening a committee meeting; I talk and act in another way and I am engaged in "chit-chat" before the official start of the meeting. When I act I have to use language to make clear to others what it is I take myself to be doing.

***Discourse analysis question*: What activity or activities is this piece of language being used to enact (i.e., get others to recognize as going on)?**

Identities

We use language to get recognized as taking on a certain identity or role, that is to build an identity here-and-now: For example, I talk and act in one way and I am speaking and acting as "chair" of the committee; at the next moment I speak and talk in a different way and I am speaking and acting as one peer/colleague speaking to another. Even if I have an official appointment as chair of the committee, I am not always taken as acting as the chair, even during meetings. I have to enact this identity at the right times and places to make it work.

Discourse analysis question: **What identity or identities is this piece of language being used to enact (i. e., get others to recognize as operative)?**

Relationships

We use language to signal what sort of relationship we have, want to have, or are trying to have with our listener(s), reader(s), or other people, groups, or institutions about whom we are communicating; that is, we use language to build social relationships. For example, in a committee meeting, as chair of the committee, I say "Prof. Smith I'm very sorry to have to move us on to the next agenda item" and signal a relatively formal and deferential relationship with Professor Smith. On the other hand, suppose I say, "Ed, it's time to move on." Now I signal a relatively informal and less deferential relationship with the same person.

Discourse analysis question: **What sort of relationship or relationships is this piece of language seeking to enact with others (present or not)?**

Politics (the distribution of social goods)

We use language to convey a perspective on the nature of the distribution of social goods, that is, to build a perspective on social goods. For example, if I say "Microsoft loaded its operating system with bugs," I treat Microsoft as purposeful and responsible, perhaps even culpable. If I say, on the other hand, "Microsoft's operating system is loaded with bugs," I treat Microsoft as less purposeful and responsible, less culpable. How I phrase the matter has implications for social goods such as guilt and blame, legal responsibility or lack of it, or Microsoft's bad or good motives.

Discourse analysis question: **What perspective on social goods is this piece of language communicating (i. e., what is being communicated as to what is taken to be "normal," "right," "good," "correct," "proper," "appropriate," "valuable," "the ways things are," "the way things ought to be," "high status or low status," "like me or not like me," and so forth)?**

Connections

We use language to render certain things connected or relevant (or not) to other things, that is, to build connections or relevance. For example, I talk and act so as to make what I am saying here-and-now in this committee meeting about whether we should support affirmative action in hiring connected or relevant to (or, on the Building tasks other hand, not connected or relevant to) what I said last week about my support for the new government's turn to the right. Things are not always inherently connected or relevant to each other. I have to make such connections. Even when things seem inherently connected or relevant to each other, I can use language to break or mitigate such connections.

Discourse analysis question: **How does this piece of language connect or disconnect things; how does it make one thing relevant or irrelevant to another?**

Sign systems and knowledge

There are many different languages (e. g., Spanish, Russian, English).

There are many different varieties of anyone language (e. g., the language of lawyers, the language of biologists, the language of hip-hop artists). There are communicative systems that are not language (e. g., equations, graphs, images). These are all different sign systems. Furthermore, we humans are always making knowledge and belief claims within these systems. We can use language to make certain sign systems and certain forms of knowledge and belief relevant or privileged, or not, in given situations, that is to build privilege or prestige for one sign system or knowledge claim over another. For example, I talk and act so as to make the knowledge and language of lawyers relevant (privileged) or not over "everyday language" or over "non-lawyerly academic language" in our committee discussion of facilitating the admission of more minority students.

***Discourse analysis question*: How does this piece of language privilege or disprivilege specific sign systems (e. g., Spanish vs. English, technical language vs. everyday language, words vs. images, words vs. equations) or different ways of knowing and believing or claims to knowledge and belief?**

3.2 An example

We will turn now to a an example of discourse analysis used to uncover the seven building tasks at work in a piece of data. However, it important at the outset to keep several things in mind. First, since we will be dealing with only a small piece of data, taken from a much larger corpus, we will be formulating *hypotheses* about this data. These hypotheses would need to be confirmed further by looking at more data and, perhaps, engaging in the collection of additional data. Much of discourse analysis—much of science, in general—is about formulating and gaining some confidence in hypotheses which must be further investigated, rather than gaining any sort of "definitive proof," which really does not exist in empirical inquiries. We must always be open, no matter how confident we are in our hypotheses, to finding evidence that might go against our favored views.

Second, discourse analysis is always a movement from context to language and from language to context. We gain information about a context in which a piece of language has been used and use this information to form hypotheses about what that piece of language means and is doing. In turn, we closely study the piece of language and ask ourselves what we can learn about the context in which the language was used and how that context was construed (interpreted) by the speaker/writer and listener(s)/reader(s). In this brief example, we can engage in this two-way process in only a limited way.

The data comes from a project in which a university history professor (I will refer to her as "Sarah Miller," not her real name) wanted to work with middle school teachers, to engage their students in oral history. She wanted the children to interview their relatives and neighbors to gain information about the history of their local neighborhoods and the city in which they lived. These oral histories were intended eventually to inform an exhibit in the city's historical museum.

The university at which the professor taught — which I will call "Woodson" — was a small elite private university that was over a hundred years old. The city in which the university resided — which I will call "New Derby" — was largely a working-class industrial city. The teachers that the professor dealt with were public school teachers with working-class origins. There were historic "town-gown" tensions between the university and the city and, in particular, tensions between people who taught at the university and people who taught in the public schools, tensions over status and commitment to the city. The members of the university faculty had not been born in the city and often did not stay there, moving on to other jobs in other cities; the public school teachers had invariably been born there and intended to stay there.

The data printed below comes from the first meeting of the group that was going to work on the oral history project in two schools. The meeting, held at one of the two schools to be involved in the project, was attended by four teachers from the two schools, the university professor and two of her research assistants, and a representative of a group that was helping to the fund the joint work of the professor and the teachers, as well as a couple of other people. The speaker is one of the teachers (I will call her "Karen Jones"). She has been asked by the person chairing the meeting (the representative of the funding agency) to give those at the meeting some background on what had transpired prior to this first official meeting.

The history professor had called the curriculum coordinator at Karen's school-a woman we will refer to as "Susan Washington" — to ask for help on her project and to gain access to the school. The "Summer Institute" Karen refers to was a workshop on research collaborations between university educators and local school teachers sponsored by the Education program at the university. The funders of the oral history project, who were also helping to support the Ser Institute, had hoped that Professor Miller and the teachers she was going to work with would attend the Institute.

So, at last, here's the data. To make matters clearer, I leave out many details from the transcript, things like pausing and hesitation, details which are, of course, themselves also meaningful and would be included in any fuller analysis. I capitalize words that were said with particular emphasis:

1. Last year, Susan Washington, who is our curriculum coordinator here had a call from Sarah at Woodson
2. And called me and said
3. We have a person from Woodson who's in the History Department
4. And she's interested in doing some research into black history in New Derby

5. And she would like to get involved with the school

6. And here's her number

7. Give her a call"

8. And I DID call her

9. And we BOTH expected to be around for the Summer Institute at Woodson

10. I did participate in it

11. But SARAH wasn't able to do THAT

While not all building tasks will be as readily apparent in all pieces of data, we can always ask questions about each one to see what we get. One device that helps us think about what something means is to ask in what other ways it could have been said or written. Once we see what alternatives existed, we can ask why the person said or wrote it as they did and not in some alternative way. So let's look at each of the building tasks in turn.

Significance

How does Karen make the fact that Sarah wasn't at the Summer Institute significant? This event could have been treated as unimportant, of little significance. However, Karen treats it as a significant happening. Karen uses her words to create a clear contrast between herself and Sarah, and Sarah's failure to attend the Summer Institute takes on significance in terms of this contrast. Karen portrays herself as responsible and as someone who did what she was told to do. She stresses this by saying "I DID call her," instead of just "I called her." She says that both (stressing "both") she and Sarah "expected" (intended) to be "around for the Summer Institute," implying, perhaps, that Sarah may have "been around," but, nonetheless, not bothered to come. She then stresses that she herself did participate (note, again, "I DID participate in it" instead of "I participated" or just "I went"). Karen concludes "But SAFAH wasn't able to do THAT." Here she uses "but" to create a contrast between her own behavior and Sarah's. She stresses both "Sarah" and "that," thereby emphasizing the contrast between herself and Sarah yet more. And she focuses on Sarah's "ability" ("wasn't able to do"), rather than just saying "But Sarah didn't come" or "Sarah couldn't come." All these details make us see that Sarah's absence from the Institute is treated by Karen as a significant or meaningful fact. She does not say exactly what she finds significant about this fact, but leaves this to be inferred by her listeners.

Activities

What is Karen using language to do here? What social activity is she attempting to enact? It appears that Karen is trying to contrast her responsible behavior and commitment to a project that she didn't ask to be on (note that she says Sarah contacted the school and, in turn, the curriculum coordinator told Karen to call Sarah) with Sarah's less responsible behavior and lesser commitment to a project she herself had requested and set in motion. Karen's social activity here is one of positioning herself in certain ways in front of the group and for the project to come and positioning Sarah in other ways. Note the pattern: "I DID," "we BOTH expected ...," "I DID ...," "But SARAH wasn't able to do THAT" Karen sets herself up as a "do-er" and Sarah as not a "do-er." Of course, Karen could have formulated her language quite differently had she wanted to. She could, for example, have said something like: "I called Sarah and, while we both had expected to be around for the Summer Institute, I was able to attend, but Sarah couldn't make it." Notice that this way of putting matters backgrounds the expectation they each had of being available to attend the Institute (placing it in a subordinate clause attached to "I was able to attend, but Sarah couldn't make it," rather than making it a main clause as Karen does). This formulation does not emphasize doing on Karen's part by using "did" and it formulates Sarah's lack of attendance in a way that does not stress her inability to come, but makes it sound as if something came up over which she had less control ("couldn't make it"). This alternative way still does not, of course, completely mitigate the contrast, but it softens it, nonetheless.

Identities

What identity is Karen trying to take on or enact? We have already seen how Karen enacts in her language an identity as a responsible do-er. In addition, she contextualizes this agentive/responsible identity in terms of her depiction of the dialog with the curriculum coordinator. The coordinator says "We have a person from Woodson ...," sounding as if they have a problem on their hands. She turns to Karen as the responsible party to handle the matter: "Give her a call." The dialog with the curriculum coordinator leaves the implication that Karen is the teacher with the most expertise or responsibility to deal with a university professor who wants to do research on "black history in New Derby" and "get involved with the school."

Relationships

What relationship is Karen trying to enact in regard to Sarah? From what we have said so far it is clear that Karen is enacting a distanced, but not particularly deferential, relationship to Sarah. The contrast, of herself as "do-er" and Sarah as not a "do-er," that she creates accomplishes this, but so does the fact that she uses Sarah's first name both in her introduction to her dialog with the curriculum coordinator and in her concluding remark that "Sarah wasn't able to do that." Note, too, that in her portrayal of the dialog with the curriculum coordinator, Karen uses the phrase "a person from Woodson who's in the History Department," rather than something like "a Woodson history professor" or "a professor from Woodson's History Department." We should note, too, that these references to the historian are made while she is sitting at a small table with the rest of the group, waiting for her turn to talk. We could ask, as well, about what sort of relationship Karen is attempting to create with the group as a whole and with the project they are embarking on.

Politics

What sorts of implications for the distribution of social goods does Karen's language have? Of course, one social good at stake here is Karen's and Sarah's reputations as responsible, trustworthy people. Another is their reputations as "do-ers" or people who fail to do what is needed. Yet another social good at stake — one that is not readily apparent to anyone who does not know the situation better — is who has "rights" to school children. At a much later meeting of the group, the other teacher from Karen's school (and her dose friend) eventually makes it dear that teachers feel that they "own" their children (e. g., she refers to them as "my children") and that researchers like Sarah should go through teachers (contact them directly) to gain access to their children, not go through an authority figure such as the curriculum coordinator. While this became clear only in a later meeting, it helps explain some of how Karen's language is designed in this short except. The other teachers in the room well know that the way in which the professor (albeit inadvertently) causes the curriculum coordinator to "order" Karen to call her in order to get into Karen's class was a breach of protocol and they can clearly hear this in her language.

Connections

How is Karen connecting things or making them relevant to each other? How is she disconnecting them or making them not relevant to each other? It is clear by now how Karen renders her attendance at the Institute and Sarah's lack of attendance connected and relevant to each other ("I DID ... , we BOTH expected, I DID, but SARAH wasn't able to do THAT"). Furthermore, she implies that this contrast is relevant to the initial call Sarah made to the school in the way in which she directly juxtaposes Sarah setting the project in motion with that phone call (without Karen's own initiative) only to fail to attend the an initial event that was meant to facilitate the project and Karen's involvement.

Sign systems and knowledge

How is Karen privileging or disprivileging specific sign systems (languages, styles of language, non-verbal sign systems) or specific ways of or claims to know and believe? This short excerpt is really the beginning of a long struggle enacted in and through language as to whether teacher knowledge or university professor knowledge in regard to history, teaching history, classrooms, children, and the community is to be privileged - and when, where, and why. This process already starts with the contrast between the use of the curriculum coordinator's first and last name (Susan Washington) and the professor's first name only. It is hinted at in the way in which the curriculum coordinator is depicted as saying "a person from Woodson" and "interested in doing some research in black history in New Derby." Both descriptions are vague. "A person from Woodson" makes it sound as if the curriculum coordinator does not really know the professor and does not cede her the authority of her rank and title. "Some research in black history in New Derby" makes it sound as though either the professor is vague about what research she wants to do ("some research on black history") or the coordinator doesn't know or care much what it is exactly (and, it just so happens, the curriculum coordinator is an African-American). In fact, everyone knew from the outset that the professor wanted to do oral history with children studying their own neighborhoods and families-that is, in fact, why Karen was involved, since she already did oral histories with the children in her class. We should keep in mind that what the curriculum coordinator says in Karen's story is Karen's depiction for this meeting - with Professor Miller sitting there - of what was said, not necessarily what actually was said.

It is clear that all the building tasks are integrally lined to each other and often mutually supported by the same words and phrases. We have generated some hypotheses from this small piece of data, based on mutual considerations of context and language-in-use. In turn, these hypotheses would guide our search through additional data. Our confidence in these hypotheses will rise if we look through more and more talk from this same group of people in this and subsequent meetings and we gain more and more evidence for our hypotheses — more and more examples that appear to best explained by our hypotheses. If we see these hypotheses further confirmed in other sorts of data — perhaps in other encounters among university professors and teachers in this and other cities — then our confidence will rise yet more. If, in the end, no equally good competing hypotheses are available, then we accept our hypotheses, at least until disconfirming evidence appears, and work on their basis. This is just how all empirical research works. Unlike mathematics, there are no hard "proofs" to be had here.

Our hypotheses make predictions about what we expect to find in further data or in a closer look at our original data. For example, by the end of our excerpt at line 11, we certainly have evidence that Professor Miller could have heard this excerpt as a criticism of herself. She could have heard line 11 as implying she did not have good reasons for not attending the Swimmer Institute. We would certainly want to look closely at Professor Miller's reaction at this point, both verbally and non-verbally (which is why it is good to videotape and not just audiotape data).

When we go back and look further at our recordings, we see, from both verbal and non-verbal cues, that Professor Miller attempts to interrupt Karen at just the point at which Karen stresses the word "that" at the end of line 11. The professor gives a small laugh and says, in a low voice, "I heard . . . how did you get." Karen speaks right through the attempted interruption, cutting it off, saying "Well, so Sarah and I talked a little bit about what her plans were and sort of what our expectations were." We don't know, of course, what the professor wanted to say, but it is clear that she had heard the end of line 11 as a point at which she wanted to stop Karen and interject something. In the end, in the research from which this data came, the hypotheses we have begun to formulate here were richly supported by more and more data as the project went on. These hypotheses, in turn, helped discourse researchers understand how and why the project, at various points, was failing and allowed them to help make things work a bit better. Could they make it "perfect"? Of course not. Some of the problems and issues (largely to do with status, power, and institutional conflicts) our hypotheses point to are entrenched problems in the real world and would require substantive social and institutional changes to remove. But that doesn't mean we can't do anything and it doesn't mean we can't start on the process of institutional change.

In Chapter 7 I will elaborate on the seven "building tasks" I have introduced here and their relevance for discourse analysis. But in the next three chapters, I want to develop several "tools of inquiry" — ways of looking at language-in-use that will help us study how these building tasks are carried out and with what social and political consequences. ①

References

[1]Brown G. & Yule G. Discourse Analysis [M]. Cambridge: Cambridge

① 摘自 Gee J. P. An Introduction to Discourse Analysis: Theory and Method (2nd edition) [M]. London: Routldege., 2005.

University Press. 1983.

[2]Coulthard M. Advances in Spoken Discourse Analysis[M]. London: Routledge, 1992.

[3] Coulthard M. Advances in Written Text Analysis [M]. London: Routledge, 1994.

[4]Fairclough N. Critical discourse analysis: the critical study of language [M]. London: Longman,1995.

[5]Fairclough N. Wodak R. Critical discourse analysis[C]//Discourse as Social Interaction. London: Sage, 1997.

[6]Fowler R. Language in the News: Discourse and Ideology in the Press [M]. London: Routledge, 1991.

[7]Gee J. P. An Introduction to Discourse Analysis: Theory and Method (2nd edition)[M]. London: Routldege., 2005.

[8]Halliday M. A. K. & Hasan R. Cohesion in English [M]. London: Longman,1976.

[9]Labov W. Language in the Inner City: Studies in Black Vernacular English[M]. Philadephia: University of Pennsylvania Press,1972.

[10] Schiffrin D. Approaches to Discourse [M]. Oxford: Blackwell Publishers Ltd, 1994.

[11]Schiffrin D., Tanen D. & Hamilton H. The Handbook of Discourse Analysis [M]. Oxford: Blackwell Publishers Ltd, 2001.

[12]Searle John. Speech Acts: An Essay in the Philosophy of Language [M]. Cambridge: Cambridge University Press, 1969.

[13]van Dijk T. Handbook of Discourse Analysis[M]. London: Academic Press, 1985.

[14]van Dijk T. Discourse as Social Interaction[M]. 1997.

[15]韩礼德. 功能语法导论[M]. 北京:外语教学与研究出版社,2000.

University Press, 1981.

[12] Swales John. Genre Analysis: English in Academic and Research Settings[M]. Cambridge: Cambridge University Press, 1990.

[15] 黄国文. [illegible]

第九章

体裁分析

导　读

最早关注体裁(genre)的是苏联学者巴赫金(M. Bakhtin)。他在20世纪20年代后期就开始研究这一问题。他指出:"语言的使用是在人类某一活动领域中参与者单个而具体的表述形式中实现的……每一单个的表述,无疑是个人的,但使用语言的每一领域却锤炼出相对稳定的表述类型,我们称之为言语体裁。"(巴赫金 1998: 140)巴赫金是在广义上使用体裁这一概念的,将文学体裁纳入语言研究。

近年来,随着ESP等领域的快速发展,体裁研究开始受到越来越多的关注。斯威尔斯(J. Swales)通过对学术论文绪论部分的研究总结出相应的理论模式,极大地推动了体裁分析的发展。杜德雷-伊文斯(Dudley-Evans)将斯威尔斯的模式推广到理学硕士论文等更复杂的学术论文研究中。布哈提亚(V. K. Bhatia)将体裁分析的模式应用到商务信函和法律文件的研究中,并取得了丰硕的成果。

1990年,斯威尔斯在《体裁分析:学术与科研英语》(*Genre Analysis: English in academic and research settings*)一书中较为详尽地开展了对体裁的研究,为体裁在民俗学、文学、语言学和修辞学中的发展指明了新的方向。他认为体裁是一种交际事件(Communicative events),具有以下特点:

- "体裁"是交际事件的一种分类。
- 交际事件分类的主要标准是一整套公认并共同遵守的交际目的,而不仅仅是语篇在语言形式上的近似性或相同点。
- 语言体裁的范例可随其原型(prototype)发生变化。
- 体裁的理据对语篇的内容和形式起着制约作用。同一交际社团或同一领域的人都承认并力图遵守这种制约性。

· 人们对交际行为的组织是否得体和成功,部分地取决于对体裁掌握和运用的纯熟程度。

总之,体裁作为语言研究的一个新兴领域,对语言教学和习得具有非常重要的指导意义和实用价值。我们相信,体裁分析也必将成为今后体裁研究的主要方向。

1. Definitions

1.1 genre

Each separate utterance is individual, of course, but each sphere in which language is used develops its own relatively stable types of these utterances. These we may call speech genre.

(Bakhtin 1952 – 1953: 60)

Genres often coincide with speech events, but must be treated as analytically independent of them. They may occur in (or as) different events. The sermon as a genre is typically identified with a certain place in a church service, but its properties may be invoked, for serious or humorous effect, in other situations.

(Hymes 1974: 61)

In a society, the recurrence of certain discursive properties is institutionalized, and individual texts are produced and perceived in relation to the norm constituted by that codification. A genre, literary or otherwise, is nothing but this codification of discursive properties.

(Todorov 1976: 162)

A genre is a group of acts unified by a constellation of forms that recurs in each of its members. These forms, *in isolation*, appear in other discourses. What is distinctive about the acts in a genre is a recurrence of the forms *together* in constellation.

(Campbell and Jamieson 1978: 20)

Genres are how things get done, when language is used to accomplish them. They range from literary to far from literary forms: poems, narratives, expositions, lectures, seminars, recipes, manuals, appointment making, service encounters, news broadcasts and so on. The term genre is used here to embrace each of the linguistically realized activity types which comprise so much of our culture.

(Martin 1985: 250)

A genre comprises a class of communicative events, the members of which serve some set of communicative purposes. These purposes are recognized by the expert members of the parent discourse community, and thereby constitute the rationale for the genre. This rationale shapes the schematic structure of the discourse and influences and constrains choice of content and style.

(Swales 1990: 58)

A general definition of genre might explain that a genre is a text or discourse type which is recognized as such by its users by its characteristic features of style or form, which will be specifiable through stylistic and text-linguistic/discourse analysis, and/or by the particular function of texts belonging to the genre.

(Malmkjær 2002: 206)

Historically, however, and largely as an inheritance from Aristotle, "genre" was defined normatively as a given category of literature, with the choices originally restricted to "dramas" and "novels."

(Strazny 2005: 379)

1.2 discourse community

Use of the term "discourse community" testifies to the increasingly common assumption that discourse operates within conventions defined by communities, be they academic disciplines or social groups. The pedagogies associated with writing across the curriculum and academic English now use the notion of "discourse communities" to signify a cluster of ideas: that language use in a group is a form of social behavior, that discourse is a means of maintaining and extending the group's knowledge and of initiating new members into the group, and that discourse is epistemic or constitutive of the group's knowledge.

(Herzberg 1986: 1)

I would now like to propose six defining characteristics that will be necessary and sufficient for identifying a group of individuals as a discourse community.

- A discourse community has a broadly agreed set of common public goals.
- A discourse community has mechanisms of intercommunication among its members.
- A discourse community uses its participatory mechanisms primarily to provide information and feedback.
- A discourse community uses and hence possesses one or more genres in the communicative furtherance of its aims.
- In addition to owning genres, a discourse community has acquired some specific lexis.
- A discourse community has a threshold level of members with a suitable degree of relevant content and discoursal expertise.

(Swales 1990: 24 – 27)

The "discourse community" concept was based on the sociolinguistic notion of the speech community, whereby similarities in speech could be accounted for by the speakers' living in a community defined by geographical space, social class, gender, ethnicity, and so on. In a discourse community, the members may be dispersed widely and of different social classes, genders, and ethnicities, but they are linked by a common set of communicative purposes.

(Brown 2006: 29)

2. Classical theories

2.1 Genre in Language Studies

Structuralist critics view literature as a self-contained system with its own codes and conventions. In contrast, another major figure, Mikhail Bakhtin, related literary language to the wider and hitherto neglected 26 Genre and Genre Analysis system of codes and expectations governing discourse in general. In "The Problem of Speech Genres," Bakhtin [1952 – 1953 (1986): 60] wrote:

Each separate utterance is individual, of course, but each sphere in which language is used develops its own relatively stable types of these utterances. These we may call speech genres … Special emphasis should be put on the extreme heterogeneity of speech genres (oral and written). In fact, the category of speech genres should include short rejoinders of daily dialogue (and these are extremely varied depending on the subject matter, situation, and participants), everyday narration, writing (in all its various forms), the brief standard military command, the elaborate and detailed order, the fairly variegated repertoire of business documents (for the most part standard), and the diverse world of commentary (in the broad sense of the word: social, political). [*italics in original*].

In language studies, in the decades following Bakhtin, the term "genre" has been appropriated by linguists who wish to explore nonliterary spoken and written discourse in which expectations of conventional use of text structure, lexis, and syntax are likely to be satisfied; for example, academic research articles, letters of application for employment, recipes, and so-called "service encounters" in which customers interact with shopkeepers in order to purchase goods. Despite common interests, there is considerable divergence in why and how these linguists use the term "genre" and undertake genre analysis.

2.2 Genre in Applied Linguistics

Applied linguists' analyses of genre share something of the approaches of both the systemic-functionalist school and the New Rhetoricians. Like the latter, they favor ethnographic descriptions of the "discourse communities" who use genres to achieve social actions (cf., the notion of a "rhetorical community" proposed by Miller, 1994). It is the needs of the discourse communities that are linked to the formal qualities of generic texts, usually described as a sequence of "moves" that recall the generic structure potential of the systemic functionalists.

One of the best-known accounts of genre in this tradition is Swales' (1981, 1990) account of research article introductions in the sciences and social sciences. He refined his model into a three-move sequence, the overall function of which within the academic community is to "create a research space." This goal is accomplished by "establishing a territory" (for example, by making a topic generalization and surveying the literature); "establishing a niche" (for example, by questioning past research or adding to its scope); and "occupying the niche" (for example, by previewing one's own research). Within the research community, the research article introduction is used rhetorically to align oneself with or against a research tradition and to frame stronger and weaker claims to knowledge. Further work along these lines has been published on business correspondence (Bhatia, 1993), quantity surveying reports (Marshall, 1987), and economics discourse (Dudley-Evans and Henderson, 1990).

Where systemic functionalists rely initially on the genre analyst's intuitions to break down a text into purposive stages, focusing mainly on multiple examples of the text type and looking for realizational patterns that justify the intuitive categorizations, the applied linguist checks his or her stages or moves against evidence garnered from the discourse community, through observation and interview.

2.3 Genre analysis

Genre analysis is an important area within English for Specific Purposes (ESP) orientated studies. The first use of the term in relation to ESP is Swales (1981), who refers to it as 'a system of analysis that is able to reveal something of the patterns of organization of a "genre" and the language used to express those patterns.'

Genre analysis is not, however, principally concerned with the classification of genres, but with the investigation of regularities of communicative purpose and language form in genres that can inform ESP materials for writing and teaching. Swales' own work has focused on the academic article, and in particular on the article introduction. In Swales (1990), he sets out his Creating a Research Space (CARS) model for the pattern of organization of the article introduction. This consists of three main moves each of which has a number of steps. The full CARS model is:

Move 1 Establishing a Territory

- Step 1 Claiming centrality

  and/or

- Step 2 Making topic generalizations

  and/or

- Step 3 Reviewing items of previous research
- *Move 2 Establishing a Niche*

- Step 1A Counterclaiming

  or

- Step 1B Indicating a gap

  or

- Step 1C Question raising

  or

- Step 1D Continuing a tradition
- *Move 3 Occupying a Niche*
- Step 1A Outlining purposes

  or

- Step 1B Announcing present research
- Step 2 Announcing principal findings
- Step 3 Indicating research article (RA) structure

This model (originally presented by Swales 1981 in a rather different form, with four moves) has had considerable influence on the development of genre analysis and on the teaching of academic writing within English for Academic Purposes (EAP). It is the first detailed example of move analysis, an approach to text analysis which Skelton (1994) defines in the following way:

Move structure analysis tentatively assigns a function to a stretch of written or spoken text, identifies that function with one, or a set of exponents which signal its presence, and seeks to establish whether or not the pattern identified is a general pattern, by reference to similar texts.

Following the initial work on the Introduction, work in the area of move analysis has concentrated on other sections of the article and on related sections in the Masters or Ph. D. thesis or dissertation. A move analysis approach has also been used for the analysis of other sections of the research article, such as the abstract (Salager-Meyer 1990), the Methods section (Wood 1982), the Results section (Brett 1994; Williams 1999), the Discussion section (Belanger 1982;

Dudley-Evans 1994), and also for the analysis of dissertations (Hopkins and Dudley-Evans 1988).

The model for the Discussion section proposed by Dudley-Evans (1994) has nine moves:

- Move 1 Information move
- Move 2 Statement of result
- Move 3 Finding
- Move 4 (Un)expected outcome
- Move 5 Reference to previous research
- Move 6 Explanation
- Move 7 Claim
- Move 8 Limitation
- Move 9 Recommendation

Writers will not necessarily use all these moves in a Discussion section, but will make their points or build their argument through the appropriate selection of the moves and ordering them into cycles.

Genre analysis has mostly been concerned with written academic texts, but its methods are equally relevant to the analysis of texts in business, professional and occupational contexts (English for Occupational Purposes or EOP). Bhatia (1993: 45 – 75) looked at two types of business letter which he calls promotional genres — the sales promotion letter and the job application letter. His conclusion is that the two types of letter follow a very similar pattern of moves and therefore constitute one genre:

	Sales promotion letter	*Job application letter*
· Move 1	Establishing credentials	Establishing credentials
· Move 2	Introducing the offer	Introducing the candidature
· Move 3	Offering incentives	Offering incentives
· Move 4	Enclosing documents	Enclosing documents

- Move 5 Soliciting response Soliciting response
- Move 6 Using pressure tactics Using pressure tactics
- Move 7 Ending politely Ending politely

Bhatia (1993: 118) also suggests a four-move pattern for the structure of legal cases:

- Move 1 Identifying the case
- Move 2 Establishing the facts of the case
- Move 3 Arguing the case
    - 3.1 stating the history of the case
    - 3.2 presenting arguments
    - 3.3 deriving *ratio decidendi* (the principle of law that the judge wishes to set down for application to future cases of a similar description)
- Move 4 Pronouncing judgement

Genre analysis is also applicable to spoken text, though the difficulty of obtaining data has meant that much less analysis has been done into oral genres. Charles' analysis of business sales negotiations is an excellent example of what is possible when spoken data has been collected (Charles 1996).

All the research findings reported above have been concerned with texts and moves. The early research under the heading of genre analysis was of this kind, but in recent years (particularly in the USA) genre studies have focused rather more on the discourse communities that use and create genres. Swales' most recent book (Swales 1998) does not include detailed move analysis, but rather describes in detail three discourse communities located in one building at the University of Michigan, and uses what he names textography (ethnography with a linguistic focus) to show the role that particular texts play in the activities of those discourse communities. Berkenkotter and Huckin (1995: 2-3) argue that early genre analysis tended to reify genres and see them as linguistic abstractions. They suggest "case research with insiders" to analyze the ways in which writers or speakers use their knowledge of genre and of the expectations of the discourse community they belong to in a strategic manner to participate successfully in the activities of a discipline or a profession.

This consideration of the context in which genres are created and used by the discourse community has added an extra, very useful, dimension to genre studies and their value in ESP work. Studies that draw on the work of sociologists of science and studies of the workplace (e.g. Myers 1989; Bazerman and Paradis 1991) have shown how 'local' discourse communities may adapt the genres they use to meet their specific communicative needs. Many genres are dynamic in that they develop or die in response to changes in society and in particular workplace or academic situations. Smart (1993) argues that the ESP teacher working within a particular situation can play an important role in helping professionals understand the tension between the convenience of following a formula or model in writing and the need to adapt the model to suit their particular rhetorical purposes. The study of change in genres has led to the growth of a specific research area investigating the ways in which key genres such as the research article have reflected change in particular disciplines over a specified period of time. Atkinson (1992), for example, showed how articles published in the *Edinburgh Medical Journal* between 1735 and 1985 have adjusted to developments in the nature of the medical profession.

More text-based research has, none the less, continued to be reported. The development of computer-based corpora has enabled researchers to look more closely and in greater detail at lexical features of genres and provided the possibility to make more detailed analyses of moves.

3. Original selecting

A Theory of Genre

Genre pervades human lives. As people go about their business, interacting with others and trying to get along in the world, they use genres to ease their way, to meet expectations, to save time. People recognize genres, though not usually the power of genres. People say, "I heard the best *joke today*," "I have to give a *lecture* at nine thirty," "I've gotten into *mysteries*," and "Do you have a *travel brochure* for the Apostle Islands?" Genres have the power to help or hurt human interaction, to ease communication or to deceive, to enable someone to speak or to discourage someone from saying something different. People learn how to do *small talk* to ease the social discomfort of large group gatherings and meeting new people, but advertisers learn how to disguise *sales letters as winning sweepstakes entries*. Outraged citizens can express themselves in *letters to the editor*, but first-year college students may struggle to dissociate their personal experience from their *research papers*. Genre has significance for people's lives.

Scholars have studied genres for centuries; neither is it a new topic in English studies. In recent years, however, views of genre have changed, shifting from a formalistic study of critics' classifications to a rhetorical study of the generic actions of everyday readers and writers. This shift is possible in part, of course, because of the work done by previous genre critics and theorists, but it represents a substantial change in what is considered interesting and significant about genre. The theorists most directly contributing to this new conception of genre come from the whole range of English studies: from literature (M. M. Bakhtin, Tzvetan Todorov, Thomas Beebee, and David Fishelov), linguistics (M. A. K. Halliday, John Swales, Aviva Freedman, and Vijay K. Bhatia), and composition and rhetoric (Kenneth Burke, Lloyd Bitzer, Karlyn Kohrs Campbell and Kathleen Hall Jamieson, Carolyn Miller, Charles Bazerman, Carol Berkenkotter and Thomas Huckin, and David Russell), to name just a few. Because genre so significantly impacts how people use language, read literature, and write and read nonliterary texts, theories of genre can contribute new perspectives and approaches to many endeavors within English studies as well as a better understanding more generally of how people operate and have operated within their societies and cultures.

This volume examines, interprets, illustrates, elaborates, critiques, refines, and extends a rhetorical theory of genre, a theory that sees genres as types of rhetorical actions that people perform in their everyday interactions with their worlds. A rather complex theory of genre has developed over the last twenty years in the field of composition and rhetoric in particular, building in North America especially on the theoretical synthesis and argument proffered by Carolyn Miller in a 1984 article, "Genre as Social Action." Miller drew from a wide range of rhetorical scholars and theorists to synthesize and then extend a semiotic theory of genre. To explain and develop different issues in this rhetorical and semiotic theory of genre, other scholars have incorporated bits from Mikhail Bakhtin's theory of speech genres, from M. A. K. Halliday's functional theory of language as a social semiotic, from Anthony Giddens's structuration theory, most recently from Soviet activity theory, and from other theories and perspectives that have proven useful and enlightening. The results today are enhanced rhetorical theories of genre, much indebted to Miller's original examination and extension of then current genre scholarship.

What I attempt in this volume is not a history of that scholarship not a detailed, blow-by-blow account of each addition to our understanding of genre. What I hope to do is to synthesize much of the existing scholarship in order to clarify where genre theory stands today; to elaborate and illustrate what I consider to be the essential ideas of contemporary genre theory so that readers may better understand our claims; to critique current theories where I see disagreements or opportunities; and to extend genre theory in order to add new directions or argue for particular perspectives. Although many scholars have advanced theories of genre upon which this book will draw, some essential assumptions have not been fully examined and some implications have not been considered. Nor has anyone attempted the perhaps foolhardy task of elaborating a comprehensive theory of genre, one that encompasses synchronic as well as diachronic perspectives, literary as well as rhetorical genres, and individual as well as social views. In making this attempt, I hope to provoke new questions, not supply all the answers.

Following current genre scholarship and therefore drawing heavily from Miller, this first chapter establishes the basic definitions and tenets I find most significant and productive in current rhetorical genre theory. Readers interested in the scholarly history of these ideas might wish to review Miller's 1984 article, in which she establishes the sources of many of the ideas that current composition theory in North America most often draws from her work. One of the ideas current in genre theory and explained in this chapter is that genre should be redefined rhetorically according to the people who participate in genres and make the forms meaningful, a shift from genre as defined by literary critics or rhetoricians to genre as defined by its users. Breaking with older, traditional notions of genre and moving toward contemporary views, this chapter explains why genre cannot be equated with classification, though genres do classify, and why genre cannot be equated with forms, though genres are often associated with formal features. More current and rhetorical theories of genre tend to follow Miller's definition of genre as typified social action associated with a recurrent situation. Agreeing with this essentially rhetorical nature of genre, this chapter draws out and extends threads introduced by Miller and other scholars to weave a detailed tapestry of genre. It amplifies Miller's challenge to the existence of recurrence as anything other than a construction, and it defines the relationship between genre and its situation as interactive and reciprocal. In fact, as David Russell does using activity theory, this chapter rejects situation as singularly defining of genre. Instead, I expand from situation to include an interaction of contexts at different levels, encompassing the impact of preexisting genres as well as situational and cultural context.

3.1 Genre as Classification and Form

At its worst, genre is a trivial and dangerous concept. It merely names what writers have created (the sonnet) and specifies formal features (fourteen lines), yet it artificially compares unique authors and works of art (Shakespeare and Donne) and stifles true creativity (forcing modern poets to break out into free verse). That negative perception leads to labeling as "genre writing" what are considered by many the least interesting literary works—formulaic mysteries, romances, westerns, and science fiction. Even at its most positive, genre is traditionally known as artificial and arhetorical, a classification system deriving from literary and rhetorical criticism that names types of texts according to their forms. No wonder that genre has become a topic of little interest to postromantic scholars, who do not care to consider such traditional topics as whether a text belongs to one genre or another, whether one type of text is its own genre or a subgenre of another, whether a new genre derives from this genre or that genre, and what comprises the essential features of a particular genre.

Such a view of genre holds little interest for contemporary language, composition, and rhetoric scholars as well, for, in the past, genre has not only been equated with literary texts exclusively but has also been divorced from contemporary understandings of how language works. Simplified views of genre encourage the very dichotomies in the study of writing that contemporary composition and rhetoric scholars have been undercutting: splits between form and content (and the related form and function, text and context), product and process, and individual and society. Treating genre as form requires dividing form from content, with genre as the form into which content is put. This container model of meaning has been superseded by a more integrated notion of how meaning is made, of the inseparability of form from content, as argued by such theorists as Kenneth Burke in "The Philosophy of Literary Form," and M. M. Bakhtin: "Form and content in discourse are one" ("Discourse" 259). Similarly, treating genre as form and text type requires binding genre to an emphasis on writing as a product, without effect on the processes of writing or, worse yet, inhibiting those processes. As a product-based concept, in fact, this view of genre seems to have more to do with reading than with writing. Genre interpretations have been popular among literary critics, those who have traditionally been more concerned with the reading of texts than with the writing of texts. Even in literature, though, the emphasis with genre has been on the product one reads rather than on the process of reading. Finally, a formal view of genre exaggerates one of the most troubling current dichotomies, that between the individual and the group or society. It makes genre a normalizing and static concept, a set of dictated forms that constrain the individual; genuine writers can distinguish themselves only by breaking out of those generic constraints, by substituting an individual genius for society's bonds. The individual and society are at odds rather than integrated. Although such simplified versions of traditional views of genre are being replaced by new versions—genre as rhetorical and dynamic, integrating form and content, product and process, individual and society—the conceptions of genre as classification system and formula have such a long history and are so well established that they are not easily dethroned. They also, of course, have some truth to them. An explanation of new theories of genre thus begins with the old.

3.2 Genre as Classification System

The conventional conception considers genre a classification system of texts based on shared formal characteristics. Since formalisms in general have sustained much of the work in linguistics, rhetoric, and literature in the past—the fields out of which genre theories have developed—it is not surprising that most genre theories in the past have been concerned with classification and form, with describing the formal features of a particular genre, describing the embodiment of a genre in a particular work, or delineating a genre system, a set of classifications of (primarily literary) texts. The emphasis on classification can be traced back to the followers of Aristotle, who turned his initial treatment in the *Poetics* of the epic, tragedy, and comedy into an infinitely modifiable classification scheme. The rhetorical division of discourse into epideictic, judicial, and deliberative can be seen as a similar classification system, one still in use by some rhetoricians today. Other writers propose broader or narrower schemes of text types: literature and nonliterature; narrative and nonnarrative; narrative, exposition, argument, description; the lyric, the sonnet; the Petrarchan sonnet. Whether called genres, subgenres, or modes, whether comprehensive or selective, whether generally accepted or disputed, these systems for classifying texts keep genre focused on static products. 1

Classifications are the effects of genre but not the extent of genre. To study genre as a rhetorical concept, one need not necessarily agree upon or even respond to many of the questions that have been raised about generic classifications—such as how many genres there are, whether x is a subgenre of y, whether this text is an instance of genre y or genre z. Tzvetan Todorov rather breezily claims, "We do not know just how many types of discourse there are, but we shall readily agree that there are more than one" (9). Though interesting in particular contexts, such classificatory questions reflect the particular purposes underlying particular classification schemes rather than the nature of genre itself. Groupings of complex items like texts are more like metaphors than equations: how texts are grouped depends on which features the classifier has selected to observe—common prosody, organization, tone, aim, or effect on the reader, for example. Daniel Defoe's *Moll Flanders*, for example, can be classified as a narrative, an episodic novel, a pseudoautobiography, or an eighteenth-century novel, depending on the classifier's interests. Even less transitional works can be classified in multiple ways: a memorandum from a departmental chair can be classified as business correspondence, memoranda, internal correspondence, or academic writing, depending on the classifier's perspective. An article in the *New York Times Book Review* can be classified as a review, an essay, a review essay, a magazine article, or journalism. Each of these works could also be classified in other ways, as purpose and interest dictate. Which of these labels are "actually" genres, which the "right" genre labels? Such classificatory questions may be interesting for the questions they raise about the nature of journalism today, the business side of academic life, or the development of the novel, but they do not define the essence of genre. As Heather Dubrow points out in her history of literary genre theory, the problem with defining genre based on *genus* (kind) is that what we will call a kind depends on "exactly what we think a genre is and hence what characteristics we take into account when deciding whether to grant that label to a given literary type". Defining genre as a kind of text becomes circular, since what we call a kind of text depends on what we think a genre is.

That conundrum does not mean that genres do not involve classification not that devising a classification scheme is necessarily a waste of time. There are purposes for which classification systems are helpful. After all, we do not reject classifications of biological species just because they reflect a principle of selection. Anne Freadman, in her classic 1987 article on genre, "Anyone for

Tennis?", lists filing systems, library classification systems, and disciplinary divisions within a university as examples of helpful classification systems (106). Similarly helpful, Aristotle's systems of classification clarified the purposes of literature and of rhetoric. The classification system that is the modes may have been created, according to Robert Connors's research, to ease the teaching of writing. Classifying texts has enabled scholars to clarify their arguments and discover new understandings, and that kind of genre work may still accomplish some purposes for literary and rhetorical scholars. But no one classification scheme delineates all genres. Genre scholars have long recognized that different classification systems serve different purposes. For a particular project, I might want to group all texts into one of three categories, comedy, tragedy, or tragicomedy; for another project, I might want to use four categories, narration, exposition, description, and argumentation; for another, just two categories, literature and nonliterature. For a project that involves working with texts in a more limited context, as in an accounting firm, for example, the classification scheme would cut smaller pieces of the world: say, letters to clients, research memoranda, internal memoranda, and sales letters. The particular labels that scholars give to genres will vary for different scholarly purposes. Rather than making the concept so broad as to be useless, as some have argued, allowing such flexibility in the definition of genre for scholars keeps the concept fluid and dynamic, able to respond to scholars' changing needs over time.

So far, I have been discussing the genre labels given by scholars and critics, but the most significant genre labels for a rhetorical definition of genre—and the classifications of most concern to rhetorical genre scholars—are the labels given by the people who use the genres. In addition to being named by analysts after the fact, genres are named as people use them, and texts are classified as they are being used. Concerned citizens write letters to their editors, students write essay examinations, teachers write syllabi, and doctors write prescriptions. Using other channels, presidents give inaugural addresses, artists paint portraits, and musicians play country songs. Most current rhetorical genre scholars base their analyses of genre not on the classifications of critics and analysts but on the ways people classify texts into genres as they use them. Carolyn Miller argues for analyzing the everyday genres that people use, and by 1997 David Russell takes as a given that participants' recognition of a genre is what rightly determines whether one genre is distinct from another ("Rethinking" 518). Genre has been redefined, then, from a classification created by critics to a classification that people make as they use symbols to get along in the world.

The cognitive origins of these common genre classifications are not well established. Of course, people classify many things, not just genres. All of language is based on classification, as words classify unique items into linguistic classes: each chair is a unique construction of materials, shapes, and designs, for example, but people call all manner of things they sit on "chair." Genre labels, too, classify unique items, but they classify symbolic actions rather than just types of texts, as I will explain further below. "Genre" itself is a label that scholars have put on one kind of classification, cutting the complexity of human cognition and of the world into this one part. Whether genres are a particular manner of classification or the same kind as all human classification is a question deserving examination by neurologists, cognitive psychologists, and psycholinguists. What we know is that language users perceive genres without being taught them apart from learning language (once they know the words, they describe themselves as telling "jokes" or "stories," for example), and different groups develop new words to describe the different genres they use. People classify unique actions under common labels, and we scholars call those labels "genres."

That the concept of genre has a reality for language users adds significance to the scholar's study of genres: studying genre is studying how people use language to make their way in the world. Examining genres as defined by language users rather than by scholars and critics gives us quite different answers to such questions as which classificatory systems are best and how many genres there are. This basis in user recognition underlies such claims as Carolyn Miller's that "the number of genres current in any society is indeterminate and depends upon the complexity and diversity of the society." With a user-based classification system for defining genre, the scholar's role in determining the proper classificatory system is replaced by another role, described by Miller as "ethnomethodological: it seeks to explicate the knowledge that practice creates." Marie-Laure Ryan earlier notes the importance of such an ethnomethodological enterprise: "The significance of generic categories thus resides in their cognitive and cultural value, and the purpose of genre theory is to lay out the implicit knowledge of the users of genres." I would add that literary and rhetorical critics are themselves people who use genres, and explicating their implicit knowledge reveals the literary and rhetorical values of our culture. Where earlier genre scholars were most interested in literary genres as defined by critics, today's rhetorical genre scholars are more often interested in everyday genres as named by their everyday users. Defining genre according to those common classifications reveals not only "something theoretically important about discourse," as Miller points out but also something important about how people think and how people act, as Miller, Ryan, and others point out. The classificatory nature of genre is an essential part of understanding genre and its significance, but such classification is defined rhetorically rather than critically, by the people who use it, for their purposes of operating in the everyday world.

3.3 Genre as Form

Although the classifications named by genre labels would seem to be based on common formal patterns, form alone cannot define genres. Theoretically, equating genre with form is tenable only within a container model of meaning, for it requires a separation of generic form from a particular text's context. Denying the container metaphor, J. R. Martin et al. write, "It is very important to recognize that genres make meaning; they are not simply a set of formal structures into which meanings are poured." Similarly, I. R. Titunik summarizes P. N. Medvedev's ideas about literary genre: "Genre is not that which is determined and defined by the components of a literary work or by sets of literary works, but that which, in effect, determines and defines them" (175). The problem of circularity also arises for form as it did for classification: A genre is named because of its formal markers; the formal markers can be identified because a genre has been named. The formal regularities we can observe in genres do not alone create the genres; they result from the genres.

On one level, genres do originate in repeated textual patterns, in forms. Readers and listeners recognize formal markers of a particular genre and identify the genre accordingly. "Once upon a time" begins some fairy tales, and "Have you heard the one about" marks some jokes. Business letters follow particular formats for inside addresses and even envelopes, and sonnets have fourteen lines. More complex discourse forms mark genres as well: contracts use a specified legal language and terminology, lab reports include required sections, tragedies follow a rise and fall of action. Such discourse markers have traditionally defined genres for many scholars and critics, and there is no doubting that certain textual forms identify certain genres. As Richard Coe argues in "An Apology for Form," the formal elements of genres are significant and meaningful, and studying the formal elements can offer insights about genres.

Practically, though, identifying reliable formal features of some genres has proven troublesome (consider the diverse forms of the novel, for example, or the essay). The formal features of some genres are at best minimal. Peter Medway has described a genre, called the architect's notebook, that students at his university write. The notebook is a particular kind of notebook physically, of a particular size, color, and material. Those studying to be architects carry the notebooks with them, and they refer to what they write as architects' notebooks. Medway's examination of the insides of these notebooks, however, revealed no common textual traits among the notebooks. Some included pictures, some did not; some used full sentences and paragraphs, some did not; some wrote about architecture, some did not. Such a "baggy genre," as Medway calls it, has little in the way of formal features to define it as a genre. One response would be to deny genre status to kinds of texts that do not have clear formal markers, and in fact some have argued against the existence of a novel or essay genre on the basis of the looseness of its textual characteristics. To deny generic labels to genres identified as such by their users, however, would seem presumptuous, especially in a rhetorical theory of genre that emphasizes the users and uses of genres. Readers say they have read a novel, and writers say they are writing essays. Architecture students say they are writing an architect's notebook.

Historically, too, identifying genres with formal features proves troublesome, for the formal characteristics of genres change over time but the users' labels of the genres do not necessarily change. Trying to solve this analytic problem by distinguishing definitive from insignificant forms has generally been unsuccessful, at best possible only after the fact and only for one historical period at a time. Rather than denying the validity of the users' genre recognition or trying to narrow it to a few forms, the task of the genre scholar is to identify what it is that makes users recognize these as genres.

Comparing genre labels to other words again may help clarify the relation of form to genre: studies of language show that speakers do not select words to classify items solely according to formal properties, that a speaker calls this rocker a "chair" not because of any formal properties of the rocker (though the rocker does indeed have a flat surface connected to an upright surface) but rather because of the speaker's perception of the rocker's function for that speaker at that time. People call a container a "cup" when they drink from it; they call a similarly shaped object a "bowl" when they spoon soup from it. Even more obviously, an emotion is not labeled "love" because of its association with heart rate or skin temperature but because of the speaker's perception of the emotion's meaning. Similarly, people do not label a particular story as a joke solely because of formal features but rather because of their perception of the rhetorical action that is occurring. At most, then, genres are associated with but not defined by textual form. The rhetorical and linguistic scholarship argues that formal features physically mark some genres, act as traces, and hence may be quite revealing. But those formal traces do not *define* or *constitute* the genre. The fact that genre is reflected in formal features does not mean that genre is those formal features.

To examine the relationship between form and genre, Karlyn Kohrs Campbell and Kathleen Hall Jamieson in 1978 reviewed substantial criticisms from rhetorical scholarship and concluded that "rhetorical forms that establish genres are stylistic and substantive responses to perceived situational demands" ("Form" 19). Any form, they note, may appear in isolation in other genres, but the "constellation" of forms in a genre, "bound together by an internal dynamic," fuses the elements so that "a unique kind of rhetorical act is created" ("Form" 20, 21, 25). That "unique kind of rhetorical act" is a genre, an action performed beyond any particular formal features. Carolyn Miller delineates Campbell and Jamieson's fusion further, describing a fusion of form with substance to create symbolically meaningful action ("Genre" 159 – 61). Campbell and Jamieson, Miller, and many genre scholars since look then not to patterns of form to define genre but to patterns of action. To understand those actions requires understanding the contexts within which they occur, contexts that in rhetorical scholarship have been called rhetorical situations. ①

References

[1] Bhatia V. K. Analysing Genre: Language Use in Professional Settings [M]. London: Longman, 1993.

[2] Cutting J. Analysing the Language of Discourse Communities [M]. Oxford: Elsevier Science Ltd, 2000.

[3] Fennell B. Mapping discourse communities [J]. Paper presented at the CCC Convention, Atlanta, 1987.

[4] Melvin S. International Encyclopedia of the Social Sciences [J]. American Sociological Review, 1968, 33(5).

[5] Herzberg Bruce. The politics of discourse communities [J]. Paper presented at the CCC Convention, New Orleans, La, March, 1986.

[6] Martin J. Process and text: two aspects of human semiosis [A]. Benson J. D. and Greaves W. S. (eds.). Systemic perspectives on discourse [C]. Ablex, 1985.

[7] 斯韦尔斯. 体裁分析——学术与科研英语[M]. 上海:上海外语教育出版社,2001.

① 摘自 Devitt A. J. *Writing Genres* [M]. Carbondale: Southern Illinois University Press, 2004.

第十章

特殊目的英语

导　读

二战以后,英语迅速成为国际语言。由此对英语教学的要求也产生相应的变化。那些希望能够阅读专业英语文献的技术人员、用英语推销产品的商人以及各种层次的学生,都希望通过学习英语来达到自己的目的。专门用途英语(ESP)就是在这个阶段应运而生的。它是一种目标明确、针对性强、实用价值高的教学手段。它两个明显的特点:首先,学习者均为成年人;其次,它被视为一种学习手段。

目前,ESP 涵盖的范围十分广阔。简单地说,它主要包括以下几个方面:

- EOP/EVP——职业英语(English for Occupational/Vocational Purposes),学习者多为工作中经常使用英语的涉外人员。其中的商务英语是目前最具潜力的领域。
- EAP/EEP——学术/教育英语(English for Academic/Educational Purposes),学习者主要为在校非英语专业的大学生和其他在学习中需要使用英语的学生。
- EST——科技英语(English for Science and Technology),作为 ESP 中的重要分支,科技英语是目前研究广泛、成果丰富的领域。这主要是因为科技发展推动下的全球化对科技文献需求量的激增。

专家们发现,不同文体、语域之间存在着很大的差异。既然语言会因语言情景的不同而变化,那么就有可能确定具体情景中的语言特色,然后依据这些特色确定学习者课程的基础。其中的体裁分析开始于 Swales 对学术论文的绪论部分所做的先导性研究工作。他从 ESP 的起源出发,介绍了 ESP 发展经历的五个阶段:语域分析、修辞或语篇分析、目标情景分析、技巧与策略和以学习为中心的方法。目前 ESP 的发展主要为“以学习为中心”的阶段,在理论探索和实证研究方面出现了大量的研究成果。相信这将成为今后 ESP 发展的主要趋势。

随着经济和科学文化的发展,英语作为国际语言的地位正在日益加强。为满足不同类型英语学习者的需要,ESP 必将发挥更加重要的作用。

1. Definitions

1.1 Language for specific purposes (LSP)

It is goal-oriented and based on needs analysis, and that it frequently has the characteristics of being constrained by time limits and being designed for adult learners.

(Robinson, 1991)

1.2 LSP testing

A test designed for language learners in specific academic, professional or vocational fields, such as tertiary students, language teachers, doctors and tour guides. Such tests rest on the assumption that language performance varies with both context and test task. While LSP tests typically claim to be testing language alone rather than content or non-language skills, in practice the boundary between language and these other skills is somewhat blurred.

(Davies 2002: 113)

1.3 English for specific purposes (ESP)

English for Specific Purposes must be seen as an approach not as a product. ESP is not a particular kind of language or methodology, nor does it consist of a particular type of teaching material. Understood properly, it is an approach to language learning, which is based on learner need.

(Hutchinson 2002: 19)

English for special purposes, also English for specific purposes, the role of

English in a language course or programme of instruction in which the content and aims of the course are fixed by the specific needs of a particular group of learners. For example courses in English for academic purposes, English for science and technology, and English for Nursing. These courses may be compared with those which aim to teach general language proficiency, English for general purposes.

(Richards 2002: 233)

1.4 Needs analysis / Target situation analysis

In ESP, the aims of the course are determined by the particular needs of the learners, and the growth of the use of English in science, technology, and business has led to both research into the nature of learners' needs (needs analysis) and the preparation of teaching materials to meet those needs.

(Malmkjær 1995: 618 – 619)

It refer to the systematic attempt to discover the needs for which a learner or group of learners requires a language.

(Clark 1999: 539)

2. Classical theories

2.1 The emergence of ESP

After the Second World War, the demand was growing for English courses tailored to specific needs, influential new ideas began to emerge in the study of language. Traditionally the aim of linguistics had been to describe the rules of

English usage, that is, the grammar. One finding of the new research was that the language we speak and write varies considerably, and in a number of different ways, from one context to another.

Swales(1985) presents an article which was published as early as 1962, but it was the late 1960s and early 1970s which saw the greatest expansion of research into the nature of particular varieties of English—for example, descriptions of written scientific and technical English. Most of the work at this time was in the area of English for Science and Technology(EST) and for a time ESP and EST were regarded as almost synonymous.

The growth of ESP, then, was brought about by a combination of three important factors: the expansion of demand for English to suit particular needs and developments in the fields of linguistics and educational psychology. All three factors seemed to point towards the need for increased specialization in language learning.

2.2 The development of ESP

We shall describe ESP in five phrases. It should be pointed out first of all that ESP is not a monolithic universal phenomenon. ESP has developed at different speeds in different countries, and examples of all the approaches we shall describe can be found operating somewhere in the world at the present time. It will also be noticeable that this area usually is known as EST. Swales in fact uses the development of EST to illustrate the development of ESP in general. He took EST as the pre-eminent position in the ESP story.

2.2.1 The concept of special language: register analysis

This stage took place mainly in the 1960s and early 1970s and was associated in particular with the work of Peter Strevens, Jack Ewer and John Swales. Operating on the basic principle that the English of, Electrical Engineering constituted a specific register different from that of, Biology or of

General English, the aim of the analysis was to identify the grammatical and lexical features of these registers. Teaching materials then took these linguistic features as their syllabus. A good example of such a syllabus is that of *A Course in Basic Scientific English* by Ewer and Latorre(1969).

In fact, as Ewer and Latorre's syllabus shows, **register analysis** revealed that there was very little that was distinctive in the sentence grammar of Scientific English beyond a tendency to favor particular forms such as the present simple tense, the passive voice and nominal compounds. It did not, for example, reveal any forms that were not found in General English. But we must be wary of making unfair criticism. Although there was an academic interest in the nature of registers of English per se, the main motive behind register analyses such as Ewer and Latorre's was the pedagogic one of making the ESP course more relevant to learners' needs. The aim was to produce a syllabus which gave high priority to the language forms students would meet in their Science studies and in turn would give low priority to forms they would not meet. Ewer and Hughes-Davies(1971), for example, compared the language of the texts their Science students had to read with the language of some widely used school textbooks. They found that the school textbooks neglected some of the language forms commonly found in Science texts, for example, compound nouns, passives, conditionals, anomalous finites. Their conclusion was that the ESP course should, therefore, give precedence to these forms.

2.2.2 Beyond the sentence: rhetorical or discourse analysis

There were, as we shall see, serious flaws in the register analysis-based syllabus, but, as it happened, register analysis as a research procedure was rapidly overtaken by developments in the world of linguistics. Whereas in the first stage of its development, ESP had focused on language at the sentence level, the second phase of development shifted attention to the level above the sentence, as ESP became closely involved with the emerging field of discourse or rhetorical analysis. The leading lights in this movement were Henry Widdowson in Britain and the so-called Washington School of Larry Selinker, Louis Trimble, John Lackstrom and Mary Todd-Trimble in the United States.

The basic hypothesis of this stage is succinctly expressed by Allen& Widdowson (1974):

"We take the view that the difficulties which the students encounter arise not so much from a defective knowledge of the system of English, but from an unfamiliarity with English use, and that consequently their needs cannot be met by a course which simply provides further practice in the composition of sentences, but only by one which develops a knowledge of how sentences are used un the performance of different communicative acts."

Register analysis had focused on sentence grammar, but now attention shifted to understanding how sentences were combined in discourse to produce meaning. The concern of research, therefore, was to identify the organizational patterns in texts and to specify the linguistic means by which these patterns are signalled. These patterns would then form the syllabus of the ESP course. The Rhetorical Process Chart below (from EST: A Discourse Approach by Louis Trimble(1985)) is representative of this approach:

Rhetorical Process Chart

Level	Description of level
A. The objectives of the total discourse	
EXAMPLES:	1. Detailing an experiment
	2. Making a recommendation
	3. Presenting new hypotheses or theory
	4. Presenting other types of EST information

续表

Level	Description of level
B. The general rhetorical functions that develop the objectives of level A	
	EXAMPLES: 1. Stating purpose 2. Reporting past research 3. Stating the problem 4. Presenting information on apparatus used in an experiment— a) Description b) Operation 5. Presenting information on experimental procedures
C. The specific rhetorical functions that develop the general rhetorical functions of Level B	
	EXAMPLES: 1. Description: physical, function, and process 2. Definiftion 3. Classification 4. Instructions 5. Visual-verbal relationships
D. The rhetorical techniques that provide relationships within and between the rhetorical units of Level C	
	EXAMPLES: I. Orders 1. Time order 2. Space order 3. Causality and result II. Patterns 1. Causality and result 2. Order of importance 3. Comparison and contrast 4. Analogy 5. Exemplification 6. Illustration

As in stage I there was a more or less tacit assumption in this approach that the rhetorical patterns of text organization differed significantly between specialist areas of use: the rhetorical structure of science texts was regarded as different from that of commercial texts, for example. However, this point was never very clearly examined and indeed paradoxically, the results of the research into the discourse of subject-specific academic texts were also used to make observations about discourse in general (Widdowson, 1978).

The typical teaching materials based on the discourse approach taught students to recognize textual patterns and discourse markers mainly by means of text-diagramming exercises.

2.2.3 Target situation analysis

The stage that we come to consider now did not really add anything new to the range of knowledge about ESP. What it aimed to do was to take the existing knowledge and set it on a more scientific basis, by establishing procedures for relating language analysis more closely to learners' reasons for learning. Given that the purpose of an ESP course is to enable learners to function adequately in a target situation, that is, the situation in which the learners will use the language they are learning, then the ESP course design process should proceed by first identifying the target situation and then carrying out a rigorous analysis of the linguistic features of that situation. The identified features will form the syllabus of the ESP course. This process is usually known as *needs analysis*. However, we prefer to take Chambers' (1980) term of "target situation analysis," since it is a more accurate description of the process concerned.

The most thorough explanation of target situation analysis is the system set out by John Munby in *Communicative Syllabus Design* (1978). The Munby model produces a detailed profile of the learners' needs in terms of communication purposes, communicative setting, the means of communication, language skills, functions, structures etc.

The target situation analysis stage marked a certain "coming of age" for ESP. what had previously been done very much in a piecemeal way, was now systematized and learner need was apparently placed at the centre of the course design process. It proved in the event to be a false dawn.

2.2.4 Skills and strategies

We noticed that in the first two stages of the development of ESP all the analysis had been of the surface forms of the language (whether at sentence level, as in register analysis, or above, as in discourse analysis). The target situation analysis approach did not really change this, because in its analysis of learner need it still looked mainly at the surface linguistic features of the target situation.

The fourth stage of ESP has been an attempt to look below the surface and to consider not the language itself but the thinking processes that underlie language use. There is no dominant figure in this movement, although we might mention the work of Francoise Grellet (1981) and others having made significant contributions to work on reading skills. Most of the work in the area of skills and strategies, however, has been done close to the ground in schemes such as the National ESP Project in Brazil etc.

Both these projects were set up to cope with study situations where the medium of instruction is the mother tongue but students need to read a number of specialist texts which are available only in English. The projects have, therefore, concentrated their efforts on reading strategies.

The principal idea behind the skills-centred approach is that underlying all language use there are common reasoning and interpreting processes, which, regardless of the surface forms, enable us to extract meaning from discourse. There is, therefore, no need to focus closely on the surface forms of the language. The focus should rather be on the underlying interpretive strategies, which enable the learner to cope with the surface forms. For example guessing the meaning of words from context, using visual layout to determine the type of text, exploiting cognates and etc. A focus on specific subject registers is unnecessary in this approach, because the underlying processes are not specific to any subject register. As has been noted, in terms of materials this approach generally puts the emphasis on reading or listening strategies. The characteristic exercises get the learners to reflect on and analyse how meaning is produces in and retrieved from written or spoken discourse. Taking their cue from cognitive learning theories, the language learners are treated as thinking beings who can be asked to observe and verbalise the interpretive processes they employ in language use.

2.2.5 A learning-centred approach

In outlining the origins of ESP, we identified three forces, which we might characterize as need, new ideas about language and new ideas about learning. It should have become clear that in its subsequent development, however, scant attention has been paid to the last of these forces-learning. All of the stages outlined so far have been fundamentally flawed, in that they are all based on description is of surface forms, as in the case of register analysis, or of underlying processes, as in the skills and strategies approach, the concern in each case is with describing what people *do* with language. But our concern in ESP is not with language use—although this will help to define the course objectives. Our concern is with language *learning*. We cannot simply assume that describing and exemplifying what people do with language will enable someone to learn it. If what were so, we should need to do no more than read a grammar book and a dictionary in order to learn a language. A truly valid approach to ESP must be based on an understanding of the processes of language *learning*.

3. Original selecting

Locating the ESP space in problem-based learning

3.1 Introduction

The restructuring of higher education in Europe in the light of the Bologna declaration has stimulated a rapid increase in the number of English-taught degree programmes, especially at master's level, as competition for students grows. However, many institutions see quality recruitment at bachelor's (or first-cycle) level as critical to the recruitment and development of "excellent" master's and research programmes. Since universities are increasingly tending to recruit master's students from across Europe (and beyond), it follows that the medium of instruction of the master's programmes has to be a language of which the students have good command; that means usually English. Universities, understandably, would like to ensure that they retain their best first-cycle students, and thus training students to study through English at first-cycle level helps to meet diverse university goals (e. g. becoming a research-led university, internationalizing the university, broadening the talent base, being an innovative university). What kind of educational approach should be implemented in the bachelor's courses, though, remains a subject of debate.

The Netherlands was one of the first countries to implement the two-cycle structure of the Bologna declaration. The Ministry of Education, Welfare and Culture seemed to have decided that early implementation could accrue first-mover advantages for the country's universities. Among the advantages we can see establishing norms and standards for "Bologna programmes" that other countries may wish to emulate, recruiting foreign students, attracting foreign academics, and attracting international research funding as a result of the strengthening of the second (master's) cycle. The previous system of a four-year *doctorandus* degree, followed by a four-year (or more) PhD programme, was rapidly switched in almost all disciplines to (usually) a three-year bachelor's degree and a one- or two-year master's degree, again followed by PhD programmes. Almost all requests from universities for delay or exemption were refused, and so in 2002 the two-cycle structure was implemented.

In some educational systems the implementation of the Bologna declaration has entailed extensive discussions not only about how to structure the two-cycle curriculum (bachelor's and master's), but also about which components of the previous degree programmes should be included in the first cycle and which not. In the Netherlands it has seemed that almost everything that was included in the previous *doctorandus* programme, except some optional courses in the fourth year, had to be compressed into the new three-year bachelor's programme, including sufficient optional courses. This process has led to a weighting of courses, with the result that some elements have been squeezed out. This has been the case, for instance, at Maastricht University where in some English-medium programmes the English for Specific Purposes (ESP) element that held a key position in the *doctorandus* programme has been dropped in the new bachelor's programme. This is perhaps an unforeseen side-effect of the Bologna process.

On the other hand, institutional strategy has led to the creation of new programmes in which the goal is to develop highly competent graduates who can also function effectively in English as professionals in the international market place. The squeeze in terms of space within the bachelor's programmes has meant that ESP training has to be integrated with the discipline that the student is studying. Training of general academic language skills, across a wide range of programmes, has been almost eliminated. The ESP elements therefore tend to be narrow-focused (usually on a single skill), short (around ten contact hours), and product-oriented (e.g. producing a specific academic paper). These elements are closely integrated into the discipline such that disciplinary experts provide input, the assignment or product is based on disciplinary course material, and often co-assessment is applied involving both content and ESP staff. The students are expected to function as novices to relatively proficient users of the disciplinary discourse, exemplifying their emergence as members of the discipline. Discourse, in this article, is assumed to be the usage of language, ideas and meanings that members of a disciplinary community consider as appropriate to that discipline. Discourse relies on shared knowledge of acceptable objects of study, agreed standards of evidence and validity, and agreed formal conventions (e.g. Porter 1986; see also Borg 2003; Jacobs 2004).

One educational approach characteristic of Maastricht University is problem-based learning (PBL) (Schmidt 1983; Schmidt 1993), which is held to stimulate the simultaneous development of knowledge, skills and attitudes. PBL is conceived as a philosophy of learning, an approach to learning and teaching, and an instructional method. However, PBL cannot be seen as static; it has changed considerably since it was first implemented at Maastricht (e.g. van der Vleuten & Wijnen 1990; Dolmans et al. 2005); yet, arguably, the greatest changes to the PBL approach applied at Maastricht have been due to the introduction of English as medium of instruction and the implementation of the Bologna declaration. (Interestingly, there are reports of Bologna leading to the application of PBL, e.g. Hernández- Encuentra & Sánchez-Carbonell 2005; Garcia-Famoso 2005; see also Heitmann 2003.) Since the start of English-medium educational programmes at the university in the mid-1980s, the enhancement of communication skills in English, the training of which has accompanied the content programmes, is characteristically integrated with the acquisition of disciplinary content. Such ESP skills training has attempted to follow the instructional precepts of PBL.

The context for this chapter lies in the gradual change at Maastricht University from Dutch to English-medium of instruction. At the start of English-medium programmes, relatively extensive support was provided for both students and staff, including observation of student and staff functioning in the educational sessions followed by feedback, extensive practice in speaking skills including vocabulary and grammar development, and training presentation and academic writing skills; in addition, staff training was provided including guidance on the instructional language materials used and lectures. However, over the years the specialist English provision has gradually been whittled away, sometimes due to changes in educational structure, sometimes due to budget cuts. The Bologna changes seem to have led to a further narrowing of the ESP provision, as the course commissioners, i. e. the faculties, demand much from short courses narrowed principally to concepts of disciplinary writing. In this context it seems wise to ensure that the short courses provided are closely aligned and integrated with student needs in the discipline under study (i. e. often a product) and with the student learning approaches (i. e. student-centred learning, usually PBL). In this light the present chapter aims to elucidate how ESP applications may adapt a student-centred approach like PBL within English-medium degree programmes. The first section sketches underpinnings of PBL and ESP. The second section compares two types of courses, adjunct and integrated, at Maastricht University, with examples of a pre-Bologna adjunct ESP course for business and economics students when the scope for ESP provision was greater and a post-Bologna integrated ESP writing course for students in health sciences, which is initially a Dutch-medium programme and shifts increasingly to English-medium. The third section discusses issues arising from this comparison with respect to the Bologna changes, concluding with the added value of PBL for ESP courses.

3.2 Theoretical background

In the literature there are few reports of PBL being applied to ESP (Barron 2002; Wood & Head 2004), although several reports have appeared in conference proceedings (e. g. Wilkinson & Geerligs 1994; Hellekjaer & Wilkinson 2001; Wilkinson 2001; Wilkinson 2002). In the cases reported ESP teachers have adapted PBL approaches to suit the particular context in which they are working. Although a "pick and mix" approach to the implementation of PBL may be seen as diluting the principles of PBL, originating in medical education (e. g. Barrows & Tamblyn 1980; Barrows 1983), any educational innovation has to be adapted and attuned as it transfers to new domains, as is the case with ESP.

PBL has variously been described as active learning, oriented to adults and focused on practice in professional contexts (e. g. Schmidt 1983; Schmidt 1993; Norman & Schmidt 1992; Camp 1996; Savery & Duffy 2001; Dolmans et al. 2005). It is a student-centred approach in which the learning is derived from confrontation with problems (briefly defined as a set of contextually-based phenomena requiring an explanation). The learning process is collaborative, with students working in small groups, and multidisciplinary, where knowledge, skills and attitudes are integrated. The theoretical model of PBL indicates that the students' prior knowledge, the problems themselves, and the tutor are factors influencing group functioning (Schmidt & Gijselaers 1990); in turn, group functioning affects interest in the topic or theme and the time students are willing to spend on the problems; the latter correlates with student achievement (Schmidt & Gijselaers 1990).

Underlying PBL are some fundamental principles of learning. Learning is determined to a large degree by prior knowledge. The activation of what students already know about the topic facilitates their learning of new information. Thus, in PBL students are first stimulated to recall what they know about the "problem" before they try to find solutions or explanations for it. Learning is also promoted if students are stimulated to elaborate on their knowledge. This second principle entails encouraging students, for example, to produce examples, make analogies, draw inferences, associate with personal experiences, summarize knowledge, compare information, and distinguish main and subsidiary issues. By constantly elaborating on the knowledge within the learning group, students are enabled to create multiple redundant retrieval paths in memory so that recall is assisted and consequently the students remember more.

A third principle is that of transfer. In essence, this holds that learning is effective when the knowledge acquired can be applied to new contexts, especially the kinds of problems encountered in professional or daily life. It is often difficult for students to apply theoretical knowledge to practical problems. PBL promotes transfer by being grounded in the problems taken from everyday professional practice. In this way, students are assumed to be more able to recognize similar problems that they meet in their profession and thus better able to transfer their problem-solving knowledge to the new context. In brief, then, it is held that the principles of learning identified by cognitive psychology (Regehr & Norman 1996), sketched above, which underlie PBL, do lead to more efficient and more effective learning and to better retention and recall (Norman & Schmidt 1992; Norman & Schmidt 2000). The PBL learning process is held to stimulate transformational learning, whereby newly acquired knowledge is integrated into existing memory schemas, which are in turn restructured and transformed (Wilkinson & Geerligs 1994).

While PBL is promoted by its proponents as leading to more effective learning, other studies question the overall effectiveness of PBL (Colliver 2000; see also Sanson-Fisher & Lynagh 2005). PBL has been shown to be more effective in knowledge retention (Norman & Schmidt 1992) compared to "traditional" approaches to learning, although the evidence is inconclusive regarding overall knowledge (Colliver 2000). PBL also seems to be conducive to better performance in practice, for example performance on medical clerkships (Distlehorst et al. 2005). In contexts where students are confronted with courses using different methodologies, some using PBL, some traditional approaches, it is difficult to demonstrate the effectiveness of PBL because of confounding from non-PBL courses. Nevertheless, the criticisms do not discount the considerable evidence that PBL does offer "a more challenging, motivating and enjoyable approach to education" (Norman & Schmidt 2000: 727).

3.3 PBL at Maastricht University

The characteristic PBL approach at Maastricht University entails students being presented with a series of tasks describing "ill-structured" problems (Schön 1987; Johansson 1997) which they tackle in small groups of usually 10 – 14 students by 60 Robert Wilkinson employing a systematic seven-step approach. The tasks describe a fuzzy problem, based on what might occur in a professional context, which the students first examine to clarify their understanding of the words and concepts; they then try to identify and define the problem; the third step requires them to analyse the problem through brainstorming what they know, usually by collecting their ideas on the board; they then systematically classify their knowledge by organizing and grouping their knowledge under thematic heading; this leads them to formulating learning objectives. After these five steps, students embark on self-study, searching sources of information in order to apply the knowledge acquired to the learning objectives. Finally, the students report back to their group what they have learned through self-study and try to synthesize their new knowledge to meet the learning objectives or solve the problem. These steps indicate the broad outlines of the learning process, as course organizers and instructors intend; however, the practical implementation is less distinct with steps 2 - 4 often conflated. Although the nature of the problems varies, and the approach has changed over time and differs somewhat from faculty to faculty, the broad lines indicated here still apply generally to education in the first two years at the university (van Til & van der Heijden 1998).

The application of PBL has not explicitly taken the language of instruction into account. The language of instruction has largely been treated as a given, that is the students are learning through their L1 or are assumed to be sufficiently proficient in the instructional language. Disciplinary language is of course acquired (especially lexis) and we may assume that the discourse of the discipline is acquired through osmosis, though it may take a very long time (e.g. Kellogg 2006). Moreover, the challenge to PBL in an L2 environment has been scarcely addressed by PBL practitioners, though Dijcks et al. (2001) have shown a perceived negative impact on content learning in medicine.

3.4 ESP

In contrast to PBL, ESP is not a theoretically grounded approach to learning. It is rather an accumulation of approaches that educators have designed for teaching the language of a set of specific disciplines or purposes to learners who are specialized or specializing in one or more of those disciplines. This is not the same as saying that theory does not underlie the approaches. In fact, ESP does rely on, for example, theories of language acquisition, theories of language and language variety (e.g. Robinson 1991), genre theory (Swales 1990; Bhatia 1993; Flowerdew 2005), and more recently theories of academic literacies (Bhatia 2004). However, it is difficult to define exactly what ESP is: Belbin (2005) recently falls back on a long-established trend dating back to Strevens (1988) of classifying the absolute and variable characteristics of ESP (e.g. Dudley-Evans & St. John 1998). In this view, the three absolute characteristics of ESP are that it is "defined to meet specific needs of the learner; [it] makes use of the underlying methodology and activities of the discipline it serves; [and it] is centred on the language (grammar, lexis and register), skills, discourse and genres appropriate to these activities" (Dudley-Evans & St. John 1998: 4 - 5). ESP is an eclectic approach, borrowing theories from learning and language learning and from the relevant disciplines according to the contextual needs of the learners to underpin its raison-d'être in a specific context (see also Räisäen & Fortanet this volume). ESP may be seen as a kind of problem-solving endeavour for the instructor, who has to select and adapt the ESP approach to the knowledge and skills needs required in the particular context. At risk of over-simplification, we might turn the thinking around and state that courses within an academic educational programme that meet these three absolute characteristics may be classified as ESP.

There is a clear difference in PBL and ESP as presented here. PBL is an educational process which, through its underlying principles of elaboration and transfer, enables learners to cope with the unpredictability of new circumstances. In essence ESP as described here is a training process which is directed to learning to produce a known outcome. ESP is essentially goal-oriented. This distinction between education and training (e. g. Widdowson 1990; see also other disciplines, e. g. medicine, Playdon & Goodsman 1997; corporate training, Tate 1997) is practical and useful; however, it may not in fact be quite so distinct (Wilson et al. 1993). Meaningful learning and the development of problem-solving abilities occur in training as they do in education, and ESP training aims to develop capacities in students to cope with new and unpredictable tasks.

3.5 Comparison of ESP course design within a PBL approach

Within a PBL approach in English-medium education, English is seen as a skill that students need to enhance, and they do so within the contexts of their multidisciplinary studies. However, English skills training may be provided as adjunct courses, that is independently of other courses that the students are studying, or as integrated courses as part of the general multidisciplinary education or linked directly to and feeding into such courses. This chapter compares the two provisions: the design, implementation, and outcomes of adjunct courses (intensive ESP training for students in economics and business, pre-Bologna) with that of integrated courses (writing skills training in health sciences, post-Bologna). This comparison also reflects the change under the Bologna process to the two-cycle system. What the examples show is how the provision has shifted from training broader disciplinary language skills where ESP training is an embedded or adjunct component in a PBL learning process to a narrow focus on training for a single product, integrated within the content programme.

Within English-taught bachelor's programmes, designers may well continue to provide series of short, integrated or dovetailed ESP courses at various moments in the students' educational studies, perhaps tailored more precisely to the needs of the students. Indeed, it would probably enhance the programmes by offering many more ESP options that are integrated with or dovetailed into the content courses. Students would then be freer to take an option at a time of their choosing: students would then benefit from ESP input and guidance at the time they felt they needed it. This development would enhance the student-centredness of ESP provision and make the learning more student-directed.

This illustrates particularly where PBL may come in. The most important component that a PBL approach can contribute is that the courses remain student-centred and focused on what the students need, even if no direct needs assessment is conducted beforehand. Secondly, the approaches used within the ESP component fit the PBL approaches that the students are used to. If institutions are to provide integrated or dovetailed ESP courses that address the language and skills needs of the students in bachelor's programmes, then a student-centred approach like PBL would seem valuable. The value of student-centred ESP, on the lines of the examples in this chapter, may increase as more and more programmes become wholly or partially English-medium, and especially as there is considerable pressure to ensure that the relevant disciplinary content is provided in the three-year degree programme. While the goals in these ESP courses within PBL are often product-centred (writing a paper), it is held that the more the product resembles the future products the professional community expects, the more likely transfer is to occur in the learner's subsequent products. A student-centred approach, even if modified from "pure" PBL (Camp 1996), in ESP training can enhance learning in English-medium degree programmes. Integrated or dovetailed ESP courses should be designed in close collaboration with content teachers to ensure that the academic literacies (Bhatia 2004) developed match those of the target discourse communities. ①

References

[1] Allen J. P. & Widdowson H. G. Grammar in Language Teaching[M]. Oxford, 1974.

[2] Ewer J. R. & Latorre G. A Course in Basic Scientific English[M]. Longman, 1969.

[3] Ewer J. R. & Hughes-Davies G. 1971. Further Notes on Development an English Programme for Students of Science and Technology [J] ELT Journal, 1971.

① 摘自 Fortanet-Gómez I., Christine A. Räisänen. ESP in European Higher Education[M]. Amsterdam: John Benjamins Publishing Company, 2008.

[4]Swales J. Episodes in ESP[M]. Pergamon, 1985.

[5]哈钦森,沃特斯. 特殊目的英语[M]. 上海:上海外语教育出版社,2002.

[6]理查兹,朗文. 语言教学及应用语言学辞典[M]. 北京:外语教学与研究出版社, 2005.

第十一章

跨文化交际

导　读

跨文化交际学(Intercultural communication,早期也称作Cross-cultural Communication)首先兴起于美国。美国是一个移民国家,除了印第安人以外,其他人都先后来自其他国家和地区。他们具有各自的文化传统和风俗习惯,在交往中难免产生问题,因此,跨文化交际理所当然地引起学者的注意。

学界把E. Hall在1959年出版的《无声的语言》(*The Silent Language*)看作是跨文化交际学的奠基之作。20世纪60年代陆续有一些有关跨文化交际的著作问世:1962年,R. T. Oliver的《文化与交际》(*Culture and Communication*);1996年A. Smith主编的《交际与文化》(*Communication and Culture*)等。1970年,在国际传播学会下成立了跨文化交际学分会。1995年,在哈尔滨工业大学召开了我国第一届跨文化交际研讨会,会上成立了中国跨文化交际研究会,并决定每两年召开一次大会。

跨文化交际研究主要涉及四大要素:一是知觉,即个人选择、评价和组织外部刺激的过程。文化知觉以信仰、价值观和态度系统为基础。二是言语过程,我们怎样交谈、怎样思想。三是非言语过程,用行动交际,这些行动表达的意义因文化而异。四是文化影响交际的语境。

跨文化交际学最突出的特点就是它的多学科性质。跨文化的哲学是变化的哲学。在跨文化的交际中应该遵循的伦理指导原则是:寻找人和文化的共同习俗,对文化差异要宽容等。

1. Definitions

1.1 culture

Culture is that complex whole which includes knowledge, belief, art, morals, law, customs and any other capabilities and habits acquires by man as a member of society.

(Tylor 1871)

The set of practices, codes and values that mark a particular nation or group: the sum of a nation or group's most highly thought of works of literature, art, music, etc. A difference is sometimes made between "High" culture of literature and the arts, and small "c" culture of attitudes, values, beliefs, and everyday lifestyles. Culture and Language combine to form what is sometimes called "Discourses", i. e. ways of talking, thinking, and behaving that reflect one's social identity.

The cultural dimension of language learning is an important dimension of second language studies. Education is seen as a process of socialization with the dominant culture. In foreign language teaching the culture of the language may be taught as an integral part of the curriculum.

(Richards 2005: 178)

In the pedagogic imagination of most language teachers around the world, the term "culture" is associated with the context in which the language is lived and spoken by its native speakers, themselves seen as a more or less homogeneous national community with age-old institutions, customs, and way of life.

(Brown 2006: 322)

Culture consists of patterns, explicit and implicit, of and for behavior acquired and transmitted by symbols, constituting the distinctive achievement of human groups, including their embodiments in artifacts; the essential core of culture consists of traditional ideas and especially their attached values; culture systems may, on the one hand, be considered as products of action, on the other hand as conditioning elements of future action.

(Kroeber & Kluckholn)

Culture is an integrated system of learned behavior patterns which are characteristic of the members of a society and which are not the result of biological inheritance.

(Hoebel & Frost)

1.2 cross-cultural & intercultural

"Cross-cultural" and "intercultural" are often regarded as interchangeable. They are, nevertheless, different. Cross-cultural research involves comparing behaviour in two or more cultures (e. g. comparing self-disclosure in Japan, the USA and Iran when individuals interact with members of their own culture). Intercultural research involves examining behaviour when members of two or more cultures interact (e. g. examining self-disclosure when Japanese and Iranians communicate with each other). ... Understanding cross-cultural differences in behaviour is a prerequisite for understanding intercultural behaviour.

(Gudykunst 2000: 314)

1.3 intercultural communication

Intercultural communication refers to communication between people whose cultural perceptions and symbol systems are distinct enough to alter the communication event.

(L. Samovar & R. Porter)

1.4 cross-cultural communication

Cross-cultural communication is usually considered to be the study of a particular idea (s) or concept (s) within several cultures that compares one culture to another on the aspect of interest, whereas intercultural communication focuses on interactions among people from different cultures.

(Brown 2006: 371)

1.5 intercultural communication competence

Intercultural communication competence is the overall internal capability of an individual to manage key challenging features of intercultural communication: namely, cultural differences and unfamiliarity, inter-group posture, and the accompanying experience of stress.

1.6 cultural identity

Cultural identity refers to one's sense of belonging to a particular culture ar ethnic group. People consciously identify themselves with a group that has a shared system of symbols and meanings as well as norms for conduct.

1.7 co-culture

Co-culture is suggested to convey the idea that no one culture is inherently superior to other coexisting cultures.

2. Classical theories

Culture and communication, although two different concepts, are directly linked. Culture is learned, acted out, transmitted, and preserved through communication. Communication—our ability to share our ideas and feelings—is the basis of all human contact. Two reasons why it is difficult locate a single definition of communication are (1) the complex nature of communication and (2) the issue of intentionality and unintentionality.

2.1 Components of Communication

There are ten components of communication: source, encoding, message, channel, noise, receiver, decoding, receiver response, feedback and context.

Source: The source or the sender is the person with an idea he or she desires to communicate. The source is the creator of the message. Because communication usually involves more than one person, more than one source of communication can exist at one time.

Encoding: unfortunately (or perhaps fortunately), humans are not able to share thoughts directly. Your communication is in the form of a symbol representing the idea you desire to communicate. Encoding is the process of putting an idea into a symbol. The symbols in which you encode your thoughts vary. You can encode thoughts into words, and you can also encode thoughts into non-spoken symbols.

Message: The term message identifies the encoded thought. Encoding is the process, the verb; the message is the resulting object. The message is made up of the ideas and feelings that the source wants to share. It is comprised of words, grammar, organization of thoughts, physical appearance, body movement, voice, aspects of the person's personality and self-concept, and personal style. Each message is unique. Even if the same message were to be created over and over again, it would differ in each instance because messages cannot be repeated or received on exactly the same way or in the same context.

Channel: The term "channel" is used technically to refer to the means by which the encoded message is transmitted. The channel or medium, then, may be print, electronic, or the light and sound waves of the face-to-face communication. For example, when two people are talking face to face, light and sound waves in the air serve as the cannels. If a letter is sent from one person to another, light waves serve as the cannel, but the paper and writing itself serve as the means by which the message is conveyed. Books, films, videotapes, television sets, computers, radios, magazines, newspapers and pictures are channels through which messages may be conveyed. In addition, people receive communication by smelling, touching and tasting. All five senses contribute to communication.

Noise: the term "noise" technically refers to anything that distorts the message the source encodes.

Noise can be of many forms:

External noise can be the sights, sounds and other stimuli that draw your attention away from the message. External noise comes from the environment and keeps the message from being heard or understood. Your heart-to-heart talk with your roommate can be interrupted by a group of people yelling in the hall, or a helicopter passing overhead. External noise does not always come from sound. You could be standing and talking to someone in the hot sun and become so uncomfortable that you can't concentrate.

Internal noise refers to your thoughts and feelings that can interfere with the message. Internal noise occurs in the minds of the sender or receiver when their thoughts or feelings are focused on something other than the communication at hand. For example, a student doesn't hear the lecture because he is thinking about lunch; a wife can't pay attention to her husband because she is upset by a problem in the office. Sometimes, beliefs or prejudices may also become internal noises.

Semantic noise refers to how alternative meanings of the source's message symbols can be distracting. Many people turn out a speaker who uses profanity because the words are so offensive to them. However, they may wonder why the speaker used profanity and their attention was drawn away from the message itself.

Receiver: The receiver is the person who attends to the message. Receivers may be intentional; that is, they may be the people the source desired to communicate with, or they may be any person who comes upon and attends to the message. Sometimes, communication occurs when one person sends ideas and the other receives them, and then the process is reversed. In that case, people are senders and receivers—both sending and receiving at the same time.

Decoding: Decoding is the opposite process of encoding and just as much as active process. The receiver is actively involved in the communication process by assigning meaning to the symbols received.

Receiver response: Receiver response refers to anything the receiver does after having attended to and decoded the message. That response can range from doing nothing to taking some action or actions that may or may not be the action desired by the source.

Feedback: Feedback refers to that portion of the receiver response of which the source has knowledge and to which the source attends and assigns meaning. A reader of this text may have many responses, but only when the reader responds to a survey or writes a letter to the author does feedback occur. When a radio interview show host receives enthusiastic telephone calls and invites a guest back, feedback has occurred.

Feedback is vital to communication because it lets the participants in the communication see whether ideas and feelings have been shared in the way they were intended. People who are having face-to-face communication have the greatest opportunity for feedback, especially if there are no distractions. Feedback makes communication two-way or interactive.

Context: The final component of communication is context. The context can be physical, social and interpersonal. Generally, context can be defined as the environment in which the communication takes place and which helps define the communication. If you know the physical context, you can predict with a high degree of accuracy much of the communication. The choice of the environment, the context, helps assign the desired meaning to the communicated words.

2.2 Communicative Competence

In the 1960s, Chomsky distinguished between "**competence**" and "**performance**".

2.2.1 Competence

Competence refers to one's underlying knowledge of a system, event, or fact. It is the non-observable ability to do something. (Brown, 2007:35) One's underlying knowledge of the system of a language—its rules of grammar, its vocabulary, all the pieces of a language and how those pieces fit together. (Brown, 2007:36) Competence often refers to the ideal speaker/hearer, that is, an idealized but not a real person who would have a complete knowledge of the whole language.

2.2.2 Performance

Performance is actual production (speaking, writing) or the comprehension (listening, reading) of linguistic events. (Brown, 2007: 36) It is the individual's ability to understand and produce language. Language production results from the creative use of a learned set of linguistic rules. In transformational generative grammar), it is the actual sue of the language by individuals in speech and writing.

2.2.3. Communicative Competence

Communicative Competence proposed by the sociolinguist Dell Hymes (1974) as an alternative to Chomsky's linguistic competence. It includes not only linguistic competence, but also includes a range of other sociolinguitic and conversational skills that enable the speaker to know how to say what to whom.

For **Savignon**, in addition to being dynamic, rather than static, and involving the negotiation of meaning, communicative competence is not restricted to spoken language, but involves writing as well. It is context-specific, which means that a competent communicator knows how to make choices specific to the situation. This ability not only to apply the grammatical rules of a language in order to form grammatically correct sentences but also to know when and where to use these sentences and to whom. It includes:

j. knowledge of the grammar and vocabulary of the language

k. knowledge of rules of speaking (e. g. knowing how to begin and end conversations, knowing what topics may be talked about in different types of speech events, knowing which address forms should be used with different persons one speaks to and in different situations.)

l. knowing how to use and respond to different types of speech acts, such as requests, apologies, thanks, and invitations.

m. Knowing how to use language appropriately

When someone wishes to communicate with others, they must recognize the social setting, their relationship to the other person(s) (role relationship), the types of language that can be used for a particular occasion. They must also be able to interpret written or spoken sentences within the total context in which they are used.

Canale and Swain (1980) further proposed that communicative competence includes:

1) *grammatical competence*:

a. the use of appropriate grammar, vocabulary, and pronunciation

b. what Chomsky calls linguistic competence and what Hymes intends by what is "formally possible."

c. the domain of grammatical and lexical capacity.

2) *sociolinguistic competence*:

a. the use of style, register, and intonation in appropriate contests and settings

b. an understanding of the social context in which communication takes place, including role relationships, the shared information of the participants, and the communicative purpose for their interaction

3) *discourse competence*:

a. the ability to combine language elements to show cohesion in form and coherence of thought

b. the interpretation of individual message elements in terms of their interconnectedness and of how meaning is represented in relationship to the entire discourse or text

4) *the strategic competence*:

a. the use of verbal and nonverbal communication strategies, such as gestures and circumlocution, to compensate for unknown language

The coping strategies that communicators employ to initiate, terminate, maintain, repair, and redirect communication.

Bachman (1990) provides a framework for Communicative Language Ability (CLA) which builds on the work of Hymes (1972), Canale and Swain (1980), and Widdowson (1989). The framework includes three components:

language competence: "a set of specific knowledge components that are utilised in communication via language" (Bachman, 1990: 66).

strategic competence: "the mental capacity for implementing the components of language competence in contextualised communicative language use" (Bachman, 1990: 67).

psychophysiological mechanisms: "the neurological and psychological processes involved in the actual execution of language as a physical phenomenon" (Bachman, 1990: 67).

However, in language use these components all interact with each other and with features of the language use situation. (Bachman, 1990:86)

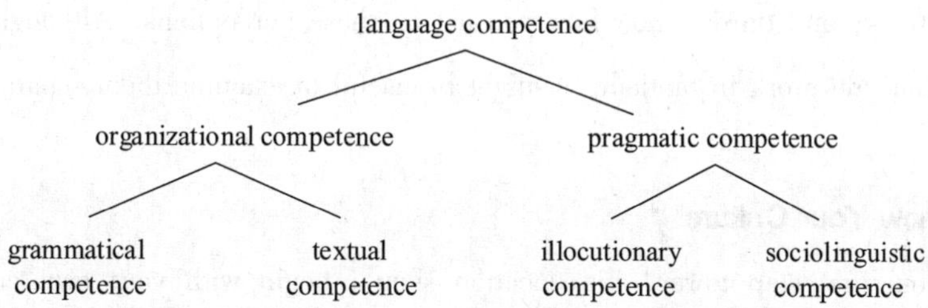

(Bachman 1990:87)

3. Original selecting

Improving Intercultural Communication

3.1 Know Yourself

In light of what we discussed in the last paragraph, it seems only fitting that we ask you to begin with *yourself* For as simplistic as it sounds, what you bring to the communication event greatly influences the success or failure of that event. Although the idea of knowing yourself is common, it is nevertheless crucial to improving intercultural communication. The novelist James Baldwin said it best when he wrote, "The questions which one asks oneself begin, at last, to illuminate the world, and become one's key to the experience of others." Baldwin's remarks serve as an ideal introduction for the portion of this book that urges you to begin your path to improvement with some self-analysis. As with many of the suggestions we offer in this section, it is easier to state the advice than to practice it. We can write the words "know yourself" with just a few strokes on our keyboard, but it will take a great deal of effort for you to translate this assignment into practice. We believe that the application of introspection should take three directions: first, know your culture; second, know your perceptions; and third, know how you act on those perceptions. Although these three concepts work in tandem, it might be useful to examine them separately.

3.2 Know Your Culture

Your first step toward introspection should begin with your own culture, regardless of what that culture might be. Remember, we are products of our culture—and that culture helps control communication. Stewart and Bennett made a similar observation when they wrote: An awareness of American culture along with examples of contrasting cultures contribute to the individual's understanding of her- or himself as a cultural being.

3.3 Know Your Attitudes

By exhorting you to examine your attitudes and perceptions, we are not referring to any mystical notions involving another reality, nor are we suggesting you engage in any deep psychological soul searching. Rather, we are asking you to identify those attitudes, prejudices, and opinions that we all carry around and that bias the way the world appears to us. If we hold a certain attitude toward gay men, and a man who is a gay talks to us, our precommunication attitude will color our response to what he says. Knowing our likes, dislikes, and degrees of personal ethnocentrism enables us to place them Out in the open so that we can detect the ways in which these attitudes influence communication. Hidden personal premises, be they directed at ideas, people, or entire cultures, are often the cause of many of our difficulties.

3.4 Know Your Communication Style

The third step in knowing ourselves is somewhat more difficult than simply identifying our prejudices and predispositions. It involves discovering the kind of image we portray to the rest of the world. Ask yourself, "How do I communicate and how do others perceive me?" If you perceive yourself in one way, and the people with whom you interact perceive you in another way, serious problems can arise. We have all heard stories of how foreigners view Americans traveling abroad. The "Ugly American" example might be old and trite, but our experiences continue to reinforce its truth. If we are to improve our communication, we must, therefore, have some idea of how we present ourselves. If, for instance, you see yourself as patient and calm, but you appear rushed and anxious, you will have a hard time understanding why people respond to you as they do. As we have noted elsewhere, our most taken-for-granted behaviors often are hidden from consciousness.

As a starting point, we suggest that you learn to recognize your communication style-the manner in which you present yourself to others. Many communication scholars have attempted to isolate the characteristics that compose a communication personality. One such inventory, which Norton has proposed, has nine characteristics. Remember, awareness is the first step to meaningful action.

Consider the Physical and Human Settings

As we stress in Chapters 7, 8 and 9, even setting carries meaning. Three attributes of the setting that can influence the encounter are timing, physical setting, and customs.

Timing

Being aware of timing can often make the difference between a successful engagement and one that produces ill feelings, antagonism, and misunderstandings. The effective communicator knows the importance of timing and has developed the skill to determine the appropriate time to talk about a subject. You know from your own experiences that there are right and wrong times to ask your parents for a loan or to ask an acquaintance for a date. Few professors will sympathize with the student who waits until the last week of the semester to announce, "I would like to come to your office and talk about the midterm examination I missed a few months ago." This indeed is poor timing!

Our use of timing is also influenced by culture. For example, as we note in Chapter 7, considering the "correct time" is a crucial aspect of doing business with other cultures. In the United States, people learn to "get down to business" quickly. However, in Japan, other Asian countries, and Mexico, the most fitting time to talk about business matters is not at the start of a business session. Ruch, discussing Mexico, highlights cultural differences in timing: "Business contacts are often made during the two- or three-hour lunch break. These are social meetings for the most part, with business being conducted in the last few minutes."

Physical Setting

We believe that physical and social context is important enough to justify three chapters in this book. The basic assumptions behind Chapters 7, 8, and 9 are that communication is rule governed and different cultures have different rules as they move from setting to setting. In the United States, during business negotiations, the two negotiation teams usually sit facing each other. However, for much of the world, this arrangement maximizes competition, not cooperation. 32 In many Arab countries, people often conduct business while sitting on the floor. And in Finland, there are major corporations that use the sauna bath as a setting for meetings. Clutterbuck describes that setting: "In the warm, informal atmosphere both sides are more open to frank discussion. The trappings of rank tend to disappear when no one has any clothes on." In America, one would nor, of course, find himself or herself sitting on the floor or conducting business in a sauna. However, being aware of the physical setting, and adapting to that setting, is often the hallmark of a successful intercultural communicator.

Customs

Your ability to adapt to the customs of each culture will, to a large extent, determine the success of your intercultural encounters. Your experience will not be fruitful if custom calls for you ro remain standing when you enter a room, but you take a seat. When, if at all, do you bow? And what is the appropriate bow? When, if at all, do you touch members of the opposite sex? And where do you touch them? What are the customs that prevail with regard to age? These and other questions need to be asked and answered so that you can fashion your behavior to meet the needs of each culture. Specific customs are found in each culture, as the following three illustrations show.

First, we turn to an important business custom in Japan-the exchanging of business cards. Adler tells us, "The Japanese must know the other person's company and position before being able to select the grammatically correct form of address. For this reason, the Japanese always exchange business *cards-meishe-before* a conversation begins."

Second, there are also subtle yet important cultural customs in the perception and manifestation of rank and status. Protocol in Germany has the junior executive walking on the left side of the senior manager. The customs of class are even more elaborate in the Middle East, as Ruch notes:

Both class and rank are quite important to Arabs despite the Muslim concept of all being equal before God. This becomes rather clear at doorways as they sort themselves out by status, the senior man going through first, being followed by the next and then the next in hierarchy.

Finally, you can avoid serious communication problems if you know that the number three and sequences that contain three items have significance in the Thai culture. In religious practices you hear repeatedly *Buddha* (the man), the *Dharma* (the teachings of Buddha) and *Sangha* (the monastic order)-a set of three. In many ceremonies, from childbirth to birthdays, the number three is very evident. Knowing about this custom can enable you to adapt your behavior (giving three small gifts before a business meeting) to Thai culture.

As we conclude this section on physical and human settings, we again urge you to be aware of your surroundings. Because we all have free choice, we can make the necessary concessions to custom, but first we must know the custom.

Seek to Understand Diverse Message Systems

In Chapters 5 and 6, we note that meanings reside in people, not in words. This basic precept of language can be stated as two positive axioms for successful communication: Whenever possible, both parties should seek a common code and/or attempt to understand cultural differences in coding systems. Admittedly, it is difficult to arrive at a common code if you and your communication partner speak different languages. To overcome this problem, our first piece of advice is that if you plan to spend some time around people from other cultures, try to learn their language. You would be far more effective if you could speak Spanish when doing business in Mexico. Because much of the world speaks English, many of us have a tendency to assume we need not learn a foreign language. The very fact that others have made an attempt to learn our language should motivate us to reciprocate. If you do not speak the foreign language of your communication partner, there still are things you can do to facilitate understanding. For example, you should keep in mind that there is more to language than vocabulary, syntax, and dialects. Language is more than a vehicle of communication; it teaches one a culture's lifestyle, ways of thinking, and different patterns of interacting. Much of Jewish culture is reflected in the wide use of stories, parables, and allegories. People, events, and circumstances are talked about in vivid narratives. For many Jews, the story is as important as the point being made by the story. And if you are interacting with Arabs, it would be useful to understand some unique characteristics of their language code. As Nydell points out:

> There are many situations in which verbal statements are required by etiquette. Meeting someone's small child calls for praise, carefully mixed with blessings; the most common are "May God keep him" or "This is what God wills." Such statements reassure the parents that there is no envy (you certainly would not add, "I wish I had a child like this!").

Knowing the characteristics of language we just mentioned for the Jewish and Arab cultures would help you communicate with people from both these cultures.

When you are speaking English with someone who is not completely familiar with your language code, there are also some things you can do to facilitate understanding. For example, remembering that most words are culture-bound, you might be extremely careful when using idioms. By definition, idioms are not capable of literal translations. Try to imagine finding meanings for the following sentences in other languages:

It's not surprising the guy couldn't get to first base with his new business: he started with two strikes against him.

Let's put this plan to the acid test by looking at the nuts and bolts of the deal.

If we stop beating our heads against a brick wall, we would not appear to be such wimps.

We need to be careful that the tail doesn't wag the dog.

Do not listen to John-he's got an ax to grind.

She's not the least bit funny-if fact, she's laid an egg.

John dropped the ball on this one, and he's sure ticked off.

If you think we're on the same wavelength, just give me a buzz, or we can play it by ear.

We need to stop dilly-dallying and get off the dime.

Confusion can be caused by a single word as well by idioms. Reflect on the literal translations of the following terms: *affirmative action*, *jazzed*, *awesome*, *interfacing*, *prolife*, *networking*, *uptight*, *stoked*, *and sexual harassment.*

In Chapter 5, we point out that the English language contains countless subcodes. Although it might be highly improper for you to use these codes if you are not a member of the co-culture, understanding them can offer you insight into both the word and the experiences behind the word. In addition, you also learn some of the differences that exist between various speech styles. For African Americans, Black English is a highly rule-governed speech style that is shared by and reflects the norms of their co-culture. Communication can be impeded when, according to Walters, someone who is speaking mainstream American English feels uncomfortable with the linguistic dissimilarity. We recommend that you realize there are different styles of "talk". One is not right and the others wrong-they are only different.

When we use the phrase *seek a common* code, we are also referring to the nonverbal codes that people use. As you learned in Chapter 6, nonverbal behaviors also shift from culture to culture. For example, in Japan, a female may cover her mouth out of shyness, but in America, we often associate this same action with fear. In China, blinking eyes at someone is impolite. And in many Buddhist traditions, it is highly improper to sit with the soles of one's feet pointed at the image of the Buddha. These differences should remind us of the two points we made with regard to verbal codes. First, the initial step in discovering a common code is learning how to read existing codes. Second, cultural differences should not keep us from looking for a common code. For example, although there are cultural variations in what makes people smile, and even in to whom they smile, one does not have to speak a foreign language to know that a *smile* carries nearly the same meaning throughout the world. Those of you who have visited other countries know the power of pointing and laughing as ways of talking.

Learning about diverse coding systems also means that you develop a code sensitivity toward the message systems used by other cultures. We have already alluded to the inappropriateness of using African American argot if you are white. If you interact with disabled people, you need to learn a list of what are called the "no-no words." *Crippled*, *gimp*, *deaf and dumb*, *deaf mute*, *abnormal*, *unfortunate*, or *victim* are examples of words that exhibit a lack of cultural awareness.

It is also employing an improper verbal code and displaying insensitivity when you use words to refer to a co-culture that are not the ones preferred by it. It would reflect respect if you used *Asians* for *Orientals*, *Native Americans for Indians*, and *African Americans* for *Negroes*. However, as we pointed out in Chapter 1 when we noted that all people are more than their culture, that there might be members of the groups mentioned in the last sentence that seek yet another term for their ethnic identification.

Develop Empathy

A famous Native American proverb tells us "We should not judge another person until we have walked two moons in his moccasins." Our next suggestion for improvement is about ' wearing those moccasins." That is, we need to develop empathy-be able to see things from the point of view of others. Many researchers in the area of interpersonal and intercultural competence believe that our success as communicators depends, to a large extent, on our "skill at establishing and maintaining desired identities for both self and others." "Identities" are actually the pictures of ourselves and the other person that we hold in our heads. We use these pictures in two ways. First, our identities help us to define the messages we receive from others; and second, they assist us in selecting the most appropriate message to send to another person. We have already discussed knowing ourselves; our focus now is on our need to develop empathy (emotional identification) and role-taking (cognitive adaptation) competence so that we can better know and adjust to the other person. After reviewing the literature on the topic of empathy, Broome concluded, "Empathy has been recognized as important to both general communication competence and as a central characteristic of competent and effective intercultural communication."

Before we begin our discussion of empathy and role taking, we need to restate two important ideas that appear in every chapter. First, as with so much of our counsel, we are again faced with a skill that is easier to talk about than to put into practice. The fact remains that however similar we may appear to be, there is something distinctive and unique about each of us. Our internal states are elusive and fleeting, and we know them only as distorted shadows. Knowing the other person, and predicting his or her reactions and needs, is a difficult and troublesome activity. And when we add the dimension of culture, we compound the problem.

Second, although we have focused primarily on culture, we also are concerned with the "interpersonal aspects" of intercultural communication. Perhaps the interpersonal dimension of communication is most evident in the area of empathy. As Miller and Steinberg noted, "To communicate interpersonally, one must leave the cultural and sociological levels of predications and psychically travel to the psychological level."

Simply put, empathy, while using knowledge about another's culture to make predications, also demands that the point of analysis be the individual personality.

A number of behaviors can keep us from understanding the feelings, thoughts, and motives of another person-regardless of his or her culture. Before we look at some of the ways to improve our role-taking skills, it might be helpful to examine a few characteristics that can impede empathy.

Encourage Feedback

The interactive nature of communication brings us to our next suggestion: encourage feedback. Feedback is the information generated by the person who receives your message. This information, be it a smile or the words "No thank you," allows you to make qualitative judgments about the communication event while it is taking place. These judgments offer useful data that enable you to correct and adjust your next message. Being able to invite feedback, even from members of those cultures that are reluctant to offer such data, is an effective communication skill. In this sense, a competent communicator uses feedback both to monitor the communication process and to exercise some control over it. Feedback clearly manifests the axioms with which we began this chapter: we can learn and adapt. Put another way, with feedback we see or hear what is happening (learn) and alter our actions (exercise free choice).

Granting that feedback is critical, we must learn to create an atmosphere that encourages other people to offer us feedback-feedback we need in order to adjust our own behavior. Therefore, let us review a number of communication skills that encourage other people to send us messages about the current situation.

We can use *nonverbal actions* as a way of inspiring others to respond to us honestly. The first step in improving our nonverbal feedback is recognizing that it takes many forms. Think for a moment of all the positive attitudes and images you associate with smiling, head nodding, leaning forward, and laughing. Although these behaviors seem very Western, they often produce positive reactions in other cultures. Each of these actions, separately or in combination with verbal messages, creates an atmosphere that tells other people we are interested in them and want to hear what they have to say.

Positive verbal behavior can also encourage feedback. Like our nonverbal messages, our use of words also takes a variety of forms. In cultures that value conversation and openness, asking questions is an excellent method of encouraging feedback about the quality of our messages. We can ask questions such as, "Perhaps we should start the meeting by introducing ourselves. Is that agreeable?" Or "How do you think we should start the meeting?" Further, questions can be used to seek additional clarification. If asked in an unthreatening manner, even the question "Do you understand?" assists in monitoring the level of comprehension. We should remind you before we leave this point that in some Asian cultures, the word no is seldom used. In Japan, for example, instead of responding negatively to your question, "they may simply apologize, keep quiet, become vague, or answer with a euphemism for no."

Our use of words also encourages feedback if we relate them directly to what the other person has just said. You know from your own experience that it is very disconcerting if you tell a friend that you do not feel well, and your friend responds that she or he just received an "A" on an examination.

Using feedback, like developing empathy, *takes time*. Rather than leaping to conclusions about what our communication partner is saying, we need to give the other person time to finish his or her thoughts. Although this notion of suspending judgments is not new, it underscores the need to avoid premature evaluations. In face-to-face interactions we often complete the thought or idea before the other person has even finished talking. If we do not cut a person off with our words or actions, we often do it in our mind, and this prevents us from making effective use of feedback. There is no positive compensation for a quick decision, particularly if we made that decision without sufficient feedback. Remember the French proverb: "Patience is bitter but its fruit is sweet."

Sometimes *silence* instead of words will inspire feedback. We have repeatedly seen that every culture has a unique communication style. Some cultural styles call for periods of silence and/or long pauses, and you must learn to respect these phases in the encounter. Giving the person this quiet period creates an atmosphere that promotes feedback once the silence is broken. There are even occasions when the silence itself is a form of feedback. As we noted elsewhere in the book, many Asian cultures do not enjoy being hurried when they are negotiating and/or solving problems. If you learn to remain silent, you will be sending them some positive feedback about the meeting.

Learn About Cultural Adaptation

Our next skill begins with this question: How do you adapt to a new culture if your exposure to that culture will take place for an extended period of time? The answer to this question is at the heart of the adaptation process. In this section, we discuss cultural contacts that are not transitory, but rather are sustained and ongoing. Immigrants, refugees, international business people with overseas assignments, military personnel, government workers, and exchange students are just a few of the people who need to adapt to a new culture for a long period of time. These people need to cope with the cultural changes brought about by continuous firsthand contact with another culture. One of the chief characteristics of the adaptation process is that elements of the original culture can never be completely erased,51 Before we begin a more detailed analysis of the adaptation process, we should point out that the word adaptation is but one of a number of words the field of intercultural communication has used to represent this concept. Kim further develops this idea when she writes, "Cross-cultural adaptation embraces other similar but narrow terms, from assimilation ... and acculturation ... to coping and adjustment ... as well as integration." We prefer the term *adaptation* for two reasons. First, it represents the most current thinking in the field; and second, it is a "middle ground" that can include all of the other points of view. To better understand this important skill, let us examine a number of the behaviors that can make the adaptation process a successful and rewarding experience.①

References

[1] Bachman L. F. Fundamental Considerations in Language Testing[M]. Oxford: Oxford University Press, 1990.

[2] Kim Y. Y. Becoming Intercultural: An Integrative Theory of Communication and Cross-cultural Adoptation [M]. CA: Sage Publications, 2001.

[3]萨莫瓦等. 跨文化交际[M]. 北京:外语教学与研究出版社,2000.

[4]严明. 跨文化交际导论[M]. 哈尔滨:黑龙江人民出版社,2006.

① 摘自萨莫瓦等. 跨文化交际[M]. 北京:外语教学与研究出版社,2000.